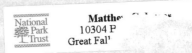

D1572715

APL—Fifty Years
of
Service to the Nation

APL—Fifty Years of Service to the Nation

A History of
The Johns Hopkins University Applied Physics Laboratory

by William K. Klingaman

Published by The Johns Hopkins University
Applied Physics Laboratory
Laurel, Maryland 20723-6099

Library of Congress Catalog Card Number: 93-077391
ISBN 0-912025-04-2

CONTENTS

FOREWORD

In the past half century The Johns Hopkins University Applied Physics Laboratory (APL) has compiled a truly impressive record of contributions to national security and made signal advances in space science and biotechnology. Nevertheless, the Laboratory is generally not well known, and even those familiar with its work are for the most part unaware of its unique institutional status among university laboratories.

It is therefore appropriate that in connection with the activities celebrating the fiftieth anniversary of the Laboratory's founding, this narrative history was commissioned to make available an account of its work to the general public, the staff, and the many organizations in government, industry, and academia who have been associated with one or another of APL's diverse programs. It describes for the first time in a comprehensive public document the development of the important national resource APL has become.

I am particularly pleased to have been invited to write a foreword to this volume. Having spent virtually an entire professional career at APL and served as its director for eleven years (1969–80), I believe profoundly that APL embodies values that will be as important to our national well-being in the future as they demonstrably have been in the past, and that these values need to be shared more widely.

William K. Klingaman, who was selected to write this volume, is a perceptive young author who has published several authoritative yet readable historical studies. Klingaman spent a year reviewing documentary sources and conducting interviews with a total of eighty individuals with special knowledge of APL and the context in which it functioned during the past fifty years.

What follows, then, is a popular history of APL from its origins in the early days of World War II to the present. Beginning with its development of the proximity fuze, one of World War II's most effective weapons, then expanding its missions to guided missiles for fleet defense and to major roles in both undersea and space systems, APL has been and is involved in a very broad variety of systems and technologies. The extraordinary record of its accomplishments, as recounted in Klingaman's narrative, stems from a number of qualities that have characterized the Laboratory's operation almost from the beginning. No single one of these qualities is unique; it is the combination of them in a single organization that distinguishes APL. An enumeration of some of these qualities may help readers to better visualize the significance of the events Klingaman recounts.

Johns Hopkins was the first university founded with the mission of public service, embodied in its School of Medicine, coequal with the mission of education and research. Not only did this focus lead Johns Hopkins to accept sponsorship of APL in wartime, but it was central to the University's decision to continue its sponsorship in peacetime and to make APL a permanent division of the University in 1948, accepting the Laboratory's continuing national security mission as part of its own.

The Laboratory's basic character was cast in the crucible of World War II under the inspired leadership of its first director, Merle A. Tuve. He instilled a spirit of teamwork and "can-do" among all the staff, along with an intense belief in the importance of the enterprise and a feeling of urgency to achieve objectives despite whatever obstacles lay in the way. Tuve's successors have worked to preserve this spirit by choosing challenging tasks of vital importance to the nation and fostering the spirit of dedication and teamwork.

The wartime fuze program was not only a remarkable engineering effort that required important technological breakthroughs; it also led APL to become deeply involved in the fuze production effort, helping train industrial teams to adapt their manufacturing processes to the new technology. After the fuzes began to come out by the thousands in an incredibly short time, key APL staff members were commissioned as Navy officers and accompanied the fuzes into the fleet. This experience established APL's operating philosophy to carry scientific and engineering developments, when needed, into the factory and the field. This unusual objective for a university laboratory has remained an important distinguishing feature of APL.

The fuze experience was applied on a larger scale in APL's development of a family of guided missiles for defending the fleet against aircraft that could launch attack missiles from beyond the range of antiaircraft gunfire. This program was carried on with the aid of an innovative partnership among universities, industry, and the Navy, first established in the fuze days under the designation "Section T Pattern" (T for Tuve). APL functioned as the central laboratory, responsible for technical direction of the work of the other team members and steering the program with the aid of technical panels. This mode of operation proved very effective in carrying out a coordinated effort by a number of independent organizations and was used by APL repeatedly over the years, notably in the areas of submarine security and the Strategic Defense Initiative.

There is probably no device that incorporates a greater diversity of technical disciplines than a modern guided missile, combining aerodynamics, structures, materials, guidance, control, propulsion, fuzing, and explosive warhead—all stressed to their limits of performance. The development of guided missiles required APL to enhance its staff's skills in system engineering to a level second to none. The Laboratory's pioneering concept of a "sectionalized" (modularized) missile proved to be a key factor in solving a critical production problem in APL's and the Navy's first operational guided missile, Terrier, and became a basis for the Navy's air defense missile arsenal. This focus on the total operational utility of the product—producibility, reliability, and maintainability as well as performance—has been another hallmark of APL from the beginning.

Throughout its history APL has focused on solutions of operational problems that went beyond fulfilling stated requirements to satisfying important needs. In so doing, it has often recommended and even urged the Navy and other sponsors to recognize unstated needs and take measures accordingly. Such initiatives led to the recognition of countermeasures as a formidable threat to air defense systems and ultimately to the initiation of a radically new system development that led to the Navy's Aegis system. Other results were the automation of the fleet's surveillance systems, the Battle Group Coordination concept, and introduction of satellite-based navigation for the Fleet Ballistic Missile system, along with a host of ship- and submarine-borne instrumentation to improve their security and war fighting capability. Few civilian organizations have been so intimately involved in operational problems of the armed forces as has APL.

The term *applied physics* captures the essence of APL's technical focus. It signifies not only a concentration on problem solving rather than on research for its own sake but also a fundamentally scientific approach to such problem solving. The emphasis has always been on the application of science and technology to solve important national problems. APL has recruited its staff from among the country's top students in the multiple disciplines required by its missions and has supplemented their skills with a vigorous staff training and graduate education program. APL's invention and subsequent development of the Transit navigation satellite system is but one example of the ingenuity and versatility of its staff.

Independence of outlook and institutional integrity have been essential assets for APL's position as a valued adviser and technical director for major government programs. These inherent characteristics have been strengthened by an unmatched record of performance in this role. APL's selection for the critical assignment as technical evaluation agent of the Navy's strategic submarine systems attests to the respect and trust with which the Laboratory is regarded in the defense community.

In addition to its national security mission, APL has enthusiastically applied its talents to nonmilitary goals, large and small. Development of the Transit navigation satellite system required far more accurate knowledge of the exact shape of the earth than was heretofore available. This geodetic research in turn has led to a major space science program, including satellites and instruments to study the earth's gravitational and electromagnetic fields, atmosphere, and oceans; our sister planets; and interplanetary space.

APL has also contributed to the areas of renewable energy, automated transportation systems, prevention of fires, and minimizing the environmental impact of power plants. For more than twenty years it has collaborated with The Johns Hopkins School of Medicine in a biomedical engineering program that has resulted in more than one hundred new medical instruments and a large body of research findings. To serve its own staff's and the community's needs for graduate education, it operates a part-time graduate program, under the academic aegis of The Johns Hopkins University School of Engineering, that has an enrollment of more than two thousand students, the largest of its kind in the country.

Today, APL is recognized as a national resource under a trust agreement between the University and the Navy, which provides for its continuity for as long as it is needed. There is no parallel for this mutuality of purpose by a university and the government.

If one were to seek a single dominant characteristic of APL, I would call it "expanding the limits." Throughout its history, the Laboratory has repeatedly and systematically challenged and sought to overcome any constraints on achieving its objectives that were not clearly fundamental and immutable. The task of designing a tiny vacuum tube that could withstand the crushing shock of being fired from a gun, which both the Germans and British considered hopeless, was seen as merely difficult. Putting the fledgling proximity fuze into mass production and distributing it to the front by the thousands in a period of months was just part of the job. As you read the ensuing narrative, you will see how this principle has led to highly successful programs to develop guided missiles, ship combat systems, space science and navigation, and submarine technology, and to the application of military knowledge to the betterment of medicine, transportation, energy, and education.

As this book goes to press, the world is undergoing radical geopolitical changes as a result of the breakup of the former Soviet Union. Clearly these changes will affect the national security of the United States in unpredictable ways. APL, which has always been characterized by its ready and enthusiastic adaptation to new challenges and environments, will need to marshal those qualities anew to help find technological solutions to such potential problems as the threat posed by regional conflicts to U.S. interests, including the serious problem of dispersal and uncertain control of weapons of mass destruction.

On the optimistic side, these geopolitical changes also hold out the hope that more of APL's resources can be directed to finding technological solutions to our many serious civilian-related problems in areas such as transportation, energy conservation, environmental cleanup, industrial competitiveness, and many others.

What is clear is that for fifty years APL has had the resilience, the versatility, and the commitment to respond to changing national priorities with great effectiveness. There is every reason to believe that the qualities that produced the achievements of the past fifty years will enable the Laboratory to meet the challenges of the future.

—Alexander Kossiakoff
February 1993

PREFACE

Fifty years ago, a small group of dedicated men and women undertook a daunting scientific and technical task: the design and production of a unique "proximity fuze" that would help protect Allied troops from enemy air attacks during World War II. From that single wartime project, the Applied Physics Laboratory (APL) of The Johns Hopkins University has expanded its activities during the following five decades to include the development of the first guided-missile systems to defend the United States Navy; the design and construction of a navigation satellite system; test and evaluation operations for the U.S. submarine fleet; space science missions for the National Aeronautics and Space Administration; biomedical research in collaboration with The Johns Hopkins University Medical Institutions; submarine security technology programs; oceanographic research; Strategic Defense Initiative experiments; and advanced research in numerous fields of chemistry and physics.

Yet even this record, as impressive as it is, does not exhaust the list of APL accomplishments from 1942 to 1992. As I have discovered while working on this history for the past eighteen months, the Applied Physics Laboratory is a very special place. Not only is it an invaluable research and development resource for the U.S. Navy and an esteemed branch of The Johns Hopkins University; it is also a vital source of specialized expertise for the nation and, in a larger sense, for the international scientific community as well.

While APL has undergone significant changes in the first fifty years of its life, the Laboratory has managed—sometimes under difficult circumstances—to maintain the spirit of creativity and dedication that motivated the original members of its staff. And for that, I salute the APL leadership and staff and wish them all the best for the next fifty years.

Finally, I would like to thank everyone who helped with this book: the present and former employees of APL who agreed to participate in the oral history interview process (all of whom are listed in the Appendix), the staff of the APL archives, the experts who kindly reviewed the manuscript and provided constructive criticism, the staff of the APL Public Information Office, and the members of the APL Fiftieth Anniversary Committee, whose patience and support were greatly appreciated.

——William K. Klingaman
December 1992

CHAPTER ONE

THE FUZE

I don't want any damn fool in this organization to save money; I want him to save time.

———*Merle A. Tuve*

It began with the Blitz and the German army's stunning victories across Western Europe in the spring of 1940. As the Luftwaffe pounded the cities of Great Britain night after night and the armored columns of the Wehrmacht swept virtually unopposed through the Low Countries, Belgium, and France in a matter of weeks, it became painfully obvious to American military and political officials watching the Nazi onslaught from across the Atlantic that the United States was woefully unprepared to fight a modern war. For the previous two decades, Congress and each succeeding administration in Washington had virtually ignored the development and production of new armaments in the name of economy and isolationism. Now, as Europe descended once again into the agony of war, the United States Army and Navy found themselves forced to rely on equipment that in large part was nothing more than surplus material left over from the First World War.

The dangers inherent in this ominous situation were especially clear to members of the nation's scientific community. More than the average American, these scientists—many of whom were refugees from the German onslaught on Europe—recognized the intimate connection

1

between technology and warfare in the twentieth century. Thus there was no shortage of volunteers when President Franklin D. Roosevelt, as part of his broad-based campaign to improve American preparedness, formed the National Defense Research Committee (NDRC) in June 1940 to coordinate scientific research on the mechanisms and devices of warfare under the chairmanship of Vannevar Bush, president of the Carnegie Institution of Washington. Within a year, nearly one-fourth of the professional physicists in the United States, most of them drawn from the academic world, had offered their services to work on NDRC projects.

While Bush was assembling and organizing his team of experts, ordnance specialists in the Army and Navy were busy drawing up a lengthy shopping list of items for the urgent attention of the NDRC. In effect, the services were attempting to overcome in a matter of months the lead that the Axis powers had attained in the previous decade. At that point, their so-called wish lists were not limited solely to items that they knew were technically feasible; one of the NDRC's first and most vital tasks would be to conduct preliminary research to determine which weapons could be produced effectively and within a short enough time to provide significant assistance to the nation's armed forces.

To facilitate the daunting research and development task that lay ahead, Bush split the NDRC into separate divisions, each with its own area of specialization; Division A, for instance, was given responsibility for armor and ordnance. Each division was then further subdivided into sections—in the case of Division A, into three sections initially—to handle specific research tasks. To make it easier to remember which group was working on what project, each section was identified by the initial of the last name of its leader. Thus the group of scientists exploring rocket weaponry at the Allegany Ballistics Laboratory in the foothills of West Virginia under the supervision of C. N. Hickman (a former protégé of the pioneering rocket expert

2

Robert Goddard) was known as Section H. Section B, headed by John E. Burchard of the Massachusetts Institute of Technology (MIT), concentrated on advanced research in armor and other means of passive defense. And the team of physicists and electronics experts working at the Carnegie Institution in Washington, D.C., on the task of developing a radical new type of fuze for antiaircraft artillery shells was designated Section T for its leader, Merle A. Tuve.

Thirty-nine years old in the spring of 1940, Merle Tuve had served most recently as chief physicist of the Department of Terrestrial Magnetism (DTM), one of Carnegie's numerous research branches. A native of South Dakota with a lifelong interest in radio and electronics, Tuve had joined the Carnegie staff in 1926 after receiving a doctorate from The Johns Hopkins University for his studies of the effects of the earth's ionosphere on long-distance radio waves, experiments that proved critical to the development of radar. At DTM, Tuve had concentrated his studies in the field of experimental nuclear physics, but when the war in Europe commenced in earnest, he had suddenly decided to abandon that work. As Tuve later explained, he and several colleagues (including Lawrence Hafstad, chief scientist at DTM) decided in February 1940 "that we would do no more physics research if the likes of Hitler were to inherit our efforts." Instead, Tuve said, "we undertook to find a way that we could contribute to the technology of modern war" in the cause of freedom.

Partly because of his background in radio technology, Tuve was drawn toward the notion of developing a new and more effective type of artillery shell, one that was armed with an influence fuze that could detect its target by reflected radio waves. As he learned in early discussions with officers of the Research and Development Division of the U.S. Navy's Bureau of Ordnance, the U.S. Navy had been trying without notable success to develop such a weapon for several years. (German and British scientists had been working on it even longer.)[1]

Their efforts had been prompted by what was generally conceded to be the extremely low effectiveness of antiaircraft fire; at that time, naval gunners required hundreds of rounds of ammunition to hit a single plane, a dismal state of affairs that clearly placed any fleet in a dangerously vulnerable position against attacks from modern, sophisticated aircraft. The use of time-fuzed shells—that is, shells that exploded with a preset time delay after being fired into the air—improved the odds somewhat but were hardly an adequate solution, since they could not respond to changes in intercept time caused by the target aircraft's changes in direction, speed, or altitude.

The concept of an influence, or variable-time (VT), fuze, on the other hand, involved a shell that could somehow sense the presence of an enemy aircraft in flight and then detonate itself at the instant when the maximum number of lethal fragments would strike the target. The notion of such a device immediately attracted Tuve, who viewed it as an opportunity to apply his extensive expertise in radio and electronics research. And so in August 1940, the Carnegie Institution signed a contract with NDRC to organize a research group under Tuve's leadership for the purpose of carrying out "preliminary experimental studies" on an advanced-design fuze for antiaircraft shells.

Unfortunately, the prospects for immediate success did not appear promising. "We got two books from Naval Intelligence, with material from the British and the Germans," recalled Elmore Chatham, a radio expert from DTM who joined Tuve on the Section T project at Carnegie early in 1941. "One book was about fifteen or twenty pages, and the other was a couple of inches thick. The big, thick one was filled with the stuff that didn't work or couldn't work with our existing technology. The other, tiny book had suggestions that offered a faint ray of hope on how it might be done."

After identifying several possible avenues of development for different types of influence fuzes, Tuve set up five separate research teams and instructed them all to conduct preliminary feasibility studies. It soon became apparent that several of these potential approaches (including an optical fuze that "looked" through a lens in the cone of the shell) simply would not work in a spinning shell within the current limits of technology; the optical fuze, for instance, displayed a disturbing tendency to mistake cloud formations for enemy aircraft.

By the autumn of 1941, Tuve and his colleagues had confirmed what they had suspected from the start: that a radio-influenced fuze represented the most viable approach. As a result, virtually the entire Section T research staff was transferred to the two teams working on the radio fuzes. Still, the problems that confronted them seemed almost insuperable. "Open the ordinary [1930s vintage] radio set on your table," suggested one writer in an attempt to explain the extent of the difficulty, "and try to imagine how you would fit it, equipped with a power plant and a transmitter as well as a receiver, into the nose of a Navy 5-inch, 38-caliber shell in a space about the size of an ice-cream cone."[2] The fuze also had to endure the shock of being fired from a gun, which subjected it to twenty thousand times the force of gravity, and withstand centrifugal forces from the spinning of the shell at speeds as high as 475 rotations per second.

Remarkably, Tuve's organization at Carnegie succeeded in developing a workable prototype fuze three months later, even before the Japanese attack on Pearl Harbor on December 7. The heart of the device was a rugged miniature vacuum tube, five-eighths of an inch long and three-eighths of an inch in diameter (about the size of an almond), not unlike the tubes used in hearing aids of that period. To ease the stress on the fuze at the moment of firing, the Carnegie team had invented an intricate suspension device known as a mousetrap (because that is what it looked like), which provided a cushion for the tungsten filament in the tube. Once aloft, the transmitter in the fuze

5

sent out electromagnetic waves on impulses at the speed of light; if the fuze passed near any target that gave a radio reflection (e.g., metal objects, water, or the ground), the reflected impulses triggered a switch that caused an electric detonator to set off the main explosive charge.

The Birth of APL

The terrible losses suffered by the U.S. Navy during the Japanese air attack on Pearl Harbor naturally made the successful development and production of a proximity fuze even more urgent. But before approving any program of mass production, Captain S. R. Shumaker, director of the Research and Development Division of the Bureau of Ordnance, insisted that the experimental proximity fuze developed by Tuve's organization demonstrate at least a 50-percent rate of effectiveness under simulated combat conditions. On January 29, 1942, the experimental Section T device underwent its first extensive tests at the Naval Proving Ground in Dahlgren, Virginia; when the guns ceased firing, 52 percent of the shells had survived the launch and managed to maintain radio output throughout flight.

Of course there were still a number of vexing technical problems to be solved. Although Tuve's teams had managed to construct a reasonably durable glass tube that could withstand the tremendous stress of firing with at least some degree of regularity, the breakage rate for these tubes was still far too high. Clearly some supplemental means of cushioning the impact of firing was needed. Furthermore, the conventional dry cell batteries employed in the early fuzes tended to deteriorate too quickly in storage; when the shells were introduced to the heat and humidity of the Pacific theater late in 1942, their batteries had to be replaced en masse about every ninety days. Safety devices also had to be built into the fuze to minimize the risk of explosion at the gun muzzle. Had one fatal accident with the fuze occurred aboard ship, the whole project might well have been scuttled.

Nevertheless, the Navy decided that the need for the fuze was so pressing that production should begin as quickly as possible, while research on the remaining problems continued. Thus began the even more daunting task of transforming an experimental device into a reliable weapon that could be mass-produced in a relatively brief time. But this job would have to be done by some organization other than the Carnegie Institution, which for all its merits simply was not suited to supervise such a project. In the first place, the Navy, having already spent $450,000 on the initial stage of proximity fuze research, was planning to issue a contract worth $800,000 through NDRC and its parent organization, the Office of Scientific Research and Development (OSRD), to fund the next phase of the project. This expansion in funding placed Vannevar Bush, who was still head of both the NDRC and the Carnegie Institution, in an awkward situation. To remove even the appearance of a conflict of interest, Bush announced that he would have to resign as president of Carnegie unless another sponsor could be found for the Section T research.

Furthermore, the Carnegie Institution had a provision in its charter that allowed expansion of its payroll for wartime work but forbade the continued employment of such personnel in peacetime; the institution—whose founder, Andrew Carnegie, had been well known for his pacifist views—was loath to add hundreds of staff members whom it would be forced to release as soon as the war was over. Besides, the number of employees involved in the project through the early months of 1942 was growing so rapidly that Carnegie already was running out of space.

So Tuve, as a graduate of The Johns Hopkins University (JHU), recommended that his alma mater replace Carnegie as the sponsor of the Section T research team. The wall of secrecy surrounding the project was such, however, that the nature of the work could not be revealed to the Board of Trustees, who were understandably wary about assuming responsibility for a contract worth nearly a million dollars when they were barred from any knowledge of what it was all about. An informal request from President Roosevelt to Isaiah Bowman, the president of Johns Hopkins and a part-time adviser to the Department of State, was required to convince the trustees to accept the arrangement. The University was also reassured by the willingness of D. Luke Hopkins, an eminent Baltimore banker who served as vice president of the Board of Trustees, to coordinate the financial arrangements and act as the University's authorized representative with the new laboratory. For the Navy, Commander W. S. Parsons was assigned as a special assistant to Vannevar Bush for Section T activities.

On March 10, 1942, The Johns Hopkins University assumed responsibility for the Section T contract with OSRD, and the Applied Physics Laboratory (APL) was formally established. The Laboratory's name came from Tuve, who wished to emphasize the practical nature of its scientific task. It should be noted that for both the

From left, Lawrence R. Hafstad and Merle A. Tuve with D. Luke Hopkins and Isaiah Bowman, fifth president of The Johns Hopkins University.

8

government and The Johns Hopkins University, this was a wartime management contract only; at the time, there were no plans to make APL an integral, permanent part of the University. Nevertheless, once the trustees of Johns Hopkins had agreed to participate, the University's administration gave the wartime endeavor its full cooperation and support.

For APL's first headquarters, the University commandeered most of the Wolfe Motor Company building at 8621 Georgia Avenue in Silver Spring, Maryland, then a relatively tranquil northwestern suburb of Washington. The Wolfe building was partitioned—the auto dealer's lobby became a temporary personnel office—and new sections were added as the staff continued to expand (by the early summer of 1942 there were nearly two hundred employees), but the "used cars" sign was allowed to remain over the lot as a sort of camouflage.

Since the APL employees were warned every week, in closed meetings at the nearby Silver Theater, to tell no one

The Wolfe building, complete with its "used cars" sign, first housed the APL staff. It had been owned by the Wolfe Motor Company, which rebuilt elsewhere in Silver Spring. APL occupied the Wolfe building on May 1, 1942, added the adjacent Navy building in 1943, and built two more stories on the main building and a central section during 1944.

9

the nature of their work, the local residents had no notion of what was happening behind the walls of 8621. Rumors were rampant; those who heard the security guard greet members of the professional staff as "Doctor" when they arrived in the morning assumed that the building was being used as some sort of experimental medical facility. Others suspected that it was just a cover for a house of ill repute. Some were merely puzzled: former APL employee James Maddox once observed an Italian-American barber several doors away gazing out his window in wonder at a black-draped, coffin-like box (containing experimental vacuum tubes) that repeatedly rose two dozen feet on a pulley and then dropped down to smash upon a thick armor plate. "They push-a them up," he murmured over and over to his customers, "and they push-a them down."

Throughout 1942, the dynamic and perennially rumpled Tuve kept pushing the project forward relentlessly, imparting his own sense of urgency to the entire APL staff in his determination to provide the Navy with an effective weapon before the end of the war. "I don't want any damn fool in this organization to save money," Tuve insisted, "I want him to save time." Sixteen-hour days were commonplace. "Time meant nothing," noted Maddox. "After eight hours, you'd do eight hours more." Throughout the day, Tuve's voice could be heard in the hallways, shouting imprecations at any material obstruction. "He was one of the finest but cussedest men you ever met," laughed Maddox. "He didn't give a damn who was there, whether it was his wife or the head of the company; if he wanted to cuss, he'd cuss. And he'd give you hell, but then he'd turn around afterward and shake hands with you."

Tuve gave his staff all the material support and inspiration it needed to accomplish its task. "He was the kind of leader who could take a man five feet tall and make him perform like he was twelve feet tall," noted Wilbur Goss, a physicist who joined APL in the spring of 1942. "The important thing was to get the job done, and he imbued

10

everyone with that spirit." Tuve never criticized his staff for attempting an experiment that turned out to be a dead end. "He was willing to accept mistakes in the pursuit of progress," confirmed Elmore Chatham. "He knew that every experimenter, when he's working, is going to have a hell of a junk pile if he has any ideas, because most ideas don't work."

As new avenues of research opened up and others reached dead ends, Tuve adroitly shifted personnel and resources from one task to another until his organizational chart resembled a collection of tangled spiderwebs. "He'd shake up the organization overnight," recalled Thomas Sheppard, a technical expert from Texas who had joined DTM after working at a radio station in East Texas. "You never knew what you'd be doing next or where." Sheppard himself spent most of the year working in the VT fuze model shop, where thirty experimental fuzes were constructed every day, each with a slightly different design. (Eventually, much of the assembly work was taken over by a team of women workers who named themselves "the wench bench.") At night, the fuzes were transported in trucks—unmarked, to avoid undue attention—to testing fields in southern Maryland (Stump Neck) and tidewater Virginia (Dam Neck and Dahlgren), where they were fired straight up into the air and then retrieved from the soft earth.

When each shell was fired, data were recorded on whether its fuze had been operating at the time it left the gun and whether it had been triggered as it approached the ground. The fuzes that failed were dug up and given a postmortem to see whether they had suffered breakage, short circuits, or some other problem. Unfortunately, as Goss explained, "There was no [certain] way of telling the reason for the failure. You had to guess, and then you said, 'Well, if that's the cause of the failure, then we'll do this to correct it.' So you made a new batch of fuzes and incorporated those changes into it, and if the new fuzes

11

worked, you could assume your hypothesis was right. It was strictly trial and error."

In the end, the problem of breakage was alleviated by cushioning the vacuum tubes inside the shell in small rubber cups, which were then embedded in blocks made of a special wax compound. To replace the original dry cell batteries, a wet cell battery was developed by employing an electrolyte in a glass ampule; after the shock of firing broke the ampule, centrifugal force spun the acid back and through the chamber, thereby activating the battery by the time the shell left the gun muzzle. As a safety precaution to protect the Navy's gunners from premature explosions of the shells, an innovative mercury switch provided a time delay before activation.

The Fuze in Combat

Even as refinements continued to be made in the basic design, the VT fuze was taken out for its first sea trial in August 1942. Again the experiment proved successful, as the cruiser USS *Cleveland* shot down three drone targets with four rounds. Buoyed by this result, the government ordered the fuze into full-scale production, and within a month a group of contractors led by the Crosley Radio Corporation was manufacturing four hundred fuzes per day. Now the time had arrived to introduce the fuze into the fleet for use in battle, but once again the veil of secrecy surrounding the project created an obstacle. Aside from a few officers at top echelons, no one in the Navy had been granted access to any detailed information about the fuze; the fact that it worked via radio waves was especially sensitive, since jamming the fuze or leading it astray with fake signals would be relatively easy once its secret was known. "We couldn't tell the Navy what it was or how it worked," lamented Elmore Chatham, "yet we had to go out there and make it work."

12

Consequently, five APL scientists (including Chatham and physicist James A. Van Allen, who later discovered the radiation belts encircling the earth) were commissioned as naval officers to demonstrate to commanders in the Pacific and Atlantic fleets the superiority of the VT fuze to conventional antiaircraft ordnance. Since the Navy was primarily occupied in the South Pacific at that time, most of the first production lots of fuzes were dispatched to that sector—five thousand fuzes by the beginning of 1943.

The first trial of the new device under combat conditions occurred in the Pacific on January 5, 1943, when a Navy task force returning from the bombardment of an enemy airfield was attacked by four Japanese Aichi 99 dive bombers off the southern coast of Guadalcanal. One of the ships in the American convoy, the USS *Helena*, had five hundred rounds of five-inch proximity fuzes on board. Unfortunately, the ship's gunners could not fire at the Japanese planes as they approached, since a group of patrolling American F-4Fs trailing the Aichis was too near the line of fire. As the second Aichi was completing its run, however, the *Helena* opened fire; seconds later, a shell armed with a VT fuze burst near one of the Japanese planes and brought it down in flames.

The following month, a dozen Japanese torpedo bombers launched a night attack on a U.S. troop convoy in the same region. Using nothing but radar-controlled antiaircraft guns firing shells equipped with VT fuzes, Navy gunners shot down five of the airborne attackers before the convoy suffered any torpedo damage. And during the ensuing siege of Okinawa, two U.S. destroyers—the USS *Hadley* and the USS *Evans*—used shells armed with the proximity fuze to fend off an assault by 156 enemy planes.

Meanwhile, the VT fuze underwent its baptism of fire in the Mediterranean in June 1943. Once again the weapon struck with deadly accuracy, as two American destroyers (the USS *Swanson* and the USS *Roe*) downed a German Junker 88 with only thirteen rounds. Use of the proximity

13

fuze in encounters with German planes tended to make U.S. officials especially apprehensive, since they felt Nazi scientists were more likely than their Japanese counterparts to decipher the secret of the weapon. So, to help disguise the nature of the VT fuze, American ships were instructed to send out decoy radio signals during an encounter, to mask the faint but distinctive signals emanating from the fuzes as they spun through the air. By the end of the year, the Navy had fired slightly more than nine thousand VT fuzes in combat in the Atlantic and Pacific theaters, with an effectiveness rate three times that of conventional time-fuzed antiaircraft ammunition.

Yet nearly 50 percent of the shells in these early generations of proximity fuzes were still failing to reach their target. These failures were due less to deficiencies in the shells themselves than to the Navy's obsolete, inadequate gun directors (the electrical systems that sighted the targets and guided the firing of long-range guns), particularly on the older ships in the fleet. Recognizing the nature of the problem, Tuve and his colleagues had already begun working on a vastly improved gun director, using a simplified version of a model developed at MIT.

Because time was short and resources were limited, the first experiments on the new gun director were done at the Laboratory's Silver Spring offices with hastily improvised test equipment, including rocking wooden platforms driven by Ford Model T engines to simulate the pitching motion of a ship's deck. By 1944 the new APL-developed gun director, known as the Mark 57, was ready for action.

Whereas its slower and more cumbersome Mark 1 predecessors had required a crew of sixteen men and an average of forty seconds to locate and track their targets using mechanical computations, the Mark 57—employing recent breakthroughs in computing technology—needed only one man and approximately 4.7 seconds to lock onto an adversary. The rapidity with which the Mark 57 could track its target took on critical importance in the Pacific theater, where Japanese kamikaze ("divine wind") pilots, cognizant of the delays inherent in the Mark 1 gun directors, had adopted a policy of changing course at least once every thirty seconds, thereby causing the Navy's old-fashioned guns to swing wildly back and forth in a futile attempt to follow the planes' flight path.

The Navy installed the first four Mark 57s aboard the USS *Missouri,* but when the battleship reached the Pacific war zone in January 1945, the fleet commander greeted the new weaponry with skepticism. Several previous "improved" gun directors had been sent to his command and failed to live up to expectations, and rather than risk action with another unproven system, he had issued an edict to the Bureau of Ordnance preventing it from placing any new directors on any of his ships. But the APL team assigned to the Pacific was so confident of the superiority of the Mark 57 that they consented to participate in a staged competition against one of the best conventional antiaircraft gunnery crews in the Pacific Fleet to persuade the commander to adopt their system.

It was hardly an equal contest. While the Mark 1 guns (on the USS *Wisconsin*) were permitted to fire virtually everything in their arsenal at the targets, the APL–Mark 57 crew (on the USS *Missouri*), firing shells armed with VT fuzes, was limited to one gun, one director, and four rounds of ammunition per target. Nevertheless, the Mark 57 clearly outperformed its rival, at one point destroying with a single shell a target three miles away. When the commander grudgingly conceded that the Mark 57 had done "pretty good shooting," Elmore Chatham, the leader of the APL target-shooting team, lost his temper. "I was incensed," Chatham recalled. "I said, 'Why, Commander, should we knock it down with less than one shot?' But he took it pretty well."

Within weeks, five more ships armed with the Mark 57 were dispatched to the Pacific, and the Navy established a special training school in Hawaii to instruct gunners in its use. None too soon, for in April 1945 the final and most spectacular Japanese kamikaze campaign commenced. Without the VT fuze and the agile Mark 57 gun control system, the odds of survival for American sailors caught in the hell of the suicidal enemy attacks would have been far poorer. By that time, however, the vital fuze was being produced at a rate of more than forty thousand per day by five separate manufacturers—Crosley, Sylvania Electric Products, Radio Corporation of America (RCA), Eastman Kodak, and McQuay Norris—supported by more than eighty subcontractors employing eighty thousand workers, 85 percent of whom were women.

A Fuze for the Army

Back at 8621 Georgia Avenue, meanwhile, a task group headed by Wilbur Goss had been working feverishly to develop a more compact version of the VT fuze that could be used in the U.S. Army's artillery ordnance for howitzer fire against enemy infantry and in the British army's three-inch guns. Specifically, what Army officials wanted was a proximity fuze that would be triggered by reflection from the ground, bursting in the air at a height that would cause maximum damage to opposing troops in any terrain. Anticipating that tremendous demand for the fuze by Allied ground forces would follow the invasion of Normandy planned for June 1944, the Army had ordered the new shells into production before the compact version of the fuze was ready. But stubborn redesign difficulties remained, and Tuve finally set a two-week deadline on Goss's team to obtain a fuze with at least a 50-percent success rate. If they had not achieved their objective by then, the project would be dropped. "There are some things that simply can't be done," Tuve told the assembled leaders of the Army fuze project, "and this may be one of them."[3]

Then fate lent a hand. The Army fuzes were being tested at the Aberdeen Proving Ground in northeastern Maryland; as soon as each batch of redesigned fuzes was ready for testing, it would be shipped up to Aberdeen and fired. But when a train derailment prevented the regular shipment from reaching the proving ground, Goss, rather than waste a day, instructed the gunners to fire a box of fuzes that had been stored at Aberdeen as part of a lower priority experiment. To limit the damage from humidity during storage, the tips of these shells had been dipped in a special waterproofing wax mixture. Soon Aberdeen relayed the stunning results to Silver Spring: the shells had compiled a success rate of 70 percent. As it turned out, the wax mixture on the nose of the shells had protected the soldering and wiring underneath from the heat and friction of firing and flight, the forces that had rendered the unprotected shells less effective. Within days, tubs of the wax mixture had been shipped to each of the plants producing the Army fuze.

None too soon, because in the summer of 1944, Germany launched a full-scale air assault against London, using its fearsome unmanned Vergeltungswaffe-1 (V-1) buzz bombs. Fortunately, Allied intelligence had spotted the camouflaged bombs in their launchers earlier, and models of the German weapon had been constructed for target practice by guns firing the compact version of the VT fuze at a specially constructed firing range in New Mexico. When the Nazi V-1 attack commenced, it was met by shells bearing the very recently arrived Army proximity fuze fired from batteries in and around London and the English Channel ports. After weathering difficulties in the initial raids, the gunners gradually gained experience and found the range: in the last week of August, 79 percent of the incoming V-1 bombs were engaged and destroyed in the air.

Despite the rush to get the Army proximity fuze into production, the Allied Combined Chiefs of Staff had hesitated to sanction its use on the continent, fearing that a dud might be recovered and dissected by the Germans and the Allied advantage might be lost forever. Furthermore, Army commanders in the field turned out to be no more eager to adopt a weapon that was unproven (to them, anyway) than their Navy counterparts were.

But the chief of the U.S. Army ground forces, General Ben Lear, continued to press for the release of what he called "the most important innovation in artillery ammunition since the introduction of high-explosive shells,"[4] and

Proximity (VT) fuze—the Mark 45, one of the later Army models of the fuze. More than twenty-two million fuzes were produced, and by the end of World War II, a third of the nation's electronic industry was engaged in fuze work.

the steady advance of Allied armies across Europe in the autumn of 1944 appeared to lessen the dangerous consequences of discovery. When the Wehrmacht caught the Allies by surprise on December 16, 1944, by suddenly turning and launching its last desperate counteroffensive in what later became known as the Battle of the Bulge, the appalling losses in the Allies' front lines convinced the Army that the secret weapon could be withheld no longer.

So the VT fuze was cut loose, with devastating results. Fire from the Allied artillery counterattack was so withering that some German troops, utterly deprived of shelter, reportedly mutinied rather than advance. "Prisoner-of-war reports are unanimous in characterizing our artillery fire as the most demoralizing and destructive ever encountered," reported one staff officer to General Levin Campbell, Army chief of ordnance. By blunting the attack of five German divisions, the fuze helped protect the access route of General George S. Patton's Third Army to the beleaguered American garrison at Bastogne. After witnessing the VT fuze in action, Patton informed General Campbell, "The new shell with the funny fuze is devastating. The other night we caught a German battalion, which was trying to get across the Sauer River. . . .I think that when all armies get this shell we will have to devise some new method of warfare. I am glad that you all thought of it first."[5]

By the close of the war in August 1945, slightly more than twenty-two million proximity fuzes had been produced. Ironically, the Army used more than twice as many shells as the Navy, though the Navy had taken over the OSRD contract with Johns Hopkins on December 1, 1944.

When the veil of wartime secrecy was finally lifted and the nation learned of the existence and effectiveness of the VT fuze, APL received a generous measure of public praise. George Kistiakowsky of Harvard University, who later became President Eisenhower's science adviser, declared that the development of the proximity fuze had been second only to the atomic bomb in its vital contribution to

19

winning the war. The *New York Times* remarked, "The Johns Hopkins group that developed the radio shell deserves the thanks of the country for having demonstrated the efficiency of cooperative research."[6] And H. Struve Hensel, assistant secretary of the Navy, noted, "For two and a half years of war, during which the only clue to its existence was what appeared to be unprecedented accuracy of gun fire, projectiles and bombs fused with this proximity device inflicted terrific damage on the enemy. It was really a device that caused devastating destruction."

To Vannevar Bush, the development of the proximity fuze—and even more important, the entire wartime Section T effort—illustrated to "an extraordinary degree the effective teamwork and professional partnership between civilian scientists and military men which lies at the heart of the safety of this country in the future."[7] Prescient words; for at the time Bush made that statement in March 1945, the partnership between APL and the military establishment had just begun.

CHAPTER TWO

BUMBLEBEE

While the intercontinental guided missile is still a blueprint, interceptor missiles are being perfected to a point that has tilted the balance well toward the defense.

———*Newsweek, February 21, 1949*

Even before the end of World War II, officials in the U.S. Navy Bureau of Ordnance (BuOrd) had come to the disturbing realization that the proximity fuze, as effective as it proved to be against conventional aircraft attacks, might not be sufficient to defend the fleet against assaults by the next generation of offensive weapons. Specifically, the Navy was concerned about the possibility of attacks by guided missiles launched from enemy airplanes beyond the range of normal shipboard antiaircraft artillery, and the sudden appearance in 1944–45 of the Japanese "Baka" bomb and the German V-2 missile created a very real sense of urgency in the service.

In July 1944, therefore, the bureau formally asked the Applied Physics Laboratory to carry out a preliminary analysis and evaluation of the problems posed by these ominous new threats and to recommend potential solutions. After several months of study and consultation, a small APL study group headed by Richard B. Roberts reported that the most promising defensive option appeared to be a supersonic, jet-powered guided missile, a

21

vehicle that would require simultaneous technological breakthroughs in numerous areas including propulsion, guidance, aerodynamics, and control. Roberts and his colleagues did not necessarily assume that such a weapon could be built; rather, they deemed it "of great military importance" to the United States to determine whether such a thing were possible. "If an intensive effort were made by a suitable technical group," they explained in their initial report of February 15, 1945, "even a negative result would be valuable, in that it would provide evidence that no nation could bring such devices into effective use against us in a predictable length of time."[1]

Armed with this recommendation, the Navy instructed BuOrd in December 1944 to proceed with the design and development of a supersonic, guided antiaircraft missile. Because this project inevitably would cut across the lines of responsibility of various organizations in the Navy and other service and government groups, the bureau decided to employ an independent agency as coordinator and supervisor. Given the remarkable success of the proximity fuze program, it is not surprising that BuOrd turned once again to the Applied Physics Laboratory. Although some members of the Board of Trustees of Johns Hopkins University continued to harbor misgivings about the expanding size and financial commitments of the Laboratory, they agreed to sign a short-term contract (NOrd-7386) with BuOrd. The new contract permitted APL to undertake this assignment, known simply as Task F, for at least seven months, contingent on the University's ability to obtain additional facilities and technical personnel.

To power a long-range supersonic missile, Tuve and his Task F team realized that they would have to devise a propulsion engine that had both greater horsepower and lighter weight than any conventional type of motor. At that time, the only possible avenues of development appeared to be either a liquid-fueled rocket or a ramjet. "We were looking for something that would fly and maintain speed out to a distance of forty thousand yards in order to destroy incoming aircraft," noted Wilbur Goss. In other words, the missile had to be fast enough—the APL task force hoped to obtain speeds of at least Mach 1.6—to strike an enemy plane before it dropped its bombs and to overtake any aircraft that tried to play cat and mouse (that is, repeatedly coming close enough to draw defensive fire and then retreating out of range in an attempt to deplete the ship's supply of ammunition). In case the incoming aircraft or bomb were maneuverable, the missile also had to be able to change its course in mid-flight. And to top it all off, the missile had to be simple enough in design that it could be produced in sufficient quantities at a reasonable cost.

Partly because it seemed too dangerous to store substantial quantities of incendiary liquid rocket fuel aboard a ship at sea, the APL report recommended the development of an air-breathing ramjet missile that could use standard hydrocarbon fuels. "The idea was just so basically simple," said Goss. Indeed, deceptively simple. But no one had ever actually built a working supersonic ramjet engine, although the feasibility of such a device had been studied for decades. Up to that time, the two leading proponents of ramjet technology had been the Hungarian engineer Albert Fous and a French engineer named René Lorin, who published his ground-breaking theoretical studies in 1913.

Someone once likened the basic concept behind ramjet propulsion to the way a squid propels itself through the water. As conceived by the APL Task F team, the ramjet engine resembled a pipe with an opening, or inlet, in its nose through which air would pass (hence the nickname "flying stovepipe"). When the engine reached supersonic speed, the air—compressed by the speed of the jet—would be slowed by a diffuser and mixed with an injected kerosene-based fuel (with the flow regulated by valves to assure the proper fuel-to-air ratio). The mixture would then burn in the cylindrical combustion chamber and the hot gas

23

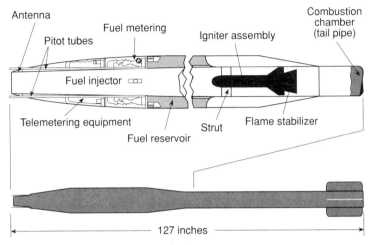

Cobra, an early ramjet test vehicle.

would discharge at the aft end, propelling the missile forward. The speed of the ramjet would be determined by the difference between the internal thrust and the external drag from the surrounding air.

One advantage of a ramjet engine is that it has no moving parts except the valves that regulate the fuel and air mixture. Furthermore, the use of air to supply the oxygen for combustion of the fuel means that the ramjet engine is burdened with only one-fifth the fuel weight of rockets powered by liquid propellants, which need to carry both fuel and oxidizers. A major drawback, and one of the reasons why ramjets had not been used in missiles before 1945, was that a ramjet engine cannot begin to operate under its own power until it has been boosted to nearly the speed of sound, and in those days developing a booster to provide such acceleration was virtually as difficult a task as building the ramjet itself.

This, then, was the challenge upon which the Applied Physics Laboratory's Task F team embarked in January 1945. At Merle Tuve's suggestion the project was code-named "Bumblebee," after a quotation Tuve had spied on

24

the office wall of an OSRD staff officer: "The bumblebee cannot fly. According to recognized aerotechnical tests, the bumblebee cannot fly because of the shape and weight of his body in relation to the total wing area. But, the bumblebee doesn't know this, so he goes ahead and flies anyway." It seemed an apt aphorism to characterize the task that APL was undertaking.

To manage the Bumblebee project, the Navy and Johns Hopkins adopted the same administrative structure that had governed the VT fuze effort. After BuOrd formulated the basic operational requirements, it assigned broad task statements to APL along with the responsibility for designing a technical program to meet the task objectives. As prime contractor with the Navy, the University assumed responsibility for the operation of APL and overall direction of the project as well as the coordination and technical supervision of the associate contractors who were brought into the project by BuOrd at the recommendation of APL. For Tuve, such an arrangement with a central outside Laboratory was essential for the Navy; as Lawrence Hafstad later recalled, Tuve liked to compare the Navy to "a big powerful machine that lacked a high speed output spindle, to give it flexibility."[2] And that was precisely what APL provided.

Since neither the Navy nor Johns Hopkins possessed a site that was both large enough and isolated enough for secret ramjet testing in the winter and spring of 1945, the APL Bumblebee team of more than three hundred men and women (led by Richard Roberts, Wilbur Goss, and Kirk Dahlstrom), commandeered a deserted stretch of beach on the New Jersey coastline at Island Beach, not far from Asbury Park. Soon an extended exercise in technical improvisation commenced. The APL crew constructed two primitive thirty-foot-long launchers out of wooden beams, wangled a standard radar system from the Signal Corps, turned an abandoned Coast Guard station into their field test headquarters, and cobbled together makeshift observation shacks so they could watch the firings from behind

25

the dunes. Their first experimental ramjet vehicles were nothing more than modified six-inch Thunderbolt airplane exhaust tail pipes with circular, cookie-cutter-type inlets, boosted by a bundle of artillery rockets that had been strapped together. (There was nothing magic about the six-inch size; it just happened to be the only size pipe available at that time.)

Given the relatively primitive state of the world's knowledge of aerodynamics in 1945, the Task F team had little choice but to proceed empirically, gradually gaining a greater understanding of the properties of propulsion and flight and sometimes demonstrating that so-called theoretical certainties were totally at odds with reality. Still operating under the pressures of wartime—originally the Bumblebee team hoped to have a viable weapon before the end of the war—the APL field test team often threw caution (and safety) quite literally to the wind.

"We couldn't be too safety conscious," recalled Max Schreiber, one of the engineers at Island Beach. "When the

"Flying stovepipe" spurts away from the Island Beach launcher. Fashioned from the exhaust pipe of a Thunderbolt fighter plane, this six-inch-diameter power plant attained a supersonic speed of twelve hundred miles per hour on June 13, 1945.

booster fin assemblies wouldn't go on the booster, we simply drove them on with a sledge hammer. We were working in a barn and kept the front doors open, facing the ocean. When somebody asked us if it wasn't dangerous to use the sledge, we'd just say . . . 'Oh no, if anything happens, it all just blows out the front door!'"[3] By the end of April, Goss and his colleagues had managed to maintain a sustained thrust in one of their ramjet test vehicles for the first time, thereby obtaining the first practical confirmation of René Lorin's theories.

Then, on June 13, an APL ramjet made its first successful flight. Soaring off the launching rack in a swirling cloud of sand and dust that could be seen three miles away, the high-powered engine (fueled by propylene oxide, a modified type of jet engine fuel supplied by Esso Research and Engineering Laboratory) sped past observers at a speed of 1,750 feet per second, traveling ten thousand yards down the beach before it finally descended with a satisfying splash into Barnegat Bay. The initial blast of the launch was so powerful that it completely demolished a protective wall of wood and sandbags that had been set up behind the ramp. "All of us who watched the firing knew what we had seen could be done again, on a larger scale," confirmed Goss. "We knew that these things would follow if we could maintain a steady progress in the understanding that comes from supporting research."[4]

Such progress was by no means assured, however, at least not under the existing affiliation with Johns Hopkins. As the war in Europe ended in April 1945 and the initial phase of the University's contract with the Bureau of Ordnance also came to a close, considerable sentiment was voiced in the University community in favor of terminating the association with the Navy. Some trustees, citing the backlash against military research in the years immediately after World War I, questioned the propriety of Johns Hopkins maintaining substantial activity in this area during peacetime. Further, they remained skeptical about the

27

prudence of operating an organization (APL) that was larger than the rest of the University—by now the Laboratory was nearing twelve hundred employees—and that was wholly dependent on continued funding by the Navy.

To assuage the trustees' concerns, Tuve proposed splitting APL into two separate parts, which he dubbed the "steer it" and "do it" groups. According to Tuve's scheme, the "do it" section would consist primarily of the associate contractors such as Bendix Corporation, Consolidated Vultee Aircraft Corporation (later Convair and currently part of General Dynamics), Curtis-Wright, and Esso Research and Engineering, which were all assisting the Section T effort. The scientific personnel at APL would form the "steer it" section. To integrate this latter group more closely into the life of the University, Tuve suggested that they spend one-third of their time on the management of APL affairs, one-third on teaching at Johns Hopkins, and one-third on their own scientific research. According to Tuve's notes of May 23, 1945, he assumed that this APL "steering" group would shrink rapidly to approximately two hundred people in the first months of peacetime.

This proposal ultimately foundered on the Navy's pressure for rapid development of a guided missile—it proved impossible to quickly reduce the technical and support staff without severely hindering progress—and on the recognition that the steering group could not fulfill its function unless it remained intimately involved with the detailed technical aspects of development. (The latter sentiment was summed up in the pithy Tuvian adage, "Only dirty hands can intelligently direct.") Nevertheless, Tuve's proposal stimulated the search for an alternative arrangement whereby the Laboratory could continue to operate with a considerably reduced commitment by the University. As the trustees explored their options, they consented to reaffirm the University's responsibility for the Applied Physics Laboratory under the existing arrangement through June 1946.

Early Ramjet Experiments

While the issue of the University's operation of APL hung fire, the scope of the Bumblebee program continued to expand. In July 1945, the Laboratory opened its own burner-test facility for supersonic ramjet engines in a remodeled radio-electronics school on a seven-acre tract at Forest Grove, Maryland, just two miles north of the APL headquarters building at 8621 Georgia Avenue. Originally equipped with three five-thousand-pound-per-square-inch air compressors imported from California, where they had been used in the construction of Shasta Dam, the Forest Grove Station got off to an inauspicious start when the flames from the first experiments set the maintenance shed on fire. After the shed was replaced by three more-substantial cinder block cubicles backed with steel-ribbed concrete walls, the tests—simulating flying velocities almost twice the speed of sound—still made so much racket that the owners of chicken hatcheries miles away complained to local authorities about the noise and vibrations.

After November, the Laboratory was also able to conduct experiments at the Navy's first modern supersonic wind tunnel station and large-scale burner lab at a twenty-five-acre site in Daingerfield, Texas. Designed by APL, the wind tunnel was constructed under the technical supervision of Laboratory personnel in a converted factory and blast furnace purchased from the Lone Star Steel Company. Operated under Navy contract by Consolidated Vultee Aircraft, the Ordnance Aerophysics Laboratory (OAL) proved an invaluable aid to APL's ramjet and aerodynamics research. Although other, smaller wind tunnel operations were also established at the University of Virginia and the Standard Oil Development Company, the Daingerfield facility remained the nation's largest and most advanced supersonic wind tunnel and propulsion test facility of its day. From the outside it looked like a series of huge connected pipes, though the test section itself measured

29

only nineteen inches by twenty-seven and one-half inches. For APL's researchers it provided excellent flow patterns with a novel type of balance system and state-of-the-art optical techniques, which allowed the study of aerodynamic principles at speeds as high as two thousand miles per hour at sea level.

In the early days, the APL and contractor personnel at OAL tested captured German buzz bombs to learn how to calculate jet engine thrust and drag precisely. Once those preliminaries were out of the way, OAL began experiments that simulated flight conditions in a laboratory environment so that researchers would be able to predict how a real missile in flight would react. First, tests were run on all the different parts of the engine, including the air inlet and combustor. Then the parts were assembled and huge quantities of air were heated and directed past the entire ramjet engine at the proper air speeds to observe the engine's performance. Finally, the resulting data were analyzed and compared with measurements made in actual test flights; then the entire process was repeated under a slightly different set of experimental conditions. According to Alvin R. Eaton, one of the nation's first supersonic aerodynamics experts, who joined APL in 1946 after completing his graduate studies at the California Institute of Technology, "We also used some early digital computer techniques, so that about sixteen seconds or so after a run, we had an initial printout of the forces and moments. There were still some subsequent corrections to be made, but it was the first capability to allow a test conductor to look at the results of one run while planning the next one. That was the idea, and that was unique."

Out at Island Beach, meanwhile, the Bumblebee ramjet tests continued at an urgent pace. To speed their progress, the Task F group split into a number of smaller task forces, each with responsibility for a different facet of missile research, including propulsion (trying out various types of fuel and different fuel-to-air ratios, for instance), controls, warheads, aerodynamics, and guidance, although guidance was clearly afforded a lower priority at that stage. Every week, each team would prepare at least one test vehicle at APL's facilities in Silver Spring; then on Monday night the crews drove up to New Jersey, carrying the test vehicles in trucks or vans for a launch on Tuesday.

Because the test vehicles often ended up in the Atlantic Ocean, each group also performed its own telemetry work to record experimental data. This work involved the transmission of information from measuring, or telemetering, instruments using frequency modulation (FM) transmitters (modified VT fuzes) located in the nose cones of the test vehicles to recording devices not unlike those employed by radio broadcasters. Simultaneously, the speed of the vehicles was measured by a series of radars while their flight was captured on film by motion picture cameras running at sixty frames per second so that the telemetry data could later be synchronized with the speed and position of the test vehicle at any particular moment.

Goss, Dahlstrom, and the rest of the senior Bumblebee scientific staff then reviewed the test results to determine how to improve the performance of the next series of experimental vehicles. According to Alvin Schulz, who joined the APL Bumblebee team in July 1945, "Usually they'd try within the next two or three days to decide what the next experiment was going to be, what they were going to change. Then they would pass the word to us as to what they wanted to measure, and we would prepare both sensing instruments and electronic telemetering to do that." But not without a few glitches along the way. "At the same time we started preparing instrumentation," added Schulz, "they would start changing their minds, which was natural for people in their position who were always coming up with new ideas."

At the start, the telemetry aspect of the flight test program provided just as much opportunity for creative improvisation as the other phases of ramjet research.

Samuel Foner, a veteran of the wartime Manhattan Project that had produced the world's first atomic bombs, joined APL in the summer of 1945 and was immediately dispatched to Island Beach as a member of the telemetry team. On his first visit to the test site, Foner found his colleagues attaching a pair of fins to a missile; but their efforts had thrown the rocket out of balance, so they had hung it from wires to restore its equilibrium and make it aerodynamically stable. As Foner approached, one of the scientists noticed that he was carrying his official APL-assigned tool kit containing screwdriver, pliers, soldering iron, and a small vise. "These guys came over," recalled Foner, "and said, 'Let's borrow that vise.' So they took it and put it in the right place [in the missile] and clamped it down, and by golly, the thing balanced. So they slipped the nose cone on it, and the next thing I know, it's shot out in the Atlantic Ocean. First tool I lost at APL."

Several months later, on October 19, 1945, Goss and his colleagues accomplished their most significant success to date, when a ramjet vehicle first accelerated to supersonic speed in free flight. The six-inch-diameter missile zoomed across the beach and out to sea at more than one and one-half times the speed of sound, developing approximately thirteen hundred horsepower in flight and traveling nearly ten miles within two minutes before landing in Barnegat Bay with an ear-splitting roar that reportedly scared a crew of visiting Norwegian fishermen nearly out of their wits. Back at the launchers, no one knew for several minutes that the missile had achieved the critical speed; but even after they received the good news, there was no great celebration, just more preparations for the next launch. "We hit the highs and the lows day by day, as things succeeded or failed," Goss observed later, "and this was just another step in the process."

APL, JHU, and the Navy—Postwar

Clearly the long days and nights at Island Beach, Forest Grove, Daingerfield, and the APL headquarters on Georgia Avenue did not reflect the mind-set of an organization that was planning to close its doors anytime in the immediate future. Although Merle Tuve had assumed that the Applied Physics Laboratory would reduce its role and size significantly once the war ended, events in the weeks following the formal Japanese surrender on September 2 were rapidly rendering his assumptions obsolete. In a memorandum to Tuve dated September 7, 1945, the Laboratory's assistant director, Lawrence Hafstad, made an eloquent case for continuing the Laboratory's work for the Navy. Drawing on his own wartime experiences and his view of the world in the immediate postwar period, Hafstad informed Tuve that he was firmly convinced that "the only field for real contributions to Society is in preventing war. . . .Peace will most likely be assured if both parties maintain military establishments which make it inconvenient and therefore unprofitable for the other to invade, but which are not large enough for either side to impose its will on the other."[5]

And for Hafstad, organizations such as the Applied Physics Laboratory had a vital role to play in the maintenance of the U.S. military establishment. The prevailing attitudes in the Army and Navy, he claimed, indicated that the "APL mechanism has proved uniquely responsive to military needs (and responsible in meeting these needs) and can in the future be of service in meeting special needs more aggressively and more adequately than either civil service or production organizations which have special limitations."[6] More specifically, Hafstad urged that APL continue the same sort of relationship with the military that

Tuve had established in wartime. "The announced Section T policy of taking needs only (not gadgets) from the military, proposing alternative solutions and accepting military choice among the alternatives is still sound," Hafstad concluded, though he urged that APL abandon as rapidly as possible its total dependence on BuOrd as a sole source of funding and assume "independent contracts with the army and the air force, etc. to spread risks."[7]

Given the military establishment's apparent commitment to increasing its funding of research and development in the immediate future, the dearth of contractors willing or (more to the point) able to fill APL's role, and the APL staff's combination of "know-how and a burning desire to do the work," Hafstad obviously believed it would be folly to simply shut down or severely restrict the work of the Laboratory. Hafstad pointed out, however, that the prevailing uncertainty about APL's future already had led some staff members to seek employment elsewhere, and he warned that unless some definitive decision were made very shortly, a further drain inevitably would occur.

Similar sentiments were voiced by a group of eight senior APL scientists, including Wilbur Goss, James Van Allen, and Walter Good, who called themselves the Young Turks Committee. In their own memorandum to Tuve, also dated September 7, this ad hoc group firmly advocated a policy of internationalism and the peaceful settlement of world disputes: "Military supremacy can be completely justified," they wrote, "only if the nation possessing it uses its leadership to bring about a regime in which this supremacy is no longer important."[8] On the other hand, the Young Turks also predicted that the Soviet Union was likely to obtain a nuclear weapons potential within five or, at most, ten years, and that in subsequent military crises—before the establishment of an effective international political organization—there would be no time for new weapons development.

34

Consequently, Goss, Van Allen, Good, and their colleagues recommended that the Section T team remain in existence as a nonprofit, privately endowed military research institute dedicated to "the discovery of basically new weapons" in close cooperation with the Joint Chiefs of Staff and the Department of Defense Research and Development Board. Clearly the Young Turks wished to emphasize the "discovery" aspect of weapons development; as they explained to Tuve, "It is the opinion of this committee that the Section T team is at its best in military research of the sort typified by Bumblebee and the early work on VT. We are at our worse [sic] in the introduction of new weapons to the Service and in the endless quibbling involved in mass production control."

Like Hafstad, the Young Turks Committee also recommended that the Laboratory expand its sphere of potential sponsors beyond BuOrd. "The present affiliation with the Bureau of Ordnance, though adequate for the present Bumblebee development, is acceptable only as an interim measure," they argued. "The Bureau of Ordnance horizon is too confined, its part in the next war too restricted to support the type of basic military research required."

For its part, the Navy clearly desired to continue its relationship with the Applied Physics Laboratory in some form. On October 18, Secretary James Forrestal urged Johns Hopkins president Isaiah Bowman to accept the Navy's offer to extend contract NOrd-7386 for another year (through June 30, 1947), to "enable certain research activities of the Applied Physics Laboratory of The Johns Hopkins University and its group of associated contractors to be carried forward effectively during a critical period of transition from war to peace." In Forrestal's opinion, "These activities are of the utmost importance to the security of the nation, and this extention [sic] will afford an opportunity for those individuals who have the necessary technical background and experience to extend and consolidate the highly significant results already attained, and will allow time for adjusting the entire program into a peace-time framework." Forrestal's rationale for requesting the continued help of APL is of vital importance for understanding the later development of the Laboratory:

> As you know [continued Forrestal], through the operation of the NOrd type contracts at the Applied Physics Laboratory and at the various association "Section T" contractors, a mechanism has been provided whereby technical direction of work in broad areas of scientific research and in the related applied fields, by groups outside of the Navy establishments, can be carried on under the guidance of interested and qualified technical men who are associated with, but not directly a part of, the Navy. Technical work related to national defense carried on by outside organizations is clearly necessary as a supplement to activities within the Navy, but no definite mechanism providing for a suitable continuation of this relationship during peace-time has as yet been created by the Navy Department or any other Governmental Agency. Until such a mechanism can be established, it is extremely important that there be no interruption, not only of the Bumblebee and VT fuze projects, but of the relationship which has been so effective during the war period.[9]

Less than two weeks later, Bowman informed Forrestal that the Johns Hopkins Board of Trustees had authorized him to extend the University's contract with the Navy for an additional year. At the same time, Bowman insisted that the contract specifically enable Johns Hopkins to guarantee employment for a number of key personnel (who were still formally on leave from their previous academic or industrial employers) for definite periods of time. Bowman also reminded Forrestal that APL would require funds for additional space and facilities to carry out its responsibilities successfully. In reply to this not particularly subtle request for financial assistance, Forrestal blandly assured Bowman, "It is certainly to be hoped that you will be successful in finding the necessary funds for this purpose."

As the structure of the peacetime relationship between the Applied Physics Laboratory and the Navy gradually began to take shape, APL took another giant step into the future by obtaining the services of four extraordinary scientists, all of whom would play critical roles in the future life of the Laboratory. In the spring and summer of 1945, a team of rocket propulsion experts from the Allegany Ballistics Laboratory—known during wartime as the Section H group of Division A—visited APL to lend their expertise (and their rockets) to the Bumblebee project. Two of those consultants were Ralph Gibson, the British-born vice-chairman and deputy chief of Section H and the wartime director of research at the Allegany Ballistics Laboratory, and Alexander Kossiakoff, his assistant director of research. After observing the relatively crude, unsophisticated rockets the Bumblebee team was working with at Island Beach, Kossiakoff and Gibson realized that the Applied Physics Laboratory would need more than short-term help in the field of rocketry.

Although Gibson, Kossiakoff, and their colleagues had intended to return to their prewar teaching jobs in the academic world (Kossiakoff was on leave from the Catholic University of America; Gibson was on the faculty of the Carnegie Institution), they decided to make a slight change in their plans once they became acquainted with life at APL. "The experience in wartime was really pretty exhilarating in terms of what you could do, if only you have the resources and the organization," noted Kossiakoff. "We had been pretty well touched by the excitement of development, as opposed to scientific research."

Besides, added Kossiakoff, the vibrant atmosphere that infused the Applied Physics Laboratory seemed quite remarkable: "Tuve had created an organization supported

37

by D. Luke Hopkins, who was then the business manager of the place. It was a total team effort. They had somehow created a situation where all the administrative people essentially worked to support the technical program. . . . They got it done. The other thing we noticed was that there was a spirit of urgency. These people didn't know the war was over." And, in contrast to Allegany's more traditional and formal relationship with the Army, "the Navy treated APL at the time as a member of the government-contractor-APL team. The whole question was, 'How do you get the job done?'"

So APL hired Gibson, Kossiakoff, and two of their Allegany colleagues, Frank T. McClure and Richard B. Kershner, as a sort of package deal, though Kossiakoff has said, "I don't think any of us thought of it as a long-term association." Shortly thereafter, Gibson became APL's director of contracts, technical supervisor of Task F, and head of what was known internally as the Blue team, an informal association of APL personnel and contractors engaged in the more basic, theoretical aspects of super-sonic guided-missile research. Gibson's counterparts as leaders of the Red team, the APL-contractor coalition that was oriented toward the experimental development of technology, were Richard Roberts and Wilbur Goss. By dividing its efforts in this fashion, the Laboratory kept the lines of long-term research moving steadily forward without sacrificing the short-term results that the Navy required.

Bumblebee Test Vehicles

At approximately the same time, APL established a series of technical panels for the Bumblebee project, consisting of specialized experts from the Laboratory and associate industrial and university contractors, each dealing with a major aspect of missile development: propulsion, guidance, aerodynamics, launching, or composite design. Meeting once every two or three months, these panels helped ensure a smooth and continuous flow of information, created the same sort of team atmosphere that had characterized the wartime VT fuze effort, and provided a regular channel for technical advice from experts in industry and the academic community.

By the autumn of 1945, each Bumblebee task group was also developing its own experimental test vehicle. There were burner test vehicles (BTVs) designed for fuel and combustion research experiments, supersonic test vehicles (STVs) for controls experiments, and "flying stovepipes" and (later) Cobras for the ramjet model tests. Even at this early stage, each APL group was also working with an industrial partner; Douglas Aircraft (later McDonnell-Douglas), for instance, built the ramjet airframes, while Consolidated Vultee Aircraft fashioned the STVs. Although the research program may have appeared to be danger-ously dispersing its resources by going off in several different directions at once, APL's Bumblebee team always intended that all these separate vehicles would eventually come together in a prototype ramjet missile.

On November 21, 1945, the first STV, a 360-pound missile, was launched at Island Beach. Intended to serve as an interim vehicle for studying such factors as acceleration, temperature, and pressure while a reliable ramjet was being developed, the original STV carried three separate jet motors designed by the Allegany Ballistics Laboratory, two for launching and one for sustaining flight. The purpose of the initial series of tests was merely to check the proper performance of the launching assembly, but before the missile could be fired, a series of intricate adjustments had to be made to the launcher, each one requiring a corre-sponding adjustment on other parts of the vehicle. One participant's account of these last-minute changes provides a firsthand glimpse into the high degree of Rube Goldberg-type improvisation that still characterized the world of guided missiles in late 1945:

I spent most of Tuesday setting up T10E1's [the rocket motors] and attaching them to the pressure heads of the launcher. There were available some very temporary wood blocks to fit into these pressure heads and in addition I cemented extra cork onto the front and cork spacers of the ACL-1 charge. To do this it was necessary to remove the closures which were on the T10E1's.

It was then necessary to screw these two T10E1's onto the pressure heads of the launcher. Fortunately the threads fit well. It was relatively easy to screw the first head and motor together . . . however, the assembly of the second one was more complicated. It was necessary to invert the launcher with its one motor, to put wedges between the cork strips of the charge and T10E1 motor so that when the motor was inverted and screwed on to the launcher the charge would not fall out, and finally to screw the motor onto the head. This was eventually accomplished.[10]

Alas, all to little avail. Upon ignition late that afternoon, the missile left the ramp and immediately proceeded on a downward trajectory, dove behind a sand dune, hit the beach, and burst. The sustainer rocket broke away from the assembly and spun through the air like a corkscrew, scattering the surprised test crew to seek shelter wherever they could find it.

Not an auspicious beginning, perhaps, but the situation was far from bleak. According to Kossiakoff, who was also present at the test as an observer from the Allegany Ballistics Laboratory, the rocket and the launcher both appeared to be well designed; the problem lay mainly in the cradle that attached the rockets to the missile. Indeed, Kossiakoff later declared he was quite impressed with the richness of concrete flight performance data obtained from the APL-designed telemetry equipment during even such short flights as this. By using information gathered on the twenty separate telemetry channels, one could determine exactly what had happened and take steps to correct any deficiencies. And it was no surprise, given the still rudimentary state of aerodynamics and combustion research, that there were additional deficiencies aplenty; the tail pipes of the test vehicles kept melting, for instance, thereby increasing drag and preventing the vehicles from attaining the required acceleration. But during the next few months, the Bumblebee team continued to break new ground as it launched and recorded data from a host of experimental STVs and Cobras from new and more extensive test facilities at Fort Miles, New Jersey, and Camp Davis, North Carolina.

Once the missiles were launched, they would eventually require some sort of guidance system to lead them to their targets; otherwise, they were practically worthless, little more than a particularly expensive form of self-destructive ammunition. In a speech to members of the Institute of Aeronautical Sciences, Gibson graphically illustrated the guidance problem facing the Bumblebee team. "Consider," Gibson suggested, "a bomber flying at 600 miles per hour or 800 feet per second being attacked by [conventional] gun fire in which the average time of flight of the shell is 15 seconds. . . .Between the time the shell leaves the gun and arrives at the predicted point of aim the bomber travels 2-1/2 miles. In order to reach the point of aim the bomber must fly with an accuracy of one part in 10,000, or, in other words, if he is careless and his course deviates by as little as half a degree, he will miss the shell by 106 feet."[11]

There were three basic methods of automatic control for the APL Bumblebee team to consider. The first was a command guidance system, whereby ground radar stations tracked both the target and the missile and then computed the course adjustments required to bring the missile into contact with its quarry. Because almost all the directional computations were done on the ground, missiles using this system needed only sufficient intelligence to receive and obey commands. The drawback—and it was a significant one—was that a separate radar would be required to guide each missile, in addition to the radar tracking each target.

The second option was a radar-based, *beam-riding* guidance system. In this procedure, the radar initially picked up the target and determined the direction in which the missile should be launched. The radar also generated two guidance beams—one a wide *capture* beam that enabled the missile to find the right beam direction, and the other a narrow *guidance* beam that led the missile to its target. The missile guidance signals were picked up by a radio receiver in the missile's tail section and then translated into control commands to adjust the vehicle's course. Although a beam-riding system required missiles to possess a more sophisticated "intellect," it greatly simplified the work of the ground station.

The third and most technologically challenging method of automatic control employed a homing guidance system, using an antenna in the nose of the missile to receive a reflected radar signal directly from its target and, in Gibson's words, "recognize its quarry and go after it." In 1945 this type of control appeared to carry with it definite range restrictions, and it appeared to be useful only in the terminal phases of the missile's course; optimally, it could be combined with a beam-riding system to provide both initial and mid-course guidance.

By the end of 1945, APL scientists were concentrating on the second option, developing a beam-riding system that could at least serve as an interim step while they continued to work on an effective homing mechanism. Like the other parts of the Bumblebee program, the beam-riding research would provide the Laboratory with essential data that would fuel further improvements for the next several years.

Merle Tuve, though, would not be present to witness those developments. On February 15, 1946, Tuve resigned

42

as director of the Applied Physics Laboratory to return to the Carnegie Institution as director of the Department of Terrestrial Magnetism. His replacement at APL was his longtime associate, Lawrence Hafstad. Clearly Tuve had never been comfortable as the leader of a large scientific organization performing defense-related research in peacetime; once he returned to DTM in 1946, he presided over a staff of only fifteen professionals who were studying the structure of the earth's interior.

Rockets for High-Altitude Research

Before Tuve left, however, he helped establish a very special, albeit temporary, APL research program that, given his lifelong interest in geophysics, was probably much dearer to his heart than the Bumblebee project. In the closing months of World War II, the U.S. Army had captured two hundred carloads of partially assembled Vergeltungswaffe-2 (V-2) rocket parts—enough for eighty motors—from the German rocket research center at Peenemunde. After Army Ordnance and General Electric engineers managed to put together twenty-five complete rockets, the Army (which was primarily interested, of course, in the military applications of the missiles) offered several leading research universities, including Johns Hopkins, the opportunity to place scientific instruments in the empty warheads of the rockets to obtain measurements from the earth's upper atmosphere.

Tuve readily accepted the Army's offer, especially since several of his staff members already were vitally interested in high-altitude research. One of those was James Van Allen, who, like Tuve, was on leave from the Carnegie Institution; Van Allen, of course, had been one of the APL scientists drafted into the Navy to instruct the Pacific Fleet on the VT fuze. On April 16, the first V-2 in the Army's program was launched from White Sands Proving Ground in Las Cruces, New Mexico. The rocket, far larger and more

43

powerful than anything American scientists had yet developed, was an awesome sight, standing forty-seven feet high. Powered by twenty-eight tons of thrust, the V-2 could accelerate to a speed of five thousand feet per second and reach an average altitude of 70 miles and a maximum altitude of 114 miles.

But the rocket, of course, could not remain for long in the upper reaches of the atmosphere. To obtain the data Van Allen wanted, the rocket had to rise more than twenty-two miles above the earth, and from the time it passed that level on the way up until it came hurtling back down, the measuring instruments (sensors, spectrometers, and Geiger-Mueller counters that "looked" out of small doors on either side of the nose cone) had only about five minutes to obtain their data. During that brief time, the signals emitted by the counters were simultaneously marked on slowly rotating steel cylinders within the nose and transmitted via radio waves to receiving stations on the ground (including a station on the roof of APL headquarters on Georgia Avenue). Since the missiles inevitably crashed when they returned to earth, the steel cylinders were constructed to withstand extreme conditions; one V-2 nose cone was lost in the desert for nearly two years before it was finally recovered and its data retrieved.

Van Allen and his team of APL physicists, including S. Fred Singer, Howard F. Tatel, and Robert P. Petersen, proved particularly adept at designing experiments to take advantage of the limited window of opportunity provided by the availability of the V-2s. On July 30, a rocket bearing APL instruments soared a hundred miles above the earth's surface, setting a high-altitude record and bringing back a wealth of information about the cosmic ray particles that constantly bombard the earth. According to Van Allen's findings, the secondary particles (known as mesons) formed by the collisions of cosmic protons with the earth's upper atmosphere were far more abundant than previously believed and were especially concentrated at a height of

44

one hundred thousand to two hundred thousand feet. Since the energies of these particles could range up to millions of times greater than those produced by nuclear fission, there was considerable public concern at the time over the possibility that they could somehow be harnessed to form a "cosmic ray bomb," but scientists quickly issued assurances that such a weapon was totally impracticable.

Although APL continued to enjoy access to selected V-2 launchings, the limited supply of these rockets persuaded Tuve to recommend that the Laboratory develop its own simpler, relatively inexpensive alternative. Such a project would also enable the Laboratory to obtain first-hand experience with liquid rockets as potential guided-missile boosters. Once again APL employed the familiar Section T contractual arrangement with the Navy and associate contractors whereby the Bureau of Ordnance funded the project, APL provided the design and technical supervision, and associate contractors—in this case, Aerojet Corporation, Douglas Aircraft (later McDonnell-Douglas), and the Jet Propulsion Laboratory of the California Institute of Technology—performed the actual engineering and production work. The result was the Aerobee rocket, a twenty-foot-long, 1,650-pound liquid-fueled missile, much smaller than the monstrous V-2, with no moving parts or guidance equipment and capable of soaring to a height of seventy-five miles at speeds of thirty-five hundred miles an hour, far higher and faster than the Army's Wac Corporal, the only other American rocket in existence at that time.

An Aerobee could carry as high as seventy miles into the atmosphere a payload of 150 pounds of equipment sealed in its eighty-eight-inch-long, pressure-tight nose cone. The first of these missiles was launched on November 24, 1947, but lasted only thirty-five seconds in flight. The flight of the second Aerobee on March 5, 1948, however, proved highly successful, providing valuable new data on the intensity and distribution of cosmic rays above the appreciable atmosphere.

Perhaps the most aesthetically significant APL high-altitude experiment occurred on July 26, 1948, when a V-2 rocket carrying APL photographic equipment took a sequence of high-quality aerial photos of the earth from a height of sixty miles. Although the experiment had been designed to demonstrate the potential for employing rockets for reconnaissance over inaccessible areas, there was a much more artistic by-product of the flight. Once the film had been recovered and developed—remarkably, not a single roll was lost from the impact of landing, because of the special protective aluminum casing surrounding the cameras—an APL team led by Clyde T. Holliday constructed a composite photograph that formed a dazzling panorama of four hundred thousand square miles, showing a view that stretched all the way from Nebraska to Mexico. It was the first view of earth ever taken from space, and there would not be another for more than a decade.

To provide a far more expansive testing range in a variety of latitudes for both the V-2 and the Aerobee, the Navy converted a seaplane tender, the USS *Norton Sound*, into a seagoing rocket laboratory in 1948 and dispatched the ship to the Pacific Ocean. A year earlier, the Navy had launched a V-2 rocket from the deck of the aircraft carrier *Midway* to prove that ships could fire such weapons. With its deck protected by a special metal sheath, the *Norton Sound* launched numerous APL rockets in 1948–49, obtaining through telemetry still more data on cosmic ray intensity and other atmospheric phenomena, including the dimensions of the ozone layer and the extent of solar radiation.

By January 1951, when the high-altitude program came to an end, APL had obtained data from thirty V-2 and Aerobee rockets launched from sites around the globe in all seasons of the year. The demise of the program coincided, not incidentally, with the departure of Van Allen from the Applied Physics Laboratory for an academic post at the University of Iowa, where he later completed the research that would earn him international recognition for the discovery of the radiation belts that surround the earth.

The Kellex "Partnership"

By this time, Merle Tuve had long since resigned from APL and the Laboratory had become associated with the Kellex Corporation, the industrial partner chosen by The Johns Hopkins University Board of Trustees to manage APL's administrative and engineering affairs, thereby diminishing the University's financial and management responsibilities. A subsidiary of the M. W. Kellogg Company, a petroleum engineering firm based in New York, the Kellex Corporation had been involved in one part of the Manhattan Project at Oak Ridge, Tennessee, during the war. Now, as the federal government sorted out its peacetime policies and responsibilities for nuclear weapons development, the directors of Kellogg were searching for some way to keep the Kellex technical staff together and profitably employed. The personal friendship of D. Luke Hopkins with Earnshaw Cook, a Kellogg executive, sealed the alliance between Kellex and the Applied Physics Laboratory.

On paper it seemed a rational and mutually beneficial arrangement. Much of the APL engineering and support staff was transferred to Kellex with assurances that the Laboratory would still be run as a single organization; the only change anyone would notice would be the Kellex name on the paychecks. The unique character of the Applied Physics Laboratory that had developed in the first five years of its life was not to be disturbed. As President Bowman assured Ralph Gibson, "The maintenance of APL/JHU as a branch of the University with a broad distribution of responsibility and freedom of operation is an important objective which must not be sacrificed by too great a spread of the administrative procedure characteristic of Industrial Organizations." Moreover, Bowman continued, "The main-

47

tenance of a scientific organization at a high level of competence and flexibility is regarded as a most important aspect of the JHU participation."[12]

In fact, the transition to the new order did not take place quite so smoothly. For one reason, Johns Hopkins and Kellex neglected to clearly define their respective areas of responsibility, an oversight that quickly and predictably raised a host of jurisdictional disputes with regard to technical direction of programs and accountability for materials, equipment, facilities, and personnel. Second, Kellex was indisputably an industrial organization with a traditional American corporate management style; that is, management treated its employees as employees and not as members of a cooperative team. Third and perhaps most significant, within a year many if not most of the APL senior technical staff had lost confidence in the motives of the Kellex Corporation—which admittedly intended to remain a profit-making concern—with regard to the future of the Laboratory.

One expression of the staff's concern may be found in an internal memorandum written by Gibson at the end of November 1947. At that time, Gibson was serving as acting director of APL in the absence of Lawrence Hafstad, who had been granted leave four months earlier to accept a temporary post as executive secretary of the Department of Defense Research and Development Board. After outlining a series of specific complaints against Kellex executives ("Repeated instances of Kellex employees obtaining the impression that Kellex was in charge of the Applied Physics Laboratory or at least soon would be," "A remark by Cook . . . that Kellex would be ready to take over direction in a few months," and so forth), Gibson concluded that "the mere fact that a serious lack of confidence exists makes the necessary cooperation impossible. As a matter of fact, the two-headed organization as it now exists, is intrinsically bad and inevitably tends to create friction and difficulty. In addition, it is not wholly satisfactory to the Navy."[13]

48

Clearly Gibson feared that Kellex could never fulfill the role of an independent, objective technical and scientific adviser in whom the Navy's Bureau of Ordnance could place its complete confidence. Hence, if Kellex should assume control of APL, the Laboratory's unique relationship with the Navy would soon falter or collapse altogether. Since Gibson was only acting director, however, he possessed limited authority to resolve these difficulties. With Hafstad preoccupied with his new assignment outside the Laboratory and D. Luke Hopkins having withdrawn to concentrate on other matters at the University, a temporary vacuum existed at the top levels of APL leadership.

Birth of the Research Center

At the working level, however, most of the APL-Kellex staff remained unaware of the mounting friction between Ralph Gibson and Earnshaw Cook, and the various research teams of the Bumblebee program continued to break new ground every day. By this time, most of the flight tests were being run either at Camp Davis, North Carolina, or the China Lake (California) Naval Ordnance Testing Station. Every now and then, life at a test site could get downright exciting. "There were occasions where some of the things which were intended to work didn't quite do exactly what they were supposed to do," explained Sam Foner. "For instance, we had some tests that were intended for straight flight, and all of a sudden the thing took a sharp turn, and somebody asked, 'Was it supposed to do that?' and we said, 'Heck, no.'

"We had another case," continued Foner, "where a subsonic test vehicle—wasn't ours, but it belonged to another outfit—the thing took off and was climbing up in the sky, and then someone said, 'I think it's coming down to the launching pad.'

"Now, the point is that when something is up there, maybe a couple thousand feet, and it's coming down,

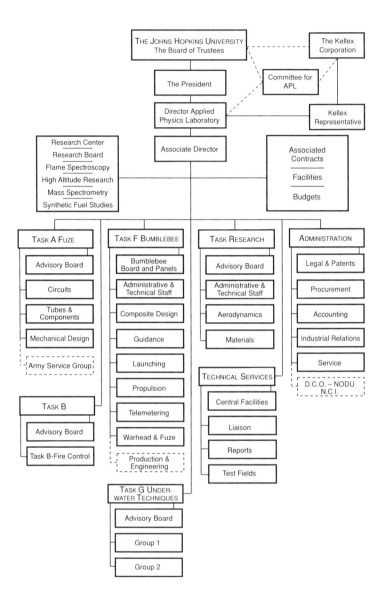

Organization chart for APL in 1947. The dual management structure proved to be unsatisfactory, and the relationship with Kellex was terminated on March 26, 1948. APL subsequently became a permanent division of The Johns Hopkins University.

50

where are you going to run? This thing has no mind of its own; in fact, it's sort of like a SCUD, you could have been as safe here as over there. You don't know what it's going to do. But accidents were surprisingly rare with these things."

Such incidents, of course, were nothing more than the inevitable concomitants of experimental research. Only those who lacked a true appreciation of the complexities involved in the Bumblebee program viewed the occasional failures as disappointments rather than as opportunities to learn something new about the forces acting on the surfaces of a test missile. Richard Ellis, an engineer who joined APL's telemetry group in 1946, recalled that Richard Kershner—then serving as leader of the Bumblebee controls group—liked to say, "If you have a success, you really haven't learned much, because you don't know anything more than you did before."

"If we had a failure," recalled Ellis, "we said, 'What's the thing we've got to learn that we didn't know?'" This unwaveringly positive attitude so infused the whole APL effort that it even affected some of the Navy personnel associated with the Bumblebee project. For instance, Admiral A. G. Noble, the newly appointed chief of the Bureau of Ordnance, visited the Inyokern Naval Ordnance Testing Station in October 1947 to witness the launch of an STV-2 (an advanced version of the original supersonic test vehicle), and while Noble confessed he was disappointed with the results of the test, he came away from the exercise with a deepened appreciation for the difficulties inherent in the undertaking. "I have had some opportunity to look over the A.P.L. and am greatly impressed," Noble wrote to Isaiah Bowman, "not only by the work which is being done there, but by the splendid attitude and morale of the technical people."[14]

As each round of aerodynamics and propulsion tests brought a working supersonic missile closer to reality, more of the Task F force shifted to work on guidance systems. (In fact, the Laboratory's Bumblebee leadership confidently reassigned some of its aerodynamics experts to other tasks, on the assumption—premature, as it turned out—that all the critical design problems had been solved.) In January 1947, APL engineers had already flown a subsonic test vehicle along a fixed radar beam for sixteen seconds. Later that year, two more test missiles flew along a slowly moving beam for nearly a minute, and in March 1948 several STV-2 vehicles rode a radar beam at supersonic speeds.

By 1948 the propulsion experiments with the initial test vehicles had proved sufficiently successful that research commenced on the more advanced burner test vehicles. Moreover, the Laboratory's telemetering systems had evolved from four-channel devices to a far more sophisticated, hundred-channel analog multiplex system. "Compared to now, it was pretty crude," noted Richard Ellis, "but for the time, it was a pretty sophisticated system. In a relatively short time, about a year, we had a very elaborate telemetering system going."

Certainly the Navy's commitment to the Bumblebee program never faltered. As Secretary Forrestal announced in his annual report for the 1946–47 fiscal year, so much "rapid progress in the field of guided missiles" had been made during the previous twelve months that the Navy now found it necessary to develop advanced ship designs to accommodate the new weapons. Moreover, in a statement directly relevant to the future of the Applied Physics Laboratory, Forrestal firmly supported the concept of Navy-sponsored "free research" not necessarily related to any specific weapon system. "Instead of being pointed toward direct solution of some practical problem," Forrestal declared, "its intention is to explore and understand more fully the laws of nature both animate and inanimate. From free research new and powerful ideas spring. These ideas in turn lead to applied research and finally to development."[15]

Forrestal's words struck a responsive chord at APL. For some time, members of the professional staff (particularly Gibson, Kossiakoff, and McClure) had been considering the formation of a special Laboratory division in which innovative research in the basic sciences—on tasks not necessarily directly related to the main programs of APL—could be carried out by members of the professional staff, free from any pressure to achieve immediate results. Such a division could also provide a pool of professional staff members who could be drafted by other parts of the Laboratory to help out in times of crisis. So, on April 1, 1947, the Research Center of the Applied Physics Laboratory was formally founded "to provide fundamental understanding in fields of present and potential importance to the Laboratory . . . to establish APL as a contributor to scientific knowledge, . . . [and] enhance the professional competence of the staff by serving as a doorway to science."[16]

Initially, the work of the Research Center was directed by a steering committee whose members included Gibson (chairman), Kossiakoff (executive secretary), McClure (who became the first director of the center in April 1948), Richard Kershner, Alvin Eaton, and James Van Allen, among others. It was under the Research Center's broad umbrella that Van Allen conducted most of his high-altitude investigations. Other early projects included experiments in flame spectroscopy, synthetic fuels, and mass spectrometry—specifically, the investigation of the intermediate chemical reactions that occurred in the flames that propelled APL's ramjets and rockets.

The establishment of the Research Center was just one aspect of the Laboratory's rapid growth in the immediate postwar years. The Bumblebee program was expanding with each passing month, and a team of APL researchers continued to work (albeit on a reduced scale) on improvements to the proximity fuze. As a result, the Laboratory found it necessary to search for additional office and research space. In February 1947, Johns Hopkins University purchased a 150-acre tract in Laurel, Maryland, with the intention of erecting a field station on the site; unfortunately, preliminary tests indicated that the soil conditions and poor drainage precluded any such construction, and so the search resumed for additional quarters in the Silver Spring area.

APL—A Permanent Part of Johns Hopkins

Meanwhile, the mounting tension between Kellex and the professional staff of APL came to a climax in early 1948, when Ralph Gibson was offered a position as director of the Atomic Energy Commission's prestigious Oak Ridge, Tennessee, nuclear research laboratories. The Applied Physics Laboratory had recently considered an overture from Oak Ridge to work on a nuclear-powered missile flight program; after lengthy discussions, the combination of APL's manpower and space limitations plus the prevailing uncertainty over the federal government's policies toward nuclear power had convinced Hafstad and Gibson to reject the proposal.

But the prospect of losing Gibson (along with a number of disaffected key technical staff) forced President Bowman to confront the APL-Kellex issue directly. After failing to obtain satisfactory assurances about the future course of the Laboratory from the top executives of Kellex Corporation, Bowman—with the reluctant concurrence of Luke Hopkins—decided to terminate the University's dual-management relationship with Kellex. Although Bowman seldom needed help from anyone to make up his mind, his decision was made easier by the fact that a number of the University trustees who had doubted the wisdom of the 1945 decision to continue supporting the work of the Applied Physics Laboratory had now changed their minds and welcomed the opportunity to serve the national interest through APL.

54

Doubtless this shift in sentiment occurred primarily because of the steadily worsening relations between the Soviet Union and the United States. By the early spring of 1948, it was clear that both the Truman administration and the American public supported an expanded national defense budget to keep the nation prepared in case the cold war erupted into open conflict. "If there is another war," declared Lawrence Hafstad in one of his last public statements as director of APL, "all indications show that it will be shorter, more violent, and 'much faster breaking' than those of the past. Only that nation can survive which is adequately prepared for just that kind of war. Next time the gadgets must be ready when the shooting starts."[17]

Bowman readily agreed. On March 26, 1948, the partnership between The Johns Hopkins University and the Kellex Corporation was officially dissolved. Although some consideration was given to the idea of turning APL into a separate corporation associated more loosely with the University, Bowman and the Board of Trustees elected to make the Applied Physics Laboratory a permanent, regular division of the University, thereby creating a unique relationship between these two organizations that had— and still has—no counterpart in any other major university research center in the nation.

To govern and review APL's activities, many of which involved highly sensitive national security matters, the University's Board of Trustees formed a special standing committee—the Trustees Committee on the Applied Physics Laboratory—consisting of about a dozen trustees along with the chairman of the full board and the president of the University as ex officio members. At least twice a year this committee would meet with the leadership of the Laboratory, usually with high-ranking Navy officials present as well, to receive progress reports and consider prospective new tasks.

Along with the Trustees Committee, Bowman also wished to establish an advisory board to provide him with guidance on matters concerning APL, much as similar bodies did for other divisions within the University. Hence the APL Advisory Board was formed in April 1948, with the Laboratory's director, associate director, and assistant directors serving as permanent members and another half-dozen members elected by the senior staff serving for specified terms. For consistency with other divisions of the University, these elected members had to be chosen from the more senior members of the APL senior staff—equivalent to the senior faculty elsewhere in the University—and so the Laboratory's Principal Professional Staff was formally established to identify those eligible for election to the Advisory Board. Just as candidates for tenured faculty were nominated by their departments and appointed by the president of the University, so candidates for APL Principal Professional Staff were—and still are—nominated by the director and appointed by the president on the recommendation of the Advisory Board.

Four months after APL officially became a full division of the University, the U. S. Army announced that it had signed a contract with Johns Hopkins for the establishment of an operations research group on the University's Homewood campus in Baltimore to study tactics and supply problems and to evaluate the comparative cost of various methods of waging war. The Navy, though caught in an interservice competition with the Army and Air Force for budget dollars, also renewed and expanded its previous contract with the Applied Physics Laboratory. And with no time to spare, for the outbreak of the Korean conflict lay just over the horizon.

CHAPTER THREE

THE FIRST MISSILES

The easiest thing in the world is to think up something for somebody else to do. What you really need are people with ideas who push them and pester you with them.

————*Ralph E. Gibson*

Early in April 1948, several weeks after The Johns Hopkins University reassumed full responsibility for the Applied Physics Laboratory, Lawrence Hafstad resigned as director of APL to devote his full attention to his position as executive secretary of the Department of Defense Research and Development Board. Using the power vested in him by the JHU charter, Isaiah Bowman wisely decided on April 12 to appoint Ralph Gibson, who already had been serving as acting director for nearly a year, to the directorship.

For the next twenty-one years, Gibson led the Applied Physics Laboratory through an era of great turmoil and immense change in both the international environment and the U.S. defense structure. More than any other individual, Gibson shaped the character of the Applied Physics Laboratory during these years, imparting to the organization his own philosophy about the appropriate role and responsibilities of a university-affiliated defense research establishment.

57

Born in 1901, Gibson was raised on the island of Islay, off the coast of western Scotland, and educated in Edinburgh, where he received a graduate degree in chemistry from the University of Edinburgh in 1924. He arrived in the United States a month later and spent the next sixteen years conducting experimental research at the Carnegie Institution of Washington and teaching part-time at George Washington University. It was from the director of Carnegie's Geophysical Laboratory, Arthur L. Day, that Gibson learned his most valuable lessons about the administration of a top-flight research laboratory. "The laboratory wasn't very large," Gibson observed several decades later, "but it became world famous during his [Day's] regime in a very informal way. Nobody cared when you showed up for work in the morning and nobody asked when you left at night. As long as you were interested in doing your work, as long as you were turning out results that were in the fields of interest to the laboratory as a whole, Day left you alone, providing equipment and facilities, and always taking an interest in your work and encouraging you to carry on."[1]

After his appointment as director of the Applied Physics Laboratory, Gibson adopted precisely the same philosophy of management, creating an environment in which the professional staff could operate with sufficient guidance but with minimal interference from the top levels of administration. Because Gibson believed that "the urge to do research is, in essence, an addiction," he felt safe in permitting trusted colleagues to manage their own projects, with the understanding that the focus ultimately was always on results. "It is rather foolish to say, 'You must produce a good thing in a year,'" Gibson once observed. "You have to wait a little longer. But eventually the time comes when you must discriminate between indolence and genius."[2]

Although he was a more contemplative and far less mercurial personality than Merle Tuve, Gibson perpetu-

From left, Isaiah Bowman, fifth president of The Johns Hopkins University, who accepted for the University the role of sponsoring the Applied Physics Laboratory in 1942; Ralph E. Gibson, who guided APL through the missile era and into the space age as Laboratory director during two postwar decades; and Vannevar Bush, chairman of the National Defense Research Committee, which marshaled the nation's scientists to respond to war and defense needs.

ated the wartime atmosphere that Tuve had created whereby everyone at APL—scientists, engineers, and clerical and maintenance staff—felt themselves valuable members of a cohesive unit. "He was a genius at getting people to work together," recalled Alvin Eaton. "He created an environment in which people could do things. He never interfered, but he was a fantastic listener—he did more listening than talking—and in the process of listening he was actually able to help people in the development of logical thought, and certainly in the development of logical programs."

Gibson readily delegated authority to the leaders of the various task groups (under his regime the professional staff, and not financial managers or bureaucrats, managed the Laboratory) and at the same time kept himself informed about every aspect of APL's operations by regularly traversing the hallways of the Laboratory's various facilities, poking his head into offices, and stopping to chat with people in the hallways. "He directed the Laboratory by walking around," noted Alexander Kossiakoff, who had served as Gibson's top aide at Allegany. "He'd go everywhere and talk to everybody." An accomplished musician, an avid gardener, and an inveterate pipe smoker, Gibson also heartily encouraged the extracurricular activities sponsored by the Laboratory, including the annual holiday concert performed by the APL chorus.

From the end of March 1948 through December, when The Johns Hopkins University Board of Trustees took the final steps to formally accept the Laboratory as a full-fledged division of the University, Gibson presided over the transition as the Kellex staff departed and the experiment in dual management was officially terminated. Although a small part of the Laboratory's professional staff left to join Kellex (which subsequently became part of the Vitro Corporation, with headquarters in Silver Spring), most of them chose to remain under Gibson's leadership.

"During the reconstruction, Gibson was the unifying force," Kossiakoff recalled. "He earned the loyalty of the people who were there to begin with." Kossiakoff himself, who had been serving as technical supervisor of the Bumblebee launching group, was named assistant director of the Laboratory effective August 1, 1948. (His place in the launching group was taken by William H. Avery, a highly respected propulsion expert who also had served with Gibson at the Allegany Ballistics Laboratory during the war.) Together, Gibson and Kossiakoff formed a leadership team that remained together for more than twenty years; Gibson provided the spiritual leadership and usually represented APL in its dealings with the Navy and the rest of the outside world, while Kossiakoff served as the Laboratory's operations director.

At the time Gibson assumed the directorship permanently, the Applied Physics Laboratory consisted of approximately 720 employees, half of whom were on direct task assignment (e.g., the Bumblebee project, high-altitude research). Another 150 were engaged in technical support and administration of specific tasks, while the remainder formed the general administrative staff, including maintenance, security, and service functions. Since the Laboratory found itself on the cutting edge of research in a brand-new field of technology, it is not surprising that the average age of the professional staff was remarkably young. Because Gibson was such a highly visible and well-respected force—a father figure, really—in the Laboratory, the director's personal philosophy of world affairs and national preparedness naturally set the tone for the entire organization. And Gibson had no doubt at all about the necessity for continuing defense research on an extensive scale during the postwar years.

In a lengthy memorandum he wrote near the end of his tenure at APL, Gibson maintained that the rationale for the Laboratory's existence could be expressed in a quote from the New Testament, the twenty-first verse of the eleventh chapter of the book of Luke: "When a strong man armed keepeth his palace, his goods are in peace. But when a stronger than he shall come upon him, and overcome him, he taketh from him all his armor wherein he trusted and divideth his spoils." Gibson wrote, "The 'palace' of immediate interest to us is the United States of America—or its extension, the 'Free World,'" and the "'goods' [include] a high national standard of living, the right to 'life, liberty, and pursuit of happiness,' [and] the privilege of free enquiry by intellectuals and freedom of expression of the results of enquiries. . . . We need only to remember," Gibson added, "the plight of the universities in countries whose military power has been insufficient to protect them from invasion and consequent economic disaster." Specifically, Gibson argued that the United States Navy represented the most vital link in the structure of national defense, since it possessed "a flexibility for demonstrating the credibility of the power of the United States in peace and war, a flexibility which surpasses that of the other two operating agencies, the Army and the Air Force."[3]

At the close of 1948, such a powerful and flexible force seemed especially essential. The United States and the Soviet Union were still engaged in a heated confrontation over access to the city of Berlin; much of southern and central Europe was still in chaos, struggling to recover from the devastating effects of the recent war; civil conflict raged in China, and open warfare had broken out between the Arabs and the new state of Israel in the Middle East. Obviously Gibson had ample reason to believe that the Navy might well need to demonstrate its power in the very near future. "Christmas 1948 finds the world still in a state of confusion and fear," Gibson wrote to the APL staff in the first of many annual Christmas messages. "We realize more and more that generations of hard work will be required to achieve a state where men of good will can live in peace. Our share in this work is a contribution to the preservation of the peaceful institutions from which progress toward peace stems."[4]

Terrier: From Test Vehicle to Missile

It was this spirit of dedication, created by Tuve and maintained by Hafstad and Gibson, that made the Applied Physics Laboratory the leading guided-missile research and development center in the United States by the beginning of 1949. In fact, the Navy was the only service that had a comprehensive, coordinated missile development program at that time, largely because it was fortunate enough to have APL to provide it with technical direction.

62

Certainly officials at the Navy's Bureau of Ordnance shared Gibson's concern over the apparent international threat to American strategic interests. At a meeting on April 23, 1948, Navy representatives informed APL that the Chief of Naval Operations—who was also locked in a battle in congressional hearings with Army and Air Force officials for a share of the dwindling postwar defense budget—wanted the Navy to obtain a working guided missile as quickly as possible. The complex ramjet missile, which required innovative technical advances in a broad range of disciplines, was still in the early stages of development and hence nowhere near ready for production, though testing on the six-inch Cobra models had been satisfactorily completed and the team had moved on to development of an eighteen-inch-diameter experimental prototype missile (XPM).

In response to the Navy's request, a number of APL scientists, led by Henry H. Porter, proposed that the Laboratory transform the solid-rocket-powered STV-3, heretofore merely a test vehicle for obtaining aerodynamics data and developing guidance systems for the ramjet, into an effective interim weapon. Further research indicated that this concept was indeed feasible, although numerous engineering problems remained to be solved, including the accuracy of the STV-3's guidance system, the reliability of the missile's components, and the effectiveness of its warhead. Nevertheless, the Navy decided to take the gamble and approve the development of a short-range beam-riding missile based on the STV-3. Consolidated Vultee Aircraft Corporation, which had previously developed and built the airframes for the STV series, was awarded the contract to engineer the new vehicle under the technical direction of APL.

It was understood at APL and within the Navy that this program would not divert resources from the longer term ramjet project; in fact, the Bureau of Ordnance and APL still hoped to have a prototype XPM available for evaluation approximately one year after the STV-3. Nevertheless, the Navy earmarked two million dollars to begin the construction of launchers and radar for shipboard use of the new solid-fuel rocket missile. To head this new development program, Gibson appointed Richard Kershner, who had been leading the guidance research effort. It was Kershner who dubbed the new missile "Terrier" for its tenacious ability to hold to the center of the radar guidance beam. (During this era, all APL missiles were given names beginning with the letter T, since the Laboratory was still operating under a Section T contract with the Navy.)

According to a former colleague, it had long been Kershner's private plan to turn the STV into a viable weapon; in fact, Kershner reportedly had provided the test vehicle with all sorts of capabilities beyond those originally deemed necessary, so that when the Navy started to search for a missile that could be operational in the near future, "there was Kershner with a rocket ready to launch." When the Navy gave APL the go-ahead for Terrier, a rivalry—usually good-natured—began at the Laboratory between the advocates of solid-fuel rocket missiles and the supporters of the ramjet.

In any event, the decision to proceed with Terrier gave further impetus to all the various Bumblebee research teams, since the Navy wanted Convair to produce a total of fifty prototype missiles in the next several years. These would be done in a sort of stepwise evolution, with each lot more sophisticated than its predecessors, ending eventually in a fully operational weapon. Meanwhile, the APL warhead group, headed by Colonel H. S. Morton, continued to work on a shell that would break up into sufficiently sizable fragments that while moving at optimum velocity could inflict critical damage on a target aircraft.

Perhaps the most persistent and perplexing aerodynamics problem the Bumblebee team had to solve involved the so-called reverse roll phenomenon, which had been observed while the STV-2 was being tested at supersonic speeds. Quite simply, the vehicle repeatedly rolled in the opposite direction from which it should have rolled, according to existing theory. For months, no one at 8621 Georgia Avenue or at the wind tunnel facility in Daingerfield could figure out how or why the missile violated the known principles of aerodynamics. Puzzled, the Bumblebee team called Alvin Eaton, who recently had been transferred to the Research Center, back to Daingerfield for a meeting of the Bumblebee aerodynamics panel.

One evening, Eaton and two of his colleagues from the panel were sitting in a hotel bar in Longview, Texas, just down the road from Daingerfield. "We were in difficult shape," remembered Eaton, "because we didn't understand what was happening. After a drink, they decided that they would challenge me, that I had to work this out or the problem might not be solved in a timely way. They left the bar, and I stayed there with napkins and a pencil, drawing diagrams. And it finally became apparent that no existing theory would ever explain the phenomenon. It was possible to show that something else had to be involved.

"It finally occurred to me," Eaton continued, "that the something else was really obvious, that if one had surfaces deflected at supersonic speeds, next to a body, there would be strong modifications of the flow field there, and one would develop positive and negative pressures in such a way that there would be a field of swirl around the body which was just nonexistent in theory. At supersonic speeds, it had been assumed that lift and pressures behaved in a very different way across the body."

Undaunted by the late hour, Eaton roused several Convair engineers out of bed and set up tests using lampblack and oil and tiny silk tufts to demonstrate the existence of this field of swirl. As the members of the aerodynamics panel watched the next day, everything worked just as Eaton had predicted—that is, the existence of the field was verified—though his explanation still met with resistance from certain obdurate members of

65

the academic community both in the United States and abroad.

The results of Eaton's test had critical implications for the design of future missiles. Since the start of the Bumblebee project, there had been an ongoing debate over the most effective way to control a missile. One option was canard steering, the straightforward type of control used in an automobile; that is, the vehicle turns in the same direction as the steering mechanism. The second possibility was rudder steering (familiar in ships, of course), which uses a control mechanism in the back to turn the ship in the opposite direction from the rudder. The third option, known as wing steering, is a composite method that uses a steering device on the sides of the vehicle to control its path, with tail surfaces providing stability. For Eaton, the reverse roll test "completely convinced me that there were limits to wing and canard control in missiles." Many others in the Bumblebee group, however, remained skeptical about the viability of tail control, and so both the ramjet experimental missile (now designated Talos, after the Greek demigod who defended Crete) and the original Terrier missiles continued to employ wing steering for the time being.

A Missile Czar

While the technical staff sought to overcome engineering difficulties in the field, Gibson and Kossiakoff had their hands full fighting the battle of the budget with Navy officials, who themselves were laboring under restrictions imposed by Congress and the Truman administration. During the previous several years, the total defense budget had been slashed from $30 billion to $14.2 billion. In addition, the Navy was still trying to determine its role in a postwar world in which the United States' primary antagonist, the Soviet Union, possessed no surface navy of any moment. Within the U.S. Navy, debates raged over the relevance of battleships built to fight battleships, the relative merits of cruisers and submarines, the ability of the fleet to transport troops safely to Europe or Asia, and the role (if any) of the Navy in any contingency plans for strategic bombing. While it was generally acknowledged that great strides had been made in the antiaircraft defense of carriers (in large measure because of the work of the Applied Physics Laboratory), it was by no means certain that the fleet could successfully operate within the range of land-based aircraft in the hands of an enemy that possessed planes in quantity and the will to commit them in massive assaults.

Naturally, all this uncertainty created an unsettled budgetary situation. For fiscal 1949 and 1950, the Navy's funding of the Bumblebee program had fallen slightly; the 1950 APL budget from the Bureau of Ordnance, for instance, included $10.8 million for Talos and $2.7 million for Terrier. In its budget for fiscal 1951, as developed in the autumn of 1949, BuOrd threatened to slice its support even thinner, despite Admiral Noble's assurances that "a research and development program of the present kind had his full and enthusiastic support."[5] When Gibson learned in the spring of 1950 that the bureau intended to allocate only $8.5 million for Bumblebee for fiscal 1952, he warned Noble that immediate steps would have to be taken to curtail the program unless additional funds were forthcoming.

They were. At the end of June 1950, just two weeks after Gibson issued his warning to Admiral Noble, North Korean forces invaded the Republic of Korea. Within a week, American troops supported by warships and Air Force units were on their way to Korea. Convinced that "there is, and will continue to be, grave danger of war between the USSR and its satellites, on the one hand, and the U.S. and its allies on the other,"[6] the Truman administration abruptly reversed the downward trend of military spending. At the Applied Physics Laboratory, the immediate effect of the Korean conflict was a decision by the Navy to skip some intermediate models of the Terrier and freeze the design so that a prototype Terrier missile (known as the "Lot 4," since it was the fourth in the series of successively more advanced Terriers) could be produced in 1951.

Events soon radically accelerated this plan, however. Ever since the end of World War II, the three main branches of the U.S. armed services had been striving independently to develop their own guided missiles. In an attempt to put an end to waste and duplication of effort, and to put the missile research effort on a more coordinated basis, Secretary (of Defense) George C. Marshall announced on October 25, 1950, that he had appointed Kaufman T. Keller, president of the Chrysler Corporation, as director of guided missiles (in effect, a missile czar) to provide the secretary's office with "competent advice in order to permit me [Marshall] to direct and coordinate activities connected with research, development and production of guided missiles."[7]

The appointment of Keller, the head of one of the nation's largest mass-production industrial corporations, indicated that the Department of Defense had decided to shift the missile program from the experimental stage into a development-production mode. Although he was serving only part-time in his Defense position, assisted by a full-time deputy director from the armed services, Keller promptly began getting a handle on his new responsibilities by touring research facilities across the country.

When he arrived at APL, Keller was given a tour and a status report on the Terrier program. He also received some unsolicited automotive advice from Wilbur Goss at the concluding meeting between Keller and the top staff of the Laboratory. "It was at the end of the session, the end of a long and tiring day, just prior to breaking up," Goss recalled. "I had been having trouble with a Plymouth that leaked water every time it rained, and I had been back to the dealer time and time again. So just in a frivolous manner, knowing that he was head of the Chrysler Corporation, I said, 'There's just one problem that we haven't talked about in our discussion today about Terrier and production, Mr. Keller, and that's waterproofing. From my experience with my Plymouth, I'm sure you realize how serious a problem that can be.' Well, it turned out that Keller didn't take kidding lightly. The next morning, I began getting calls from all over the East Coast. They brought me a new car, they took my old one away to be waterproofed and fixed up, and I guess they spent about two days sealing up every nook and cranny on the car."

Very shortly after his appointment, Keller decided that the only way to uncover all the problems involved in producing guided missiles was to actually force the missiles into production. So he chose the three that seemed to be closest to completion—the Navy's Terrier and Sparrow, and the Army's Nike—and ordered an initial production run of one thousand of each missile. Keller also insisted that the companies involved establish production lines capable of turning out one thousand of each missile per month by March 1953. When the Navy awarded a contract to Convair to build the one thousand Terrier missiles that Keller wanted, BuOrd officials made no provision for APL involvement or direction, apparently because they felt that the Laboratory, the original developer of the missile, would never stop trying to "perfect" its product.

To provide Convair with an adequate facility to engineer and mass-produce the missiles, the Navy also awarded the corporation a contract to construct a guided-missile plant at Pomona, California, about fifty miles east of Los Angeles. But since no one had ever mass-produced guided missiles before, the confusion that soon ensued on the West Coast should have surprised no one.

The Terrier Production Crisis

In the absence of any executives experienced in missile production, the task of organizing and managing the Terrier production program fell to the Convair (formerly Consolidated Vultee) research and development engineers who had helped design the missile, largely because they were virtually the only ones in the company who had any detailed knowledge about it. In short order, however, these engineers, most of whom had very limited management training, found themselves supervising hundreds of new and inexperienced employees who had been hired to do the product engineering.

That approach simply did not work. Development items were released to production prematurely, without adequate testing. Making matters worse, many components (including the guidance package and the servos) that already had been designed for the Lot 4 missiles were redesigned for production by Convair, creating new problems that became apparent only as the missiles came off the assembly lines. Further, many of the components were built in the new Pomona facility by recently hired factory personnel who had no experience in this area. "You were trying to force a small, essentially research and development engineering organization to expand by an order of magnitude in the period of a year or not much more, and go into production," observed Kossiakoff. "Nobody was in a position to say, 'Hell, this is a stupid idea.' You just did your best. . . .It was essentially trying to do a job that had never been done before, by people who had never done anything remotely like it, in an incredibly short period of time, with no opportunity for organizing, training, learning, or much else."

By the spring of 1952, it was clear to many at APL that the Laboratory needed to get actively involved in the production process. As a first step, two engineers were dispatched to California to work with their Convair counterparts to complete the design of the beam-riding receiver. But the problems went far deeper than any one component. Missiles that had been assembled for final factory checkout were failing their acceptance tests, revealing a multitude of instabilities, unreliable parts, and other deficiencies.

In late November, the seriousness of the situation led Navy officials to establish a Terrier task group consisting of contractor and service personnel (the APL representative was Alexander Kossiakoff) to lend temporary on-site management assistance at the Convair plant. To provide further emergency assistance to Convair engineers and factory managers at the working level, APL sent a team of twenty-five experienced engineers, headed by Thomas Sheppard, to help identify and solve technical problems.

During the next six months, sufficient progress was made to enable Convair to produce a limited number of missiles that passed acceptance tests. Nevertheless, as the APL personnel in California grew more intimately acquainted with the process and problems of Terrier production, they became convinced that nothing less than a major engineering redesign was necessary to provide the Navy with an effective missile capable of being produced in large quantities.

For instance, each missile still required an inordinately prolonged time for final assembly and checkout. Persistent quality control problems on the production line forced numerous adjustments to practically every missile as it came off the line. Making matters worse, because each part of the missile was interdependent with the other parts, an attempt to fine-tune one component almost invariably affected another part adversely, leading to a virtually interminable sequence of last-minute adjustments.

"The missile had been designed by an aircraft company as if it were an airplane," explained Sheppard. "In an airplane, you can have access to the parts and get in and work on things. But not so with a missile. There's not enough space, and it's wired and bolted together. . . .If the guidance system failed, you had to disassemble the missile to remove the receiver, and in so doing you would have to disassemble the hydraulic system to get to the receiver. Then you put that back together and now the hydraulic system doesn't work. Meanwhile, the control system has a failure, so you have to tear everything apart again, perhaps disrupting something else. You could never get the darn thing working together for long enough to pass the composite test."

In short, the Terrier had been designed to minimize space and weight requirements rather than to facilitate production. To overcome this roadblock, Kershner and Kossiakoff proposed that the Terrier missile be "sectionalized," that is, designed as an assemblage of functionally independent sections. "You'd have a separate rocket section," explained Sheppard, "a separate power section, a warhead section, and guidance and control sections, each of which did not require individual tuning." Each section would be self-contained, standardized, easily tested, and interchangeable, with specific tolerances built in. If a problem occurred in the hydraulics section, a weapons officer could simply remove that module and install another hydraulics package without disturbing the rest of the missile.

Unfortunately, Convair did not accept this fundamental change as necessary or desirable. So APL proposed to demonstrate the viability and advantages of the sectionalization principle by carrying out a pilot program of sorts. The Laboratory agreed to design a group of missiles for production, to oversee and actually partici-pate in the fabrication of the individual sections, and to carry out the necessary flight tests of the completed missiles. When the Navy had accepted this proposal, the Laboratory established a special task force, directed by Kershner and led by Roland W. Larson, to design, build, and test ten missiles that soon became known as the Terrier 1B.

Although this program was a major departure from APL's traditional scope of activities because it took the Laboratory away from its usual concentration on research and development, it proved a resounding success. Inspired by Kershner's motto, "We have plenty of time if we work fast enough," the task force accomplished all its objectives on schedule and within the estimated cost. Eight of the nine 1B missiles that were actually launched were fully successful, far exceeding the flight reliability of the production Terrier missiles (which now became known as Terrier 1A). Even more important, the project clearly demonstrated the superiority of the sectionalization principle.

This experience, undertaken with considerable apprehension on the part of some members of the Laboratory's leadership, had unforeseen and highly serendipitous consequences several years later. It created in APL a cadre of staff with the ability to build high-quality, sophisticated electronic equipment that could withstand both the thrust of a rocket and the vibrations of a missile in flight— precisely the sort of expertise that would soon prove invaluable when the Laboratory reentered the field of space research under the leadership of Richard Kershner. Though the Terrier 1B was never produced on a large-scale basis for use by the fleet (the Navy decided to wait until the technical advances then under development could be incorporated into a production model), subsequent models of the Terrier—including the 1C, and especially the Terrier II—incorporated the 1B's basic design approach, particularly the sectionalized, modular concept, as well as many of its specific features. Indeed, the concept of a modularized missile, which soon became a standard feature in other weapons programs at APL and elsewhere, permitted evolutionary improvements to be introduced to each new generation of missiles with an ease that never could have been achieved with the original design.

Certainly the results of Terrier flight tests in 1953-54 validated the improvement program that had been led by APL. Although the first Terrier launches in the spring of 1952 had fizzled because of electrical failures and roll problems, by April 1953 fully two-thirds of the Terriers launched had successfully intercepted the target, while an additional 9 percent had displayed good beam-riding capabilities. During the last six months of 1954, a total of 211 Terrier missiles were fired, again compiling an overall guidance success rate of 67 percent.

Initial shipboard launch tests of Terrier I missiles had been carried out on the USS *Norton Sound* in 1951 after the ship's radar and fire control systems had been altered, under APL supervision, to enable the ship to handle Terrier missiles. By mid-1953, Terriers fired from the battleship USS *Mississippi,* which had been modified by the installation of two dual-arm missile launchers in place of its aft gun turrets, were regularly destroying target drones in tests at sea, some by direct hits. Two years later, after the Terrier was deemed ready for use in the fleet, the cruiser USS *Boston*—armed with Terriers—became the world's first combatant guided-missile ship when it was recommissioned as CAG-1 at a special ceremony at the U.S. Naval Shipyard in Philadelphia on November 1, 1955.

By developing the Navy's first effective guided missile in a remarkably short time and under trying conditions, APL had once again demonstrated its value to the service and had perhaps rescued the Bureau of Ordnance from a potential disaster with the Terrier 1A fiasco. In fact, naval officials were sufficiently impressed with APL's performance during the Terrier crisis that they initiated informal discussions with the Laboratory to determine its willingness to assume additional duties.

Specifically, BuOrd wanted to know whether APL would consider assuming responsibility for engineering supervision of the entire Bumblebee missile program. At a November 13, 1953, meeting between representatives of

Terrier missile roars off the battleship USS Mississippi, *which was modified in 1952 to permit testing of Terrier under realistic at-sea conditions.*

BuOrd and Kossiakoff and Walter Verdier of APL, a proposal was floated to give the Laboratory "engineering supervision, preparation and approval of specifications, approval of waivers drawings, preparation of classification of defects and similar functions."[8]

During the next week, Gibson and a small group of top-level APL personnel indicated their willingness to consider such a service, pending the resolution of specific details. Actually, the Laboratory already was performing certain of these duties as part of the Talos program, and BuOrd had also given APL technical responsibility for the research and development phases of the Terrier II missile program, as well as technical responsibility for the Convair engineering program when Terrier II reached that stage.

75

USS Boston, *world's first operational guided-missile ship. Note Terrier launchers on aft deck.*

Not everyone at APL agreed that the Laboratory should undertake such an expansion of its responsibilities, but the mere fact that the bureau had initiated the inquiry reflected a deep and abiding confidence in APL's expertise and judgment. Thus far, the Navy had made virtually no attempts to micromanage the Bumblebee program or make any decisions that it was not technically competent to make. Certainly the Navy provided the Applied Physics Laboratory with far more freedom to carry out its mission in the 1950s than it would in subsequent decades.

Talos on Land and in the Fleet

When the Navy gave Terrier the go-ahead for production, it did so on the assumption that the Applied Physics Laboratory's research on the Talos ramjet missile would not be adversely affected. Indeed, after Keller had studied the ramjet program, he recommended that thirty Talos missiles be produced while additional experimental research and

76

component development work continued, particularly on the homing guidance system. In 1951, funding for the Talos program rose to $11.38 million and the APL Talos effort continued to gather momentum, incorporating advances in the propulsion system, autopilot, and guidance, particularly the homing system.

On October 28, 1952, the first Talos XPM, weighing 7,455 pounds, was launched. By the following year, the eighteen-inch-diameter XPM had given way to the twenty-four-inch developmental missile known as the Talos 6A, which could accurately deliver a five-hundred-pound warhead against targets up to fifty miles away. Given such range, an effective homing system was especially critical for the Talos, since beam-riding guidance was simply not sufficiently accurate at distances greater than twenty miles. Hence a semiactive "interferometer" homing system had been devised to take over from the radar beam as the missile neared its target and guide it the rest of the way by sensing signals reflected from the target.

Even though snags remained (most notably, the homing system still displayed an annoying tendency to malfunction), the missile looked so promising by 1953 that it attracted the attention of the Air Force as well as the Navy. For the Air Force, the notion of a land-based Talos system presented an intriguing option for the defense of its Strategic Air Command (SAC) bases against enemy bombers, and so it commissioned independent studies that indicated Talos was indeed a viable candidate for continental defense.

It became an even more attractive option once APL had devised a solution to one of the most persistent Talos design problems. When a homing-guidance Talos approached two or more missiles or planes flying several hundred feet apart it tended to get confused, because it received signals from both targets and could not decide which one to attack. Armed with a conventional warhead with a limited "kill" range, the missile might not destroy either target. So in the summer of 1952 the Laboratory turned its attention to developing a Talos missile that could carry a tactical nuclear warhead.

During a conversation with a former student who had become an assistant director at the Atomic Energy Commission, Wilbur Goss had learned that low-yield, tactical nuclear weapons for Navy fighter aircraft had recently been given a high priority. To accommodate a nuclear warhead in Talos, an APL research team under the direction of William H. Garten completely redesigned the front end of the missile, removing a portion of the electronic equipment and reducing the thickness of the shell to permit the insertion of a one- or two-kiloton nuclear weapon. Although there was no longer room for a homing device, neither was there much need for it, given the tremendous destructive radius of the warhead.

Again the Laboratory worked with the same sense of urgency that had marked its wartime research on the proximity fuze. On December 15, 1953, less than eighteen months after the program began, APL successfully flight-tested the first Talos missile bearing a simulated nuclear warhead. (Garten made sure that all the contractors involved in the engineering of the missile were physically present at the site, just in case anything went wrong.) Initially, twelve of these missiles—known as the Talos Whammy or, more formally, the 6AW—were produced, though virtually all the wrinkles had been worked out of the system by the time the first six had been fired. The Air Force, which was not entirely satisfied with the Army's Nike missile as a defense for its bases, was sufficiently impressed with the Whammy's performance to propose the allocation of $50 million for a tactical prototype Talos and the production of two hundred missiles by 1955.

Unfortunately, interservice rivalries put the land-based Talos project temporarily on hold, but in 1954 the Navy did award a contract to the Bendix Corporation to begin producing a ship-based Talos missile. No existing ship could handle this weapon; indeed, the size of the missile and the associated shipboard guidance equipment (originally, Talos needed nine double-relay racks full of electronic gear) had always been Talos's principal disadvantage. Consequently, the Navy also announced that it was funding the conversion of a World War II cruiser, the USS *Galveston*, to enable it to launch a Talos 6A. Although the first production missiles were delivered by Bendix in late 1955, six months after the first series of successful Talos flight tests at the White Sands Proving Ground, the conversion of the *Galveston* required an additional three years.

Drawing on its experience in the production of the Terrier missile, including the attendant difficulties between Convair and the Laboratory, APL enjoyed excellent relations with Bendix, the prime contractor for Talos, throughout the entire life of the Talos program. "We ironed out our difficulties at the very beginning," noted Goss. "Dr. Gibson and I had a meeting with the heads of the Bendix Corporation, and we all agreed to agree. That meant that if two people at the lower level couldn't work out their problems, they agreed to disagree, and it would go up to the next level and they would reach agreement there. And if it ever got up to the president of the Bendix Corporation and Gibson, it would then be settled. There would be no continuing dichotomy between the two organizations. We were going to operate as if we were one organization. And we did that throughout the entire program. It was hard to tell during the development phase whether these people who were in the program were being paid by Bendix or by the University."

Cannonball and Triton

If the Terrier and Talos developmental programs were the Applied Physics Laboratory's most significant long-term ventures in the early 1950s, they represented only a portion of the Laboratory's activities during those years.

79

From antitank missiles to transistors and the capture of free radicals in chemical reactions, the professional staff at APL engaged in a wide variety of projects that continually advanced the frontiers of technology and scientific research.

One of most intriguing of all the Laboratory's programs involved the so-called Cannonball missile, known within APL as D-40. As conceived by Randolph S. Rae of APL, the Cannonball was a sphere made from steel sheet; twenty inches in diameter and weighing 150 pounds, it could be fired by infantry or amphibious troops to destroy oncoming tanks. A very early application of guided-missile technology to antitank warfare, the Cannonball and its flight pattern must have seemed a bit unconventional at first glance. One bemused observer related his impressions of a Cannonball test launch: a launched ball suddenly sprouts "little bursts of flame, [from the central jets] rises about three feet off the ground, and takes off across the fields and hedgerows like a scared rabbit. As you watch in fascination, the dancing ball swerves a bit, rises a little more, and plunges through the bullseye of a target 2000 yards away."[9]

Between 1952 and 1955, the Cannonball smashed its way through the development and field testing phases and subsequently made a brief appearance as a submarine-based missile. By mid-1955 it had attracted interest from both the U.S. Marine Corps and the U.S. Navy, and funds were provided for the construction of fifteen missiles to be carried aboard submarines. In the late 1950s, however, when the budget-conscious Eisenhower administration began winnowing the field of prospective missiles for production, the Cannonball program was canceled.

Equally fascinating, albeit perhaps too sophisticated for its time, was a long-range Navy bombardment missile known as Triton. An outgrowth of the most advanced Talos development research, Triton was designed to carry a powerful warhead to targets several thousand miles away; in fact, it was supposed to be able to hit within six hundred

80

yards of its target at ranges up to two thousand miles. The APL team that began working on Triton in 1950 planned to devise a propulsion system that would enable the missile to cruise at a speed of Mach 2.7 (later increased to Mach 3.5) at altitudes greater than seventy thousand feet.

As we shall see, the Triton project never made it past the preliminary stage, partly because of competition from the rival Polaris missile, yet a number of significant advances came out of the Triton program. The most notable was the design of an intelligent radar map-matching guidance system—developed in part by the Goodyear Rubber Company—that permitted the missile to correct its course in mid-flight by observing the terrain directly below and comparing the data with references and checkpoints on a map stored in its computer. Several decades later, a more sophisticated version of this guidance system would be employed in the Tomahawk cruise missile.

Recognizing the revolutionary impact that the nascent transistor technology of the early 1950s would have on electronics, the Laboratory launched a four-year effort in 1954 to adapt transistors to the electronic circuitry of the Bumblebee guidance systems. "Transistors were pretty crude and unreliable in 1954," recalled Alvin Schulz, who led the APL transistor team, "but they were coming along." Schulz's primary task was to develop a transistorized version of the vacuum tube receiver in the beam-riding nuclear warhead Talos missile. "We expected in the long run to have more reliability with transistors than with vacuum tubes," explained Schulz, "which of course turned out to be the case."

Working in close cooperation with the International Telephone and Telegraph Development Laboratory in New Jersey, where the vacuum tube receivers were being produced, the APL team completed the primary design for the transistorized model and then turned the job over to the contractor. By 1958, when Schulz's group disbanded to work on individual missile systems, it had completed the Talos transistorized receiver and its members were busy teaching classes in transistor theory to the rest of the staff at APL, including the members who would soon form the nucleus of the Laboratory's spacecraft development program.

Meanwhile, another Applied Physics Laboratory task group had devised an especially lethal type of non-nuclear warhead for the Navy's antiaircraft missiles. Even though guidance systems were steadily becoming more accurate, they still could not ensure a direct hit; hence the challenge for the Laboratory lay in devising a warhead with a maximum effective "kill" radius, especially at high altitudes.

After staging numerous damage trials against drone aircraft at New Mexico A & M University's testing range in the desert, the APL warheads group decided in 1952 to develop a shell whose casing would unfold at detonation into a continuous ring of steel, slashing through any obstacle in its path

Science and Technology

Occasionally the Department of Defense (DoD) required the Laboratory's expertise to help with specific, short-term projects. In 1951, for instance, APL was asked to perform an instrumentation study on the first hydrogen bomb test (code-named "Mike") at Eniwetok Atoll in the South Pacific. Specifically, DoD wanted the Laboratory to determine the free-air pressure of a thermonuclear bomb. When a nuclear weapon is exploded in the air, it produces an initial shock wave; but when that wave strikes the ground, a secondary wave comes off and reinforces the initial blast. Since ground measurements would pick up both the direct and the reflected pressures, it was necessary to use airborne instrumentation to measure the force of the initial bomb pressure alone.

82

Samuel Foner, who had been working in the APL Research Center since 1947, was chosen to design the instruments for the Eniwetok blast, and Foner asked Richard Ellis and several other technicians from the Laboratory to assist him. "Sam came up with the concept," recalled Ellis, who was the only APL staff member at the blast site. "In simple terms, you put up a wire holding instruments, with the wire being supported by a special kind of balloon. On this wire you have a series of switches, and as the shock wave moves out, it hits these switches. Every time it hits a switch, you get a signal that is essentially the time of the arrival of the shock wave at that point. Now, to measure the pressure, you need to know the ratio of shock velocity to sound velocity. So at each switch location, you also put a microphone.

"A very short time before the main bang, you set off a small charge of TNT—a quarter-pound, or something like that—and it makes a big bang. By the time it moves out fifty feet or so, it's no longer a shock wave, it's a sound wave. And so you get 'bing, bing, bing, bing,' as the sound hits each microphone. Then a second or two later, you set off the bomb, and then the shock wave moves past each switch. On the record you get these blips that are the sound arrivals, and then the clicks of the shock arrivals. You measure the distance between station one and station two for the sound, and then measure the distance between those stations for the shock, so you have the velocity of sound and shock. From that, you can calculate the actual shock velocity extremely precisely."

It took six months to develop the concept and test the instrumentation at the Aberdeen Proving Ground. To guard against equipment failure, a great deal of redundancy was built into the system; Ellis took multiple transmitters, receivers, and recording instruments out to Eniwetok. When the bomb was detonated on November 1, 1952, Ellis (who was stationed at an observation post twenty miles away) noted that "everything worked. We

83

had so much data we didn't know what to do with it. In fact, every piece of equipment we set up worked." When the Pentagon received the final APL report, it learned that the shock waves from the blast were even more powerful than they had expected. "Mike" had blown a mile-long, 175-foot-deep canyon in the ocean floor. The fireball from the explosion, four miles wide and five miles high, would have vaporized the city of San Francisco. The island of Elugelab, where the bomb had actually been detonated, broke in two and sank, still smoldering, beneath the surface of the ocean.

Foner's participation in the hydrogen bomb test was a diversion from his ongoing work in the Applied Physics Laboratory's Research Center, where a staff of approximately fifty APL scientists from a wide range of disciplines was engaged in a variety of experimental and theoretical projects under the chairmanship of Frank McClure. An intense man who did not suffer fools graciously, McClure was a brilliant scientist as well as a forceful leader. "I've worked with a lot of very bright people," noted Joseph Massey, who worked with McClure for twenty-four years, "but I thought Frank came the closest to being a genius of anyone I've ever worked with."

In the early years of the Research Center's existence, Gibson entrusted McClure with broad authority to initiate virtually any program that might produce useful scientific results, subject only to review by the in-house Research Board of which McClure was chairman. It was assumed from the start that practical applications of many of the Research Center's projects would occur only in the distant future, if at all. Considered an inevitable part of the price for advancing the frontiers of scientific knowledge, this "basic" research was to be pursued with a minimum of bureaucratic interference. "We never wrote reports, we never wrote proposals," recalled Edward Cochran, a chemist who joined APL in 1956. "It was just a matter of going out there and doing good science."

Doubtless the existence of the Research Center made APL appear more attractive to the Board of Trustees of Johns Hopkins University; in fact, the Laboratory encouraged collaboration between the Research Center staff and the faculty of Johns Hopkins and other universities. Shortly after the formation of the center, for instance, that association bore fruit when R. A. Alpher of APL and George Gamow, a professor at George Washington University, published a paper formally proposing for the first time the "big bang" theory of the origin of the universe.

In the first decade of the Research Center's existence, its programs included Van Allen's high-altitude atmospheric research, studies in flame spectroscopy, microwave and low-temperature spectroscopy, the development of synthetic fuels, and the quest to detect and identify free radicals in complex chemical reactions. Certainly the free radical research investigations were among the longest running programs in the history of the Laboratory, as they continued in various forms for more than thirty years. Originally conceived by McClure and Kossiakoff, the free radical experiments were led in the early years by Samuel Foner and Richard L. Hudson. In simple terms, free radicals are transient molecules, the intermediate products of certain chemical reactions. Their extreme reactivity makes them difficult to observe because they react extremely quickly with other molecules and then vanish, often within one one-thousandth of a second.

Because conventional mass spectrometers could not detect such active particles, Kossiakoff and McClure proposed the development of a molecular beam apparatus to isolate the reactive intermediates—catch them on the fly, as it were—before they collided with other molecules. Foner subsequently designed a customized mass spectrometer

Richard L. Hudson and Samuel N. Foner with the modulated molecular beam mass spectrometer they designed to detect very reactive, short-lived chemical intermediates. They used this instrument for the first detection of the elusive and long-sought-after HO$_2$ free radical in 1953.

that could provide the transition between the high-pressure environment of the original chemical reaction and the low-pressure area (reduced by a factor of up to one million, to prevent collisions) where the radicals could be ionized and detected.

One of the most significant results of this work involved one of the simplest chemical reactions in nature: the combination of hydrogen and oxygen to produce water. Chemists had long speculated that the free radical HO$_2$ (one atom of hydrogen joined to two atoms of oxygen) had to be one of the intermediate products of this reaction. No one had ever managed to detect it, however, until 1953, when Foner and Hudson succeeded by using a modified version of their molecular beam mass spectrometer. "I think getting the HO_2 free radical really put us on the map," observed Foner, "because we had found something people had been looking for and speculating about for years."

At first glance, the relationship of free radical research to the main lines of the Laboratory's naval weapons research may not have seemed entirely clear. But it had long been Gibson's firm belief that any organization that endeavored to make technical advances without understanding the fundamental scientific principles involved ("You have to understand the science," Gibson liked to say) was doomed ultimately to fail. The free radical program, for instance, originally grew out of the Laboratory's combustion research for its guided-missile programs, specifically from the search for a more efficient propellant.

Similarly, McClure asked Joseph Massey in 1952 to undertake microwave research for no other reason than "to have those capabilities if we ever need them." "And we did subsequently," noted Massey years later. "So it was sort of a shot in the dark. We didn't know if we were going to need these techniques that we would learn by starting this particular research project, but it was a store of information and capabilities that the Navy had. And it was the same way with many projects over the years that have originated in the Research Center."

The Move to Howard County

All in all, the inventory of APL's projects in the early 1950s formed an impressive list of accomplishments. Some of the top professional staff, however, argued that the Laboratory should concentrate its talent and resources on fewer assignments instead of heading off in so many different directions at once. Wilbur Goss, for one, complained to Ralph Gibson on March 27, 1952, about what he called "a disastrous trend in this Laboratory—namely, the

87

continued acceptance of new assignments without a corresponding curtailment of the old. The resulting dilution of the senior technical staff," explained the leader of the Talos project, "can in [a] short time reduce the usefulness of APL."[10]

Goss recommended instead that APL scale back its commitments, particularly the fledgling Terrier II research and development effort, which he claimed could safely be left to Convair to prosecute at its own pace with the help of excess APL staff. The Laboratory's work on Terrier II, Goss feared, was delaying the completion and early deployment of both Terrier I and Talos at a time when the Navy urgently needed those weapons. "Were time scale no object," Goss concluded, "none of what I am saying would make any sense. At the core of the guided missiles field, however, is the timeliness of a development."

Others, such as Henry Porter, another of the original leaders of the Bumblebee program (and in 1953 still the official head of the Laboratory's Bumblebee operations), shared Goss's concern that APL was losing its preeminence in the development of guided missiles. Unlike Goss, however, Porter argued (in a memo dated June 11, 1953) that research on the Terrier II system should be pressed with all due speed, while Terrier I could safely be left to Convair. For Porter, it was the Laboratory's decision to get more involved in the production end of the missile procurement cycle—that is, the seemingly interminable attempt to keep Convair on track, plus the fabrication of Terrier 1B—that represented a dangerous diversion of effort.

But to fulfill its mission to the Navy, the Applied Physics Laboratory could not afford to slight either the development of advanced missile systems such as the Terrier II or the rapid deployment of the first-generation Talos and Terrier missiles. Indeed, the essentially creative nature of the Laboratory made growth and the initiation of new programs virtually inevitable: every successful research

88

project opened up new avenues of opportunity for future development, and as each task neared completion it carried within it the seeds of further research, showing the way toward an even more advanced prototype.

It was not surprising, then, that the staff of the Laboratory continued to grow throughout the early 1950s. After dipping to its lowest postwar level in 1949 (680 members, including approximately 300 professional and scientific staff) the total number of APL personnel rose to 1,156 in May 1955. Most of this growth occurred in the supporting staff, which totaled 734 employees in 1954. Of the 412 professionals on the APL payroll in May 1954, 84 held doctorates, 87 had master's degrees, 187 held bachelor's degrees, and 54 had no formal college degree. In terms of academic training, by far the largest percentage of professionals were engineers (more than 50 percent), followed by physicists, mathematicians, and chemists.

Opportunities for adding extra office space at the Laboratory's headquarters at 8621 Georgia Avenue had long been exhausted. As a temporary solution, additional space had been rented in two nearby buildings in Silver Spring, but this sort of physical dispersion— with propulsion and other technical research going on at Forest Grove Station as well—soon proved unsatisfactory and downright inefficient. So the search continued for new quarters outside Silver Spring but within the Washington Baltimore metropolitan corridor.

By mid-1951, an APL facilities committee headed by Walter Verdier had located a sizable tract of gently rolling farmland in Howard County, Maryland, about fifteen miles northeast of the Georgia Avenue building. "It was a cornfield—oh, it was hot—and the only things they had were snakes and mosquitoes," recalled APL's James Maddox, who inspected the property with Verdier. But the tract was large enough (290 acres) to house the entire APL operation and provide plenty of room for growth; besides, the land came relatively cheap: slightly more than three hundred dollars per acre. And so, on October 10, 1951, The Johns Hopkins University Trustees' Committee on the Applied Physics Laboratory gave initial approval to a resolution to authorize the Laboratory to construct a $1.8-million building on the Howard County site. The University agreed to defray one-third of the cost, and the Navy agreed to amortize the remainder. By the time the Board of Trustees granted final approval in June 1952, the estimated cost had risen to $2.05 million.

Ground was broken in February 1953, and on September 1, 1954, the Laboratory accepted the first building from the contractor: a sixty-three-thousand-square-foot structure known at APL as "the new laboratory." The dedication ceremonies were held on October 16, though not without a bit of excitement provided by Hurricane Hazel. On the afternoon before the ceremony, the storm passed directly through central Maryland, knocking down power lines and blocking roadways with fallen trees.

"I remember we built a rather elaborate speaker's platform, because the president of California Institute of Technology was going to give the main dedication speech, which was supposed to be Sunday," said Arthur Stucki, who had been hired two months earlier as head of APL plant services. "We had it set up by Building 1, but Hurricane Hazel was on its way and was starting to blow everything away. It blew the gravel off the roof, it blew the trees down in the front driveway. So we got every human being we could find out here, not only our maintenance and construction people, but the scientists and everyone else—we got about fifty people and carried the platform around behind the east wing, which was much more sheltered. We had to lean into the wind to keep standing up."

The first groups to start moving into the Howard County facility in September 1954 were the Research Center and a portion of the Bumblebee operations. Within nine months, more than two hundred APL employees were

90

housed in the new laboratory. By that time the trustees already had approved a $1-million addition (the west wing) to the original building along with the purchase of a dozen prefabricated steel buildings to house the Terrier and Talos test and engineering facilities—excluding the burner laboratory, which remained temporarily at Forest Grove.

Meanwhile, APL's personnel department had inaugurated a nationwide recruiting program in the late 1940s to obtain additional top-flight scientists, engineers, and technicians. The problem of obtaining desirable new staff members and replacements grew increasingly difficult, however, largely because of the rising demand in industry and government for what was still a relatively small number of graduates with technical degrees. To distinguish itself from its competitors in private industry, APL emphasized the Laboratory's dedication to preserving "an atmosphere conducive to creative research and opportunity for work on important problems."[11]

In short, the Laboratory offered prospective staff members a unique combination: the opportunity to conduct research in a university environment along with a chance to apply the results of that research to practical problems of national importance. For scientists and engineers with a creative inclination, APL represented an extremely attractive option, and the number of Laboratory professional staff members continued to expand rapidly throughout the 1950s.

New Generations of Terriers

As the conflict in Korea approached conclusion in the spring of 1953, however, the defense budget again came under closer scrutiny, this time from the incoming Eisenhower administration. Anyone who had expected President Eisenhower, a career Army officer and the former commander of Allied forces in World War II, to display a bias in favor of increased military spending was in for a

91

shock. More than any other president of modern times, Eisenhower believed that unless the White House checked the trend of burgeoning annual increases in the defense budget, the nation would soon face the question of "whether national bankruptcy or national destruction would get us first."[12]

And the Eisenhower administration did enforce more stringent fiscal limits on the Pentagon. But its decision to rely heavily on the U.S. nuclear deterrent while cutting ground forces (the "new look policy") meant that guided-missile programs received favored budgetary treatment, though it soon became obvious that even in this situation defense funds were simply insufficient to bring every missile system then under development into production.

Despite any existing or potential budget constraints, the relationship between APL and the Bureau of Ordnance grew even stronger during these years. For BuOrd, APL remained the Navy's premier antiaircraft guided-missile organization and, more specifically, the source of creative inspiration and advanced thinking for the development of new weapon systems. As Admiral M. F. Schoeffel, then chief of BuOrd, explained very clearly to the trustees of Johns Hopkins, "the Navy's chief interest [in APL] was in a partnership with the University in research and development activity and not in the building up of another naval facility."[13]

According to Admiral Mark Woods, who served as the bureau's Terrier research and development officer from 1952 to 1954, the APL staff was in a far better position than the officers in BuOrd to recommend innovations in antiaircraft technology. "I always counted very heavily on the Laboratory to do original thinking in the field of Navy weapons," said Woods. "I've always had the feeling that in the jobs downtown [i.e., in Washington], you're so busy putting out today's fires that you really don't have the chance to do long-range thinking. In the world of guided missiles, I relied very heavily on the Lab to do original, long-range thinking, and they've always done that very well. They're a great asset to the Navy in that regard. They feel like they're a part of the Navy, and they feel like they've got an obligation, a duty to the Navy."

In fact, Woods maintained that APL personnel usually knew better than the fleet line officers themselves what sort of advanced research and development improvements could and should be made to the Navy's weapon systems. "I always felt that the Navy was not in a position to know what it wanted," Woods stated, "because they didn't know what new things were coming down the pike, what was possible. They needed people who understood the Navy and who understood what the new technologies were, to suggest things that might match. I used to get somewhat upset on active duty when people would say, 'Let's ask the fleet what they want.' Phooey! I've been in the fleet; the fleet is busy steaming and training, and so on. They don't know what they want, they haven't a clue as to what's new in the world of computers, or in the world of electronics. They want the best thing they can get—you tell them what is possible."

In the early 1950s the Navy was still relatively decentralized, with each bureau operating almost as an autonomous unit. This division and redivision of authority within the Navy presented problems for the integration of the various portions of each guided-missile system. Within BuOrd, for instance, there was one desk responsible for rockets, another for warheads, another for launchers, and so on down the line. "It was just hells of problems to coordinate and try to get a design put together," lamented Thomas Sheppard, "because the rocket people wanted to do it their way, the guidance people wanted to do it their way, and so forth. So there was a lot of difficulty in making a missile because there was not a central responsibility within the Navy."

This state of affairs also created difficulties for the APL team, headed by Robert Morton and Milton Moon, that was examining the status of integrated command-control ship-board and ground-based systems (radars, launching systems, computers, etc.) for the original Terrier ships. Obviously all the various parts of the systems had to work together in a coordinated fashion, but according to Moon, "There was just no one around who really had spent any time on that aspect of the problem." As Morton and Moon tried to steer the Navy toward the selection of compatible radar and computer equipment, they were frustrated by the lack of central authority. "You found you had to keep hitting the hot spots one at a time," observed Moon, "and eventually things began to smooth over."

To some extent, anyway. The first few guided-missile test ships in the fleet were individually customized, literally by hand, so that they could carry out their task efficiently. But once missiles and ships started to come off the production lines en masse, the lack of integrated systems would pose a serious threat to the welfare of the entire Navy.

Ever since that day at the Navy's Ordnance Aerophysical Laboratory in Daingerfield, Texas, when he demonstrated the cause of the reverse roll problem that had plagued the early supersonic test vehicles, Al Eaton had been convinced that tail-controlled guided missiles were the wave of the future. "I tried hard and unsuccessfully to talk Lab management into giving up on the [Terrier] 1B and the 1C," recalled Eaton, "because I knew that tail control would have better composite design, better control, and better performance. The control moments would be large, and you could have a design with very low static stability, so that you could swing the body around in a hurry to get quick response and high lift at high body angles. I knew that if you were interested in long range for a given missile, you didn't want big draggy wings, and you didn't need them to reach the goal of relatively high maneuverability with limited aerodynamic difficulty."

94

But since the ramjet engine designed for Talos required a missile body with variable deflection wings, both Talos and Terrier I—which, after all, had started life as a test vehicle for Talos—initially employed wing steering. Nevertheless, Eaton and a small group (all that could be spared from the other ongoing, higher priority APL projects) were given permission to conduct a series of studies and flight tests for the design of a tail-control missile that could intercept high-speed targets at extremely high altitudes. The Laboratory was also able to set up a similar program at Convair's facility in Pomona, though it remained very much a sideline for the time being.

Once the Terrier I moved into production in 1950, however, it became imperative to begin planning follow-on programs. "As time went on," said Eaton, "it became quite generally evident that the next step ought to be tail control, though that became evident with difficulty. People had to be convinced." It proved especially difficult to convince Convair of the advantages of tail control. Because the tail-controlled Terrier II was an APL innovation and employed technology in which Convair had very little expertise, it seemed evident that any decision to produce the Terrier II would inevitably lead to a diminution of Convair authority over the program.

The battle was complicated by the assumption, held by virtually everyone responsible for the Terrier program, that one step in the missile's growth would be the design of a semiactive homing version of Terrier, both to give the missile greater range and to allow it to intercept aircraft approaching at low altitudes, where shipboard radar often failed to distinguish between an aircraft and its reflections from the water. This situation presented a problem in the design of the missile radome (the radar-transparent "windshield" that covered the homing antenna within the nose of the missile, allowing the homing device to transmit microwave signals and receive the reflections from ap-

95

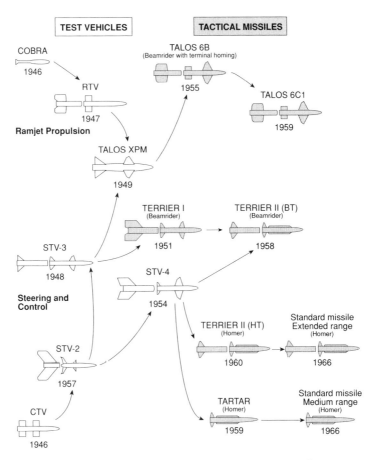

| TEST VEHICLES | TACTICAL MISSILES |

COBRA
1946

TALOS 6B
(Beamrider with terminal homing)
1955

TALOS 6C1
1959

RTV
1947
Ramjet Propulsion

TALOS XPM
1949

TERRIER I
(Beamrider)
1951

TERRIER II (BT)
(Beamrider)
1958

STV-3
1948

Steering and
Control

STV-4
1954

TERRIER II (HT)
(Homer)
1960

Standard missile
Extended range
(Homer)
1966

STV-2
1957

CTV
1946

TARTAR
(Homer)
1959

Standard missile
Medium range
(Homer)
1966

The Bumblebee family tree. Separately tested designs for steering and for propulsion in Talos, Terrier, Tartar, and Standard missiles.

proaching aircraft). Because of its unique configuration, a tail-controlled, homing Terrier required a radome that was virtually optically perfect.

As long as a homing missile stayed below supersonic speeds, a conventional fiberglass radome was quite satisfactory. But when it moved to speeds above Mach 1.7, the missile required a more sophisticated glass-like radome

96

made from an extremely durable material. As Richard Ellis explained, "The problem was to have something that could survive the impact of rain erosion. The missile had to be able to fly through clouds of heavy rain, and when you're traveling at supersonic speeds, a drop of rain is like a .45 bullet hitting you. So they needed an extremely hard material with excellent thermal and electrical characteristics." Further, the forward portion of the radome had to withstand the thermal shock of going from ground temperature to two thousand degrees Fahrenheit within three or four seconds after launching.

To help APL design a suitably durable radome, Kershner enlisted the aid of Corning Glass Corporation, which had extensive expertise in working with hardened, temperature-resistant, glass-like materials. Ralph Robinson, an APL engineer who had served with the Laboratory since the wartime years and had played a major role in the development of the various Terrier models, headed the task group that began working with Corning. Robinson started by examining every existing material that appeared promising, running samples through a variety of ingenious tests at Cornell University, Edwards Air Force Base, and Dahlgren Naval Laboratory to assess their durability. The critical test was provided by a gun-like device, about .22 caliber with a smooth bore, that shot small quantities of lightweight projectiles to simulate raindrops at extremely high velocities.

One by one, Robinson's team rejected each sample material. After three years of experiments, Corning finally offered to develop something entirely new if Robinson would give their technicians the specifications APL needed. "So they came up [in November 1955] with two materials," remembered Robinson. "They flew down to Silver Spring with these specimens, about four inches square and half an inch thick, ground just like jewel blocks. I worked into the evening to get everything ready for the test, by myself, until about ten o'clock at night. Then I heated it up to one

97

thousand degrees Fahrenheit and fired the raindrops at it. And the hair stood up on the back of my head, because I realized at that point that we had reached the promised land. We had made our breakthrough. We had a material that would withstand raindrops at Mach 3, that was manufacturable, and would do the job." The material became popularly known as Pyroceram, and as befitted a project that benefited both partners, Corning used the Pyroceram formula to produce a whole new line of best-selling temperature-resistant ceramic cookware.

The seeking device in Terrier II was adapted from the nation's first semiactive homing system (that is, one that took over in mid-flight, as the missile neared its target) designed by the Raytheon Corporation for use with the Navy's Sparrow missile. Using Raytheon's DPN-24 "seeker" as a model, the Laboratory developed its own eight-inch parabolic homing dish with a redesigned gimbal system and a modified electronics and guidance package. Ellis and his associates then fabricated a series of prototype radomes in an elaborately equipped darkroom at the Laboratory, grinding them until they were free of distortions (much as one would make a pair of prescription eyeglasses) and then carrying out a sort of "eye test" to make sure that the signal did not waver because of lingering imperfections.

Meanwhile, design improvements to a beam-riding version of Terrier II had proceeded, albeit at a slower pace due to the intensive crash program to salvage Terrier I. It was not until 1954 that the first tail-control test vehicle—a fifteen-inch-diameter missile known as STV-4—was successfully launched. That missile, however, still had large fixed wings on the sides, which presented severe shipboard storage and handling problems; ultimately, the Navy decided that the STV-4 was simply too radical a change and too costly to shift into production at that time.

But additional control design studies at APL revealed that the four wings could simply be removed and replaced with much smaller dorsal "fins" near the rear of the missile. This alternative Terrier II model—which incorporated the modular, sectionalized approach of the Terrier 1B, a reduced thirteen-and-one-half-inch diameter, and a new tail-control aerodynamic configuration that tilted the entire missile body to provide improved maneuverability—now became known as the Terrier BT (for *beam*-riding, *tail*-control).

It had always been APL policy to bring into the development process as soon as possible the industrial contractors who would perform the production engineering and actually produce the missile, and the BT program demonstrated just how much this sort of cooperation could smooth the path of development. Since much of the design and early testing work on the BT had been carried out at Pomona with the assistance of a small group of Convair engineers, a bond already had been created at the working level between Alvin Eaton's APL team members and their Convair counterparts.

Furthermore, the division of authority evident in earlier stages of missile development was resolved by assigning a responsible officer to facilitate the decision-making process. "It was a very different world then, because all the decisions could be made by a triumvirate," recalled Eaton. "We [APL] did have technical direction, which was a very meaningful term in those days. It really meant technical control from design on into production. Then there was a Navy commander who represented the Navy and had very considerable authority; and then there was someone at Pomona [in the case of Terrier II] who could represent the operation there."

This relationship proved invaluable when the initial flight tests revealed numerous bugs in the Terrier BT, most of which were nothing more than the consequences of the technical advances that made the missile so effective. For instance, the BT used a high-energy power supply to give it a longer flight time than its predecessors had, but the fuel tended to overheat and start spectacular fires in mid-flight. The prolonged flight times meant that rocket tail pipes often burned through before the missile reached its target, and the advanced, quick-response autopilot turned out to be so finely tuned that it often overreacted, sending the missile spinning wildly through the air, out of control. These gyrations were also occasionally exacerbated by occasional intense vibrations that nearly shook the thirteen-and-one-half-inch-diameter airframe apart.

Using computer models and wind tunnel studies, APL and Convair engineers identified and solved all these problems in record time. Less than three years passed—actually, two years and nine months—after the first specifications were approved for the Terrier BT until the missile went into production in 1959. (Although everyone recognized that the future lay with the homing version of Terrier II—the HT—the Navy decided to approve the BT for production to permit the fleet to take advantage of its improved performance as quickly as possible.)

Since the BT employed entirely new technology, the rapid completion of this program represented a remarkable achievement, made possible only by the willingness of the Bureau of Ordnance and the Laboratory's management to support an experimental program without undue interference. "Of course we were allowed to fail," said Eaton. "We were allowed to learn from flight failures and to continue. And we had a lot of flight failures. But by the time we got into production, as far as the missile was concerned, we were in pretty good shape."

Eventually the BT gave way to the homing version of Terrier II, which possessed greater range and better low-altitude coverage, but the BT remained a vital part of the fleet's defense after it was outfitted with a nuclear warhead. As Thomas Sheppard explained, beam-riding missiles were the preferred vehicles for nuclear weapons because of safety considerations. "You had more positive control

100

with a beam rider," noted Sheppard. "With a homing missile, you shoot it and it goes you may not know where. A beam rider, on the other hand, goes where you direct it."

The modification of the BT to a nuclear-armed missile commenced late in 1955, when BuOrd embarked on an intensive program to increase the Navy's store of atomic weapons. Recent advances in building smaller, lighter, tactical nuclear warheads appeared to make them feasible for such missiles as Terrier II (and, of course, the Talos Whammy). In mid-1956, therefore, a joint committee known as the BuOrd Field Command/Air Forces Special Weapons Project was formed, consisting of representatives of the Lawrence Livermore Laboratory; the Sandia Corporation of the Atomic Energy Commission; the Naval Ordnance Laboratory (NOL) at White Oak, Maryland; and the Applied Physics Laboratory, with Alvin Eaton serving as chairman, representing both APL and the Navy.

Working with the Livermore physicists and Sandia engineers, Eaton recalled, was definitely a challenging and rewarding experience. Neither group had previously been subjected to the type of systematic technical direction APL employed, particularly the Laboratory's techniques for efficient system integration. The difficulties involved in maintaining effective communication between the organizations was further complicated by the fact that various components of the proposed weapon system had been developed independently by different sources—the warhead came from Sandia, the missile from Convair, and the fuzing system from NOL. Later, however, when design difficulties arose, representatives of both Sandia and Livermore were impressed by the ease with which the necessary modifications could be achieved by means of the disciplined interface process established by APL. By early 1959, when the nuclear version of the Terrier BT, now renamed BT(N), was ready for flight testing, the two organizations openly praised APL's management of the program.

101

Tartar: A Terrier for Small Ships

Amid the proliferating versions of Terrier, though, there still was no guided missile small enough to be suitable for deployment aboard the Navy's destroyer fleet. In 1951–52, an APL feasibility study group recommended the development of a wingless, tail-control, eight-inch-diameter missile for this smaller class of ships, but technological limitations and the Terrier I crisis kept the project simmering on a back burner. When the immediate emergency at Pomona abated, however, BuOrd reiterated its interest in obtaining a destroyer-launched missile within five years.

In early 1957, the Navy issued Operational Requirement AD07703, calling for a highly capable air defense missile configured for use on destroyers. APL responded by forming another task force, headed by Thomas Sheppard, to study the development of a brand-new small-ship missile that combined the sectionalized, modular design of the Terrier with a homing guidance system and, most important for the destroyer class of ships, a single rocket that could supply both boost and thrust.

After Sheppard's group issued its first report in July 1954, it became apparent that the small-ship missile envisioned by APL—which was to be ten inches in diameter—was close enough to the proposed thirteen-and-one-half-inch Terrier HT design that the two missiles could be made largely identical, with numerous interchangeable sections to take maximum advantage of the advances already achieved by the Terrier program and the economies of a single production line. In January 1955, APL submitted a detailed proposal to BuOrd to design and develop a complete small-ship guided-missile system known as Tartar.

One important feature of the Laboratory's proposal was the highly compact design of the missile magazine and launcher, which could directly replace the five-inch forward gun mounts previously employed on destroyers. The detailed design of the magazine and launcher was done by a Norwegian-born APL engineer named Sverre (Steven) Kongelbeck, a man of considerable talents in a variety of pursuits. In his youth, Kongelbeck—a close friend of King Olaf of Norway—had won international athletic fame as an Olympic-class swimmer and Norway's heavyweight boxing champion; then, while working as an engineer for a diamond mine in South Africa, he reportedly had performed an emergency appendectomy on one of the local people. After emigrating to the United States, Kongelbeck had become the principal mechanical designer of the University of California's cyclotron before casting his lot with APL in 1952. There his talent for innovative design of complex mechanisms proved invaluable when the Navy adopted the Laboratory's design concept for the Tartar missile.

Although the Navy wished to proceed at once with Tartar, officials in the Department of Defense held up approval for six months because the Army was already far along in developing its Hawk missile, which was approximately the same size as Tartar and appeared (to Pentagon officials, at least) to represent a viable alternative for destroyers, thus rendering Tartar unnecessary. Only when further DoD studies revealed that the Hawk's huge delta wings and the near total lack of safety provisions for operating the missile in a shipboard environment made the Hawk entirely unsuitable for the fleet's purposes did the Navy receive permission to issue a Tartar missile development contract.

In December 1955 BuOrd awarded that contract to Convair. Given the confusion and infighting that had occurred in the Terrier I program, it was not surprising that APL asked for and received complete responsibility for technical direction of the missile development and advisory and coordinating responsibility for the development of the shipboard system. By mid-1957 the Tartar project team, led by Sheppard, had devised a new rocket motor that could provide initial thrust and then throttle down to sustaining speed. When the first Tartar control test vehicle was launched in July of that year, however, it veered sharply off course, turned almost completely around, and landed to the rear of the launcher. Undaunted, the Tartar project team returned to the drawing board, and one year later the first prototype Tartar missile successfully intercepted a target in its initial launch.

That milestone marked the end of an era at the Applied Physics Laboratory. Since 1945, the Laboratory had concentrated most of its resources on the Bumblebee and "3T" programs (the Talos, Terrier, and Tartar guided-missile systems). Now, in the latter half of the 1950s, APL entered a new phase of its history, one that would take the Laboratory far beneath the surface of the sea and out into the mysteries of interplanetary space.

At White Sands Missile Range in the New Mexico desert, left to right, Talos, Terrier, and Tartar.

CHAPTER FOUR

POLARIS AND TRANSIT

*The people who get opportunities
are those who recognize them as
they go by.*

——*Ralph Gibson*

On July 24, 1957, the top leadership of the Applied Physics Laboratory held a brainstorming session in the director's conference room to generate proposals for future projects for the Laboratory. As assistant director for technical operations, Alexander Kossiakoff presided over the meeting; also in attendance were Wilbur Goss, Richard Kershner, William Avery, George Carlton (head of the Triton Division), Alvin Schulz, and Frank McClure. Although these men often had met unofficially to exchange ideas, this was the first time they had gathered formally for such an exercise. They had come together on this occasion because the cold war was going through one of its periodic thaws, and there recently had been strong indications from the Pentagon that defense-related research organizations such as APL might wish to start taking on civilian projects to cover anticipated cuts in military spending.

During the July 24 meeting, sixteen separate projects were proposed and discussed, including "thinking machines," a rocket-powered airfoil device (code-named "Dragonfly") capable of transporting individuals over short distances, and the construction of a nuclear research reactor at the Laboratory's Howard County facility. In the

105

end, Kossiakoff asked for a vote to see which proposals appeared most desirable and most likely to receive substantial funding. As one might have expected, the projects that finished near the top of the list—the development of panoramic passive radar, high-energy fuels, an air-to-surface missile, and countermeasure controls to protect guided missiles from jamming and other forms of electronic interference—were all closely related to work already in progress at APL; most also were tasks of interest to BuOrd, still the Laboratory's primary sponsor.

Farther down the list, in ninth place, was a proposal put forth by Kershner to expand APL's limited participation in the Navy's recently established Polaris strategic submarine program. And ranked in the penultimate spot, behind suggestions to mine the ocean floor and develop a short-range antibomb missile, stood Frank McClure's suggestion to carry out studies of the earth's magnetic field.

This ballot did not necessarily reflect the APL leadership's lack of interest in either space exploration or submarine technology. Indeed, the Laboratory had already established under the auspices of the Research Center a small study group of about six people in the field of space science, and a few individuals from the Laboratory—including Kershner, Avery, and Kossiakoff—had been assisting the Navy in an evaluation of the Polaris program in its early stages. The point is, rather, that it was impossible for anyone at APL to know just how intimately the future of the Laboratory would be interwoven with submarines and the exploration of outer space. After all, the Laboratory always had viewed the antiair defense of the fleet as its primary mission. Certainly with the shock of Sputnik still several months away, the Eisenhower administration had paid little heed, in terms of budgetary support, to the need for space research. And in July 1957 the Polaris program, which eventually formed an indispensible part of the U.S. strategic triad, still remained on shaky ground eighteen months after it had received Pentagon approval for full-scale development.

In looking back, it is important to remember that Polaris had to overcome immense hurdles before it could become an integral part of the fleet. Ever since the end of World War II, a group of bright junior Navy officers had advocated enthusiastically the development of a U.S. ship-launched ballistic missile system. Because their proposals represented a radical redirection of the Navy's traditional role in the American defense structure and would have given the fleet a strategic responsibility it had never enjoyed before, they attracted violent opposition from the Army and the Air Force—both of which viewed such a system as an infringement on their turf—and from a substantial segment of the Navy establishment itself.

As the U.S. defense budget shrank in the postwar years, it became clear that any allocation of funds for a fleet ballistic missile force would trigger a corresponding reduction in the budget for regular ship construction or the nuclear submarine program, or both. For the hierarchy of the United States Navy, an institution rightly renowned for its tenacious adherence to tradition, the notion of jeopardizing the welfare of the surface fleet for a speculative submarine missile system was virtually unthinkable. In short, the regular Navy leadership placed a higher priority on the fulfillment of its day-to-day operational needs than on the long-range development of a fleet ballistic missile system, thus providing confirmation of Admiral Mark Woods's contention that fleet commanders should not be the sole arbiters of the types of weapon systems the Navy may need in the future.

Beyond the issue of funding, there was a long-standing distrust of modern rocket technology among many Navy officers. An experimental test of a liquid-fueled missile aboard a dry-docked ship in 1949 had ended disastrously when liquid oxygen had spilled across the deck, cracking steel plates and splitting support beams. (This mishap, incidentally, had also solidified support within the Bureau of Ordnance for the ramjet Talos and the solid-propellant Terrier over liquid-fueled alternatives.)

Even though there were lingering doubts about solid-fueled rockets, because of their disturbing tendency to explode in mid-flight, the Navy had agreed to sponsor a small-scale research effort, led by Captain Levering Smith, into solid-fuel missile technology at the Inyokern Naval Ordnance Testing Station. Steady progress in that field in the early 1950s, added to the contributions of APL and its associate contractors through the Bumblebee program, gradually dispelled much of the hostility within the fleet toward the deployment of solid-fuel shipboard missiles. When the Atomic Energy Commission informed the Pentagon in 1954 that it had succeeded in reducing drastically the size and weight of nuclear warheads, the feasibility of a submarine-based deterrent force appeared to improve dramatically.

The final push toward the creation of a fleet ballistic missile system came from a report by the Technological Capabilities Panel of the Science Advisory Committee. Popularly known as the Killian Committee, after its chairman, James T. Killian, Jr., this high-level group of experts had been assembled in the spring of 1954 at the request of President Eisenhower, who instructed them to assess the strategic vulnerability of the United States to a surprise attack. In its report to the president eleven months later, the Killian Committee emphasized its serious concern over the vulnerability of the U.S. strategic delivery systems (i.e., long-range bombers and land-based intercontinental ballistic missiles) to enemy attack. To reduce that vulnerability, the committee strongly recommended the development of a ship-based ballistic missile system at the earliest possible moment. To make the deterrent even less visible, the Navy decided to put its intermediate-range ballistic missiles aboard submarines, where, given the state of existing technology, they would be impossible to detect.

APL and the Special Projects Office

Eisenhower approved the Killian Committee's report in September 1955. Within three months the Navy had formed a small task force known as the Special Projects Office (the name was deliberately kept vague for reasons of secrecy) to coordinate the development of a fleet ballistic missile system. To keep the Special Projects Office (SP) free of intraservice jurisdictional squabbles, it was established as an entirely separate organization whose chief would report directly and exclusively to the secretary of the Navy. The officer chosen to head SP was Rear Admiral William F. Raborn, a former deputy director of the Navy's guided-missile program; Captain Levering Smith, later promoted to admiral, became the technical director of SP.

Initially there was considerable pressure on SP to adapt an existing intermediate-range missile—specifically, the army's Jupiter system—for submarine use. But since the Jupiter was liquid fueled and a monstrous thing besides, standing forty-four feet high and weighing 160,000 pounds, Levering Smith knew perfectly well that it was unsuitable for submarine use. So Smith formed an ad hoc committee of rocket and missile experts to provide him with an independent assessment of the technical feasibility of both the existing and the prospective systems and to point out potential trouble spots down the line. Turning to the Applied Physics Laboratory to help staff this advisory group, Smith asked Alexander Kossiakoff and William Avery, both of whom he had known since their wartime service at Allegany Ballistics Laboratory, to serve on the committee.

Bolstered by the committee's report in the summer of 1956, Smith and Raborn concluded that SP needed to develop a new weapon system; in December, Secretary (of Defense) Charles E. Wilson authorized the Navy to initiate such a program. As a first step, Raborn established a series of design committees, coordinated by Smith (who acted as a sort of technical director) and staffed by contractors such as Lockheed, Westinghouse, MIT, and General Electric. The blueprints that eventually emerged called for a missile, later named Polaris, which would stand twenty-eight feet high, weigh approximately twenty-eight thousand pounds, and possess an effective range of one thousand to fifteen hundred miles. Though smaller than the mammoth Jupiter, the Polaris booster was still far larger than anything heretofore employed in a U.S. submarine missile system. And the inertial guidance system, developed by MIT's Charles Draper, employed technology that was still largely unproven in practice.

In short, the Polaris system designed by these blue-ribbon committees was an extraordinarily ambitious undertaking. APL's Alexander Kossiakoff, for one, was certainly impressed by the technical challenges it presented. "It was just miles beyond anything that had ever been attempted," recalled Kossiakoff. "The size of the rocket was far bigger than anything we'd tested, and since solid rockets still were not well understood at that time, they were taking a sizable risk." Further, the guidance system needed to be both extremely precise and durable, able to withstand the shock of an undersea launch and subsequent acceleration. And of course the navigation reference system had to allow the submarine commander to determine the position of his boat at all times. As Kossiakoff concluded, it was not an ideal situation for the development of a weapon system: "They were expecting a lot of things that were very high risk to work out all at the same time."

That was precisely why Levering Smith wanted the best systems evaluation expertise he could obtain. As the pace of activity within SP quickened—particularly after the Soviet launching of Sputnik in October 1957 scared Congress into approving an accelerated development schedule for Polaris—Raborn suggested that Smith hire a deputy to share the work load. So Smith went to APL and asked Ralph Gibson if he could borrow Richard Kershner, who had headed the Terrier program at APL since its inception. Though Gibson would not approve Kershner's transfer on a full-time basis, he did agree to make him available at least half-time; Kershner moved into an office at SP as an adviser and technical deputy to Levering Smith.

Captain Smith could not have made a better choice, because Kershner excelled at solving what one former colleague termed "complicated hardware-people problems, making things work politically and technically." Born in Ohio in 1913, Kershner had received a doctorate in mathematics from The Johns Hopkins University in 1937. During the war he had worked with Gibson, Kossiakoff, McClure, and Avery on rocket research and development, first at the Carnegie Institution and then at the Allegany Ballistics Laboratory. A slightly built man who combined a tough, penetrating intelligence with a love of poetry (he enjoyed writing sonnets in his spare time), a refreshing wit, and a perennially rumpled wardrobe, Kershner inspired intense loyalty and affection in his associates.

"He was incredibly honest, both with himself and the people around him," noted Harold Black, who worked closely with Kershner at APL for more than twenty years. "And he had a wonderful sense of humor. He liked to find humor in serious situations." For instance, Kershner did not hesitate to poke fun at the Navy when the occasion warranted a touch of satire, though he remained a deeply patriotic man throughout his life. Kershner also possessed the rare ability to cut through a maze of obscure jargon to summarize clearly the fundamental issues posed by any scientific problem. "He was an incredibly clever and insightful man, and so quick," recalled Carl Bostrom, who joined Kershner at the Laboratory in 1960. "He could grasp whatever anyone was saying, and extend it. He'd say,

111

'Well, what you really mean is . . . ' or 'From that you can see that this would be true. . . .'"

But above all, Kershner was a genuinely warm human being who knew how to lead and motivate a research organization. One of Kershner's trademark managerial techniques at APL, from the early Terrier days to Polaris and later to the space program, was to encourage his staff to obtain hands-on experience with the hardware they were developing, an approach that usually generated enthusiastic response among engineers and scientists. "He was a hell of a leader," said William Frain, who also joined Kershner in the APL space program in the early 1960s; "he had remarkable ways of challenging you." "People really wanted to deliver for that guy," agreed long-time associate Ralph Robinson, "because there was never any question that Kershner was behind you one hundred percent."

Early Polaris Tests

With Kershner serving as Levering Smith's part-time technical deputy, the role of APL in the Polaris program began to expand. As the Polaris system approached its initial test stage in late 1957, Smith asked the Applied Physics Laboratory to evaluate the ground and flight test preparations. This was an extremely vital role in the SP scheme of development, because the office had decided to conduct the most rigorous real-world tests imaginable so that any potential shortcomings in the Polaris system would be exposed at the earliest possible date. Besides, the missiles were so expensive that the tests had to be done right the first time. According to Smith, he selected APL for this critical task primarily because of the Laboratory's "very considerable breadth of science and engineering disciplines," its expertise in assessing weapons from a complete systems viewpoint, and its independent status outside the naval bureaucracy (which, along with the fact that the

Laboratory had not been directly involved in the design of the missile, ensured the sort of objectivity Smith required).

To meet this challenge, APL formally established under Kershner's leadership a small Polaris Division, which was then subdivided into two task forces. The first of these groups assumed control of the Polaris test and evaluation effort and was headed by Kirk Dahlstrom, whom Smith had personally requested to supervise the telemetry analysis. (Dahlstrom was known throughout the Navy as a telemetry wizard. "He could look at a telemetering record and, from the little wiggles, tell you anything," said Kossiakoff. "It was like a doctor listening with his stethoscope.") The other APL Polaris task group, led by Robert Morton, concentrated on the job of systems analysis. But at that stage, the entire APL Polaris Division was intended to be a very temporary organization, lasting only until the first five fleet ballistic missile submarines had successfully completed their initial at-sea test firings.

Right from the start, the APL teams at Cape Canaveral, Florida, should have qualified for hazardous duty. No one had ever successfully launched a missile that looked like the Polaris, with its champagne-bottle shape and huge solid-fueled engines; in fact, the Air Force, which operated the Atlantic Missile Range at the cape, had virtually no experience in solid-propelled rockets at all. Although an early series of Polaris flight test vehicles had flown almost without a hitch, the first full-scale Polaris (AX-1) launch on September 24, 1958, was a disaster. Because of the failure of a twenty-five-dollar piece of electronic equipment, the missile refused to turn out to sea and had to be destroyed several seconds after launching; remnants landed in the nearby Banana River, close to a trailer park. From that moment on, the local residents referred to the Polaris test missiles as the IBRMs—the "in-the-Banana-River missiles."

The next Polaris test missile, the AX-2, separated on the launching pad, sending its second stage soaring wildly into the air; it too had to be destroyed. But those two failures had been caused by mechanical problems that were easily identified and corrected. The next launch vehicle, the AX-3, took off on December 30 without a hitch and flew beautifully for forty-five seconds until it suddenly began to pitch and roll erratically, finally breaking up. The telemetry tapes from this flight were immediately processed and analyzed by a Polaris test evaluation team. Working with engineers from the missile's production contractor, Lockheed Missiles and Space Division, the team identified the problem as excessive heat strain on the missile's jet steering mechanism.

Before Lockheed could remedy the problem, three more Polaris test vehicles went similarly and spectacularly astray in flight. But on April 20, 1959, the AX-6, the first Polaris test missile to incorporate all the required design changes, successfully completed a three-hundred-mile journey into the Atlantic Ocean. The final step, of course, was the launch of a Polaris missile from a submerged vessel. The ship chosen for this task was the USS *George Washington*, the Navy's first fleet ballistic missile submarine. (Actually, the *George Washington* had originally been designed as an attack submarine. To save money and meet the accelerated schedule established by the Pentagon—which called for a Polaris launch no later than mid-1960—the Navy had decided to adapt the submarine and several of its brethren while they were still under construction, slicing their keels in half to insert a 130-foot weapon system section that could carry sixteen Polaris missiles.)

During the time the modified version of the *George Washington* was under assembly at the shipyards of the Electric Boat Division of General Dynamics Corporation in Groton, Connecticut, SP had assigned APL's Polaris systems evaluation group the technical responsibility for integrating and testing the various subsystems on the ship (the launcher, fire control, the missile itself), each of which had been built by a different contractor. "We wrote the requirements for the testing of each of the subsystems in the factories as well as the testing of the entire boat," recalled Robert Kemelhor, who was APL's Polaris launch system specialist. And then, of course, everything had to be tested all over again on the firing launches.

The first two full-scale Polaris launches were scheduled for July 18, 1960. A host of civilian and military dignitaries, including Eisenhower's science adviser, George Kistiakowsky; Admiral Raborn; and Admiral Arleigh Burke (Chief of Naval Operations), along with assorted contractor representatives and a seven-man team from APL, were on board the *George Washington* as it sailed out from Cape Canaveral at six o'clock that morning. Following were several destroyers, a cruiser, a submarine tender, and, at a safe distance, an observation ship carrying about a hundred reporters and photographers. Radar tracking stations up and down the Florida coast had been put on alert. "We had been practicing day in and day out for almost three months with underwater tests," said Kemelhor, who had ridden with the *George Washington*'s crew from Newport, Rhode Island, to the cape and was acting as technical adviser to the submarine's launch officer that day. "We were apprehensive because this had never been done before, and the possibility of an in-tube explosion during the launch phase of a live missile was always with us. We had made plans and rehearsed emergency actions in case of possible malfunction readouts on the launcher panel."

As the countdown to firing the first missile commenced, Kemelhor stood behind the launch officer, watching the indicators on the entire panel board. Everything went smoothly—the hatches were opened, and fifteen of the sixteen lights on the launcher panel had turned green—until T minus eight seconds. The only red light remaining was the indicator for the umbilical cord attached to the warhead. At T minus eight seconds, that cord was supposed to retract, thereby clearing the tube for the missile launch. According to Kemelhor, "The signal was given to

115

retract the umbilical, and the light on the panel went from red to green—which meant good—and then to nothing. Black." The launch officer turned to Kemelhor for help; Kemelhor immediately made a negative gesture, turning his thumb down. "We had a panic button that we could hit and stop the launch," he said, "because you could blow up the submarine if this missile doesn't come out properly. So he hit the panic button and stopped the launch."

Within seconds the skipper, Commander James Osborn—accompanied by Raborn, Levering Smith, Robert Morton, and Kistiakowsky—was down on the launch level demanding (in a not particularly calm manner) to know what had happened. Kemelhor explained that the warning system had been installed to prevent potentially catastrophic accidents, and hence when something malfunctioned, the prudent course of action was always to postpone the test. A postmortem later revealed that the umbilical cord had in fact been half on and half off the missile, apparently because a crew member had substituted a stainless steel pin for the soft shear pin that had been specially designed for the job. The original shear pin was supposed to give way so the cord could retract, but the much tougher stainless steel pin had remained in place. Consequently, any attempt to launch the missile might well have resulted in a disaster.

Given the wealth of publicity attending the planned Polaris launch, a decision was made to try to fire the submarine's second missile at two o'clock that afternoon to avoid undue embarrassment. But once again a malfunction occurred late in the countdown. This time the culprit was a loss of electrical power to an instrumentation monitor that had been inadvertently disconnected, apparently by someone tripping over the cord. At that point Commander Osborn called it a day and the *George Washington* returned to Cape Canaveral. The observation ship, however, was kept at sea for forty-eight hours so that the reporters could not file their stories.

116

After two days of tests, repairs, and alterations, the *George Washington* and its entire entourage headed back out to sea on July 20. After a slight delay, the first missile fired and, after breaking through the surface of the water at a steep angle, recovered and continued on its course. To demonstrate that this success had not been a fluke, the second missile was fired an hour and a half later. It, too, proved successful, thereby providing a much-needed boost to the Polaris program. At the time, however, APL's precise role in the program—once these initial launches had been carried out—remained somewhat uncertain.

A New Dimension

In the meantime, the Laboratory had made another vital contribution to the Polaris program, one that also opened up a whole new avenue of development for APL. As a result of the informal brainstorming sessions among the Laboratory's leadership in early 1957, a space explora-tion study group had been established, consisting of about six senior members of the staff, under the auspices of the Research Center and Frank McClure, to look into ways of applying the Laboratory's technical expertise to the field of space research.

Although this ad hoc study group never submitted any formal proposals, it did create an area of research interest and specialized knowledge within the Laboratory, accord-ing to Gibson, so that "when an idea that was really good came up, they saw it." That one "really good" idea arose in the autumn of 1957, in the wake of the Soviet Union's launching of its Sputnik satellite on October 4. The success of Sputnik caught virtually the entire world by surprise, and the staff of APL were as shocked and disturbed as anyone. More than most observers, the missile systems experts at the Laboratory—especially those who had recently been evaluating the status of the U.S. intercontinental ballistic missile programs for the Pentagon—immediately realized

117

The first submarine-launched Polaris missile emerges from the sea on July 20, 1960. The test program was planned and monitored by APL technical teams both aboard the submarine USS George Washington *and ashore in Cape Canaveral.*

that if the Soviets could put a satellite into orbit, they would not have much difficulty launching ballistic missiles that could strike the United States.

The consternation Sputnik aroused at APL was tempered, however, by the fascination that the Soviet achievement aroused in many members of the Laboratory who actually, in the words of one senior-level APL official, "thought it was pretty neat." One of those who were

118

captivated by the Sputnik episode was William Guier, a member of the Research Center staff who had joined the Laboratory in 1951. Guier, who came to APL with a national reputation for his work in computer simulations for nuclear weapons, belonged to that rising generation of bright, driven, and intensely curious young scientists whom the Laboratory was trying to attract throughout the 1950s. The crucial factors that led Guier, like many others, to join APL were the dynamic character of the Laboratory's leadership (in Guier's case, Frank McClure) and the opportunity to combine basic scientific research with vital strategic defense applications. "McClure was so clear, concise, and visionary," recalled Guier. "He was starting a small group under his tutelage, whose task was to use basic science to come up with new ideas and new weapon systems—not incremental ideas, but big-time new things. And it just sounded fascinating."

For his first six years at APL, Guier worked primarily with a "theoretical task group" led by Robert Hart, which had the enviable assignment of searching through the various departments at the Laboratory for complex weapons problems—such as the low-angle radar dilemma, and advanced guidance signals and processing—that required fundamental scientific research for their solution. Then in October 1957 came the weekend of Sputnik.

"The next Monday I came in," remembered Guier, "and I hadn't really thought about doing anything with Sputnik, but to my surprise, no one was listening to it. They kept saying you could get it on twenty megacycles, and I thought someone would be listening, with all the receivers all over this place. At lunchtime I talked with others, but no one had thought to tune in on it. So in the early afternoon, I decided I'd see if I could get that thing."

Guier had been working recently in the Research Center with George Weiffenbach, a physicist who had joined APL at about the same time. As part of his experiments in microwave spectroscopy, Weiffenbach had been

119

using a shortwave receiver that could pick up very sensitive radio signals. Around four o'clock that afternoon, Weiffenbach stuck a piece of wire into the antenna connection on his receiver, and he and Guier began listening to the distinctive "beep-beep" signals emanating from Sputnik.

They broke for dinner, and when Guier returned to the Laboratory that evening he brought with him a high-quality tape recorder he had recently purchased. Sitting in Weiffenbach's lab, the two men tuned into Sputnik once more and recorded the signals on Guier's machine. On the same track they superimposed precise time signals broadcast by the national time and frequency station (WWV), located in nearby Beltsville. But the tone from the satellite kept changing in frequency, which puzzled everyone—for about five minutes. "I remember listening to it, and it was so steady that I said, 'That's got to be the satellite,'" noted Guier; "'No human could twiddle an oscillator like that.' Then somebody asked why the frequency was constantly changing. And I said, 'Oh, for gosh sakes, that's the Doppler effect. Of course it's going to change, it's going to go down.'"

Sure enough, when Weiffenbach analyzed the tape recordings with the aid of a wave analyzer borrowed from another member of the Research Center staff, the result was "an absolutely gorgeous Doppler shift." In other words, the satellite's signals sounded higher pitched as Sputnik came closer to Washington and lower as it went away, just as a bystander would hear the whistle of a freight train change pitch as the train approaches and passes. (Actually, the differences in pitch made some listeners wonder whether the Sputnik's beeps were actually coded messages, but that notion was quickly discarded by all but the most credulous.)

While waiting for the satellite's next pass over the United States, Guier realized that the slope of the Doppler shift could help him ascertain how far away Sputnik was.

To compute the satellite's path, he and Weiffenbach used the estimated time of Sputnik's arrival over Washington as broadcast by a Moscow shortwave radio station that Weiffenbach had serendipitously picked up on his receiver. After listening and recording data for several days (and losing a great deal of sleep in the process, since most of Sputnik's passes over APL occurred at night), the two physicists discovered they could use a mechanical calculator to predict the satellite's orbit much more accurately than could the elaborate tracking system employed by the Navy's research station in downtown Washington. "We called up the Vanguard headquarters [Vanguard was then the primary U.S. satellite under development] and asked if there was any way we could help them," recalled Guier, "because we knew they were trying to track it and obviously were having trouble. And they said, 'You can certainly tell us when it's coming over,' which we did. I still remember this long pause on the phone. I told him we were computing its orbit from the Doppler shift, and the guy obviously thought I was a nut."

But when Gibson learned that Guier and Weiffenbach were tracking Sputnik more accurately, apparently, than anyone else outside the Soviet Union, he immediately provided them with twenty thousand dollars worth of support from a discretionary fund, which at least allowed them to buy better monitoring equipment. Gibson became so entranced with their research, in fact, that he kept calling them every few days to see how they were doing. Unfortunately, Sputnik I stopped sending signals after the first week because its storage batteries gave out. But Guier took his calculations and began processing them on the Laboratory's recently installed Univac 1103 digital computer, to put them on a more accurate quantitative basis.

When the Soviets launched Sputnik II on November 3, the signals from space resumed and Weiffenbach and Guier discovered that with the aid of the Univac they were able to carry out even more sophisticated experiments with

121

their Doppler data. They still were tracking the satellite more accurately than anyone else in the nation; moreover, they were doing it from a single station, thereby defying the conventional wisdom that at least two stations were needed to track a spacecraft accurately.

For nearly six months, Guier and Weiffenbach and a small team of colleagues persisted in tracking first Sputnik II and then the first U.S. satellite, Explorer I, which was launched at the end of January 1958. Finally, on March 17, 1958, Frank McClure called the two young physicists into his office. Up to that time, Guier had believed that McClure was not terribly excited about their discovery, but on that particular Monday morning Guier learned he had been mistaken. "I now know why you were doing this," McClure told them, whereupon he began outlining the implications of their work for a new system of ocean navigation.

On the previous Friday night, McClure suddenly had been struck by the realization that one could stand the whole Doppler tracking procedure on its head. As he explained to his colleagues, "If you can find the orbit of a satellite, you sure as hell can find the listening station on earth from the orbit";[1] that is, if you knew in detail the orbit of a satellite and the precise time of its passing, you could use the Doppler effect to compute your location on the ground. McClure had phoned Richard Kershner that evening to bounce the concept off him, and the two had spent the whole weekend working out the preliminary details of a navigational system that could employ this radically innovative principle. By Sunday night they had finished the job.

On March 18, one day after his meeting with Guier and Weiffenbach, McClure laid out the entire situation in a memorandum to Gibson. Although McClure acknowledged the potential importance of his discovery to the developing Polaris system, he was far more excited about its peaceful applications for naval communications. "I believe this could turn out to be one of the most important jobs APL could undertake," McClure declared.[2] Assuming

122

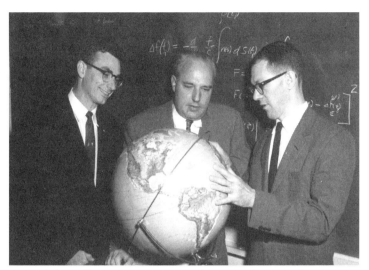

From left, William H. Guier, Frank T. McClure, and George C. Weiffenbach. Guier and Weiffenbach developed the first successful method of tracking satellites by use of the Doppler shift; McClure invented the Doppler method of navigation.

that the Laboratory could design a shipboard console-computer to receive and analyze the satellite's signals, McClure reasoned that "one could envision such a console on every ship at sea, giving the precise location of the ship on a one- or two-hour basis from a system of satellites, perhaps only ten in number. It occurs to me that the establishment of such a system might represent a wonderful cold war opportunity for the United States in providing world navigation to anyone who would make such a console a part of the equipment of his ship." Almost immediately upon receipt of McClure's note, Gibson phoned Milton Eisenhower, who had assumed the presidency of The Johns Hopkins University a year earlier, to help spread news of this breakthrough to the top levels of the civilian and military administration in Washington.

Unknown to the leadership of APL, however, a special presidential committee already had been established to

123

evaluate opportunities in the field of satellite technology. To recoup at least some of the scientific prestige lost to the Soviet Union (and recapture some of the momentum lost when the Eisenhower administration canceled an army satellite launching program in 1956), it was clear that the federal government was going to have to fund a major program to build and launch satellites. This presidential committee—which later evolved into the Advanced Research Projects Agency (ARPA) and subsequently into the Defense Advanced Research Projects Agency (DARPA)—was assigned the task of recommending the most valuable military and scientific applications for orbiting spacecraft. Since APL was virtually the only research organization in the nation with a specific proposal to use satellites for navigation, the committee's chairman, Herbert York, asked to visit the Laboratory to examine its ideas in detail.

Right from the start, the committee was intensely interested in the Laboratory's plans. The notion of using a satellite for navigation was clearly a tremendous advance over any existing system of celestial navigation, since it could operate both day and night in all kinds of weather and did not require the ship to carry any directional antennas. APL also was able to provide ARPA with a fairly complete system design (complete with block diagrams, power and weight estimates, and an accuracy analysis) even at this early stage. As devised by McClure and Kershner, the navigation system would consist of four basic elements: (1) a satellite containing a highly precise crystal-driven clock or cycle counter, a frequency generator, and a dual-frequency radio transmitter to beam signals to earth; (2) a network of tracking stations to measure the frequency of the received satellite signals; (3) an injection station, or communication channel, to permit ground engineers to insert the predicted orbital positions of the satellite (which they calculated using the previous day's tracking data) into the spacecraft's memory every twelve hours; and, of course, (4) the shipboard navigation set to receive and

124

interpret the signals broadcast by the satellite. Even before the system was built, Kershner and McClure assured the committee that it would permit a ship to identify its location anywhere on earth with an accuracy of one-half nautical mile or better.

After the second round of APL testimony (this time at the Pentagon), York was sufficiently impressed to ask Weiffenbach point blank how much money the Laboratory would need to get the project under way. Guier and Weiffenbach looked at each other for a moment and then, pulling a number out of the air, Weiffenbach nonchalantly answered, "Well, $250,000 would be a good start." "You've got it," York replied. "Start writing a formal proposal to back this up."

Transit: Navigation by Satellite

For a year and a half, ARPA funded at APL the research and development of the world's first navigational satellite. Like everything else the Laboratory developed, the satellite's name had to start with a T (for Tuve, remember), and hence it came to be known as Transit. Ironically, the concept of a navigational satellite was not greeted with open arms by the Navy hierarchy. According to Ralph Gibson, "Most of the Navy at that time thought that they could navigate accurately enough, and so they weren't particularly interested in another system. To tell the truth, the rest of the Navy couldn't have cared less. . . .Besides, they weren't sure that it would work; lots of people said that it wouldn't."[3]

Special Projects, however, knew that its Polaris submarines would require an extremely accurate navigation system, to enable them to know precisely where they were when they launched their missiles. The original Polaris inertial guidance system—known as SINS, as designed by Draper at MIT—required the submarines to surface occasionally to reset their gyros, but since the whole point of the

Polaris program was to provide a hidden deterrent force, the notion of remaining underwater and using signals from a satellite was clearly a far more attractive option. Besides, SP was used to taking chances on innovative technologies, and Raborn and Smith certainly had plenty of firsthand experience with both the scientific capabilities of APL and the personal leadership qualities of the Laboratory's top professional staff.

So SP prevailed on ARPA to increase its funding of Transit, and, in its usual fashion, SP managed the program with a minimum of red tape. "There were no constraints put upon us," observed Weiffenbach. "The only question I ever heard from them was, Do you need more money? And our answer always was no, because we wouldn't have known what to do with any more money than we had."

On the other hand, the rest of the Navy refused to accept Transit for a number of years. The Bureau of Navigation (BuNav), in particular, remained hostile to the program because Transit had superseded its own satellite navigation proposal. Unfortunately, the BuNav system involved a large radio telescope with a sizable radar dish and gimbals. BuNav proposed to launch satellites carrying simple radio transmitters that would act as targets for the radio telescope, and since most of this extensive tracking equipment had to be located above decks, the system did not particularly gladden hearts at Special Projects. Although the regular Navy's opposition to Transit did not slow the project in its early stages, largely because of SP's political clout within the service, it did have unfortunate repercussions down the road.

Like many new tasks the Laboratory undertook, the Transit project was initially assigned to a special group in the director's office until it became a separate organizational entity of its own. From the start, Richard Kershner assumed leadership of the Transit program, partly because of his existing close relationship with SP (he was still serving as Levering Smith's technical deputy at the time) and partly because he was looking for something else to occupy his restless mind after the successful completion of the Terrier development effort. Rather than bring new employees into the Laboratory to work on Transit, Kershner drafted staff members from the various Bumblebee missile systems groups. Originally, Kershner planned to build eight experimental Transit satellites, each more sophisticated than its predecessor, and he told his fledgling organization at the outset that he expected the project to take seven years from concept to a viable, fully functioning system—a prediction that turned out to be uncannily accurate.

Throughout the first eighteen months, the frenetic pace of the satellite program was reminiscent of the early Bumblebee days. "It was just go as fast as you can," noted Guier, who spent most of his days deriving equations and stuffing them into the Laboratory's Univac computer. Here the vast experience of the APL scientific and engineering staff, gained during more than a decade of intensive guided-missile systems development and high-altitude research, proved an invaluable asset to the nation. By fabricating many of the prototype components of its 3T (Talos, Terrier, and Tartar) guided missiles—recall the Terrier 1B experience—the Laboratory had learned how to make complex electronic devices that could withstand the shock and acceleration of rocket launchings. Through its involvement with the Polaris program, APL was also building up a detailed knowledge of the fleet ballistic missile submarines and their unique physical characteristics. And most important, the Laboratory's oft-demonstrated willingness to carry a technical development project from the initial design phase through the engineering and production stages now enabled APL to meet the Transit challenge in an amazingly short time.

This ability was indeed fortunate, because the Transit team had to cross uncharted territory simultaneously in a number of technical areas: designing entirely new computing hardware and software, developing more precise atmospheric models, building oscillators with sufficient stability to withstand the pressures of launch and still remain accurate, determining what effect (if any) the Van Allen radiation belts might have on the effective life of the spacecraft, and calculating how high into orbit the satellite needed to go to overcome air drag and how low it had to stay to obtain accurate readings.

Probably the most vexing difficulty arose from an unexpected quarter, when the APL Transit team confirmed that the shape of the earth, especially the northern hemisphere, was far less regular than previously believed. In fact, the earth's gravitational field appeared downright bumpy in places. This revelation obviously had critical implications for the accuracy of the proposed navigation system. "It became very obvious early on that, because the earth's gravitational field was much more complex than we had thought, one needed tracking stations pretty much all over the world to get the best out of the system," observed Ralph Gibson. "The satellite was moving in an orbit, but a much more complex orbit than the early theory would indicate."[4] To learn more about this "gravitational error" phenomenon, the Transit group instituted an intensive geodetic research effort, with massive computer programs that took weeks to write and eighteen hours to run on the weekends. Soon the Laboratory's geodesy program had grown into a significant research and satellite-building operation of its own, continuing for well over a decade.

While the first experimental Transit satellite was being constructed at APL, the Laboratory also designed and built Transit tracking stations and transported them to four remote locations: Austin, Texas; Seattle, Washington; Las Cruces, New Mexico; and Argentia, Newfoundland (the site of the famous Roosevelt-Churchill conference in 1941). A fifth tracking station was located at the APL facility in Howard County, Maryland. (The APL tracking equipment, including a Doppler antenna, was located in a specially constructed tower and control room on the roof of the main building.) In addition, the British government built and erected its own station at the Royal Aircraft Establishment in Farnborough, Hampshire. All these stations were connected by telephone and telegraph to the Transit control center in Howard County, as were the blockhouse at the Atlantic Missile Range at Cape Canaveral, the APL Computing Center, and the Parsons Auditorium at APL—the latter serving as the Laboratory's observation post.

On Friday, September 17, 1959—barely nine months after the Laboratory received the initial Transit funds from ARPA—the first APL satellite, known as Transit 1A, was ready for launch from Cape Canaveral. (The 130-pound satellite had been shipped in a plain wooden box from the Laboratory to the cape by truck, with no fanfare and little advance publicity.) All the components had been so thoroughly tested ahead of time that few among the Transit team had any doubt that the satellite would operate as designed; instead, they were far more concerned about how long it would last in the uncertain environment of outer space.

At 10:33 a.m., the three-stage Thor-Able rocket that carried the Transit 1A blasted off the launchpad. Two minutes later, APL observers in the Parsons Auditorium learned that the Howard County station was locked onto two frequencies from the satellite as it sped across the Atlantic, rising to an altitude of approximately two hundred miles. Shortly thereafter, the tracking station at Argentia reported that it too was receiving signals from the satellite. Using these signals, technicians at APL determined the Doppler frequency shift and plotted the data on large charts. For the first eleven minutes, the frequency shifts exactly matched the theoretical curves that had been calculated weeks in advance. But then, where there should have been a break in the curve signaling an acceleration from the ignition of the third stage of the rocket, the curve simply continued to follow a smooth course. Meanwhile, the Farnborough

129

station reported that clear signals had been received from the satellite for several minutes and then suddenly died away.

By that time, it had become clear to the Transit observation team at APL that the third stage of the rocket had failed to ignite, sending the satellite plunging into the sea about three hundred miles southwest of Ireland. But in those first brief minutes of radio contact, the spacecraft had demonstrated that the electronic gear designed and fabricated at the Laboratory had withstood the shock and vibration of launch and the subsequent high acceleration. Perhaps more significant, it proved that ground stations could use the satellite's signals to plot its orbit; when an APL team was able to use the Doppler shift data to predict within five miles where the third stage of the rocket had landed, Kershner declared unequivocally, "We're in."

Gibson certainly had no lingering doubts either, and so on January 1, 1960, the Applied Physics Laboratory officially established its Space Development Division, headed of course by Kershner. Initially, the division consisted of four separate task groups for research and analysis, satellite design, system engineering, and ground systems. On April 13, the second Transit satellite (Transit 1B) was launched from Cape Canaveral. A slightly more sophisticated version of its predecessor, with different radio frequencies and enhanced electrical power, the 1B also had the advantage of being boosted by a more reliable rocket, the two-stage Thor-Able-Star. To prepare for the day when two or more satellites could be launched atop a single rocket, a dummy test weight was added to the nose cone of the Able-Star.

Again the Transit tracking stations heard the signals from the satellite as the 1B soared skyward, and this time the spacecraft made it safely into orbit. Although the 1B failed to reach the planned altitude of eight hundred miles, it performed well enough to reinforce the Doppler data obtained from the 1A. Buoyed by this success, the fledgling Space Development Division solidified its position as a

130

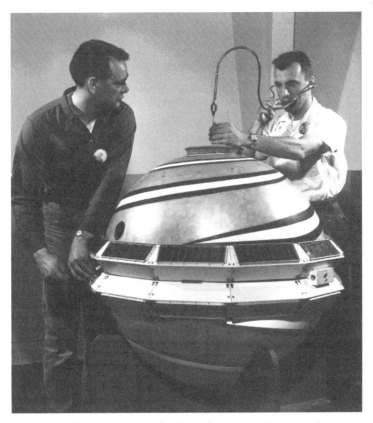

Transit 1B being prepared for launch at Cape Canaveral.

permanent and vital part of the Laboratory as it continued to design and build the remaining satellites in the experimental Transit series.

For the first time in its history, the Applied Physics Laboratory was engaged in a large-scale development task that was not directly related to the defense of the United States surface fleet. Insofar as this effort opened up a whole new set of potential sponsors—notably the National Aeronautics and Space Administration (NASA)—it proved a significant boon to the Laboratory. But as Gibson clearly recognized, the value of the Space Development Division extended far beyond any tangible benefits. "It gave us a new objective," the director confirmed, "and that's always important. Many laboratories just live with dead objectives, and then they die, too. This gave everybody a shot in the arm."[5] And that was precisely what the Laboratory needed in 1960, because its guided-missile programs had recently suffered a series of discouraging setbacks.

CHAPTER FIVE

FROM MISSILES TO SYSTEMS

*I don't know why your radar can't
lock onto that airplane; dammit, I
can see it!*

—— *Anonymous Navy captain
on board a Terrier ship*

When President Eisenhower entered the White House in March 1953, he embarked on a crusade to control federal spending and, in particular, reduce the defense budget. But as his predecessor, Harry Truman, had predicted, it was far more difficult for Eisenhower to obtain compliance from Congress and the federal bureaucracy than from the Allied armies in World War II. Despite the administration's much-publicized campaign to obtain "more bang for the buck" by reducing conventional forces and relying on a strategic nuclear deterrent, military spending proved far more resistant to reductions than the president expected. But in the summer of 1957, with the nation on the brink of another severe recession, Eisenhower renewed his determination to bring the Pentagon's budget under control.

One of the president's favorite fiscal targets had always been the military services' guided-missile programs. Eisenhower was convinced (with considerable justification) that the Army, Navy, and Air Force were still pursuing too many separate projects, developing too many individual systems that, in his words, "seemed to resemble one another quite markedly in their capabilities." The revelation that DoD had spent $11.8 billion on missile programs

133

in fiscal 1956 and 1957, far beyond the administration's target ceiling of $3.8 billion per year, angered the president. In a meeting of the National Security Council on July 3, 1957, Eisenhower insisted, "A choice must be made of the best all-round program, because we could not afford to carry on so many programs in the quest for a missile which would have the quality of perfection. . . .We cannot hope for a perfect family of these weapons designed to achieve every purpose in warfare."[1] Unfortunately, the example the president chose on that particular occasion to identify as expendable was one of APL's missiles, the Tartar, which Eisenhower claimed should be eliminated because "its estimated performance seemed to lie somewhere in between the Terrier missile and the advanced Terrier missile" (Terrier II).

Apparently the president was unaware that the Tartar was designed for an entirely different class of ship than the Terrier missiles and could not be cut out of the budget without jeopardizing the safety of the Navy's destroyer fleet. The Tartar program survived Eisenhower's assault, but his determination to slash the missile research and development budget—a decision that was seconded by Secretary (of Defense) Charles Wilson—struck the Applied Physics Laboratory in another, more vulnerable area.

The Federal Budget Pinches

By the summer of 1957 the Laboratory's Triton program had reached the advanced planning and preliminary design stage. There appeared to be few major technical breakthroughs yet to be made, and contractors already were at work developing specific components. Convinced that the Triton concept was far superior to any other long-range bombardment missile available to the Navy, Gibson had authorized an expansion in the APL Triton staff in the fall and winter of 1956. "I am sure," Gibson wrote in

September 1957, "it [Triton] would give us the operational capability of penetrating into almost all the military targets in the heartland of potentially enemy territory earlier than any other missile now contemplated."[2]

From every angle, the Triton appeared to be a formidable weapon indeed. Impartial assessments had concluded that its map-reading guidance system was far superior to any other such system then under development. Its predicted accuracy at ranges up to two thousand miles meant that the Triton, unlike other intermediate-range missiles, did not need to depend on mass destruction to be effective. And since much of the preliminary development work already had been completed, it represented a relatively inexpensive alternative to its less well-advanced competitors.

Nevertheless, in the first week of September 1957, the Chief of Naval Operations abruptly cancelled the Triton program. The decision was forced by the Bureau of Ordnance's inability to fund Triton full-scale development and production from its severely reduced budget without support from other appropriations allocated to the Navy. Rather than fund a long-range cruise missile such as Triton, the Navy chose to cast its lot with the Polaris ballistic missile.

Gibson felt the pain of Triton's cancellation deeply. From a national strategic perspective, he firmly believed that the system's demise left the United States bereft of an essential element in its continental defense. Gibson wrote to JHU president Milton Eisenhower on September 6, "We are convinced that the Navy needs a weapon system with all the capabilities of Triton, [and] the need may grow rather than decline."[3] Although the cancellation order's effect on the Laboratory was far less significant than the perceived strategic consequences for the nation, Gibson informed Eisenhower that the Navy's decision would also have a deleterious effect on the morale of the Laboratory staff:

All who worked on it [Triton] believed in it thoroughly, and knew that it was almost universally recognized to be pointed to a needed objective, well planned, ingeniously implemented and economically carried out. Yet the decision against this program has been made, not on the basis of any objective analysis comparing the operational characteristics, cost, and effectiveness of Triton with other weapons in the same operational field, but on the basis of budgetary expediency.

I am distressed, therefore, by the impact of such a decision on people whom we must ask for continued loyal, devoted, and intelligent hard work to help maintain the support of our Armed Services with the best weapons obtainable, weapons they may need desperately. The problem of maintaining morale under these circumstances is one to which we are giving urgent attention.[4]

Sadly, the cancellation of the Triton program was followed by another discouraging setback. As we have seen, the Air Force had expressed considerable interest in deploying a land-based version of the Talos ramjet missile to defend its Strategic Air Command bases, first against enemy bombers and then, in the mid-1950s, against the growing threat of Soviet intercontinental ballistic missiles. In 1955–56, Fletcher Paddison of APL had headed a study group that demonstrated the suitability of Talos for such a mission; Paddison's study eventually became part of a special report forwarded to Eger V. Murphee, the new special assistant to the secretary of defense on missile programs, who set up a special committee in the summer of 1956 to investigate the issue of continental defense.

At that time, the land-based Talos was clearly the most advanced long-range antiaircraft system in existence in the United States. Just as important, it had already gone into limited production at Bendix, the prime contractor for the missile, and hence comprised the best option for an

136

immediately available ground-to-air defense. As modified by recent technical advances, the Talos missile possessed an effective range of more than one hundred miles and could therefore cover an area greater than thirty thousand square miles. Its state-of-the-art homing system provided it with accurate guidance that did not deteriorate at long range, at the White Sands Proving Ground, it consistently scored direct hits on drone targets at ranges of fifty miles. Hence it did not have to carry nuclear warheads to ensure the destruction of an enemy missile. Its ramjet engine provided it with far greater fuel efficiency than solid- or liquid-fueled rockets of comparable size, and its capabilities at both high and low altitudes meant that a whole family of missiles would not be required to guarantee effective coverage against different methods of attack. Finally, the Talos had been designed with the most advanced technology (thus guaranteeing that it would not soon be rendered obsolescent), including numerous counter-countermeasure features that made its guidance system relatively immune to jamming and long-distance electronic sabotage.

The only other remotely comparable long-range ground-to-air missile at that time was the Army's Nike Hercules system. Unlike the Talos, the Nike Hercules (an advanced version of the original Nike Ajax missile) did not have a homing seeker, nor did it possess the degree of automation built into the Talos, which used digital computers to automatically recognize and assign targets—a feature that became increasingly important as the enemy threat became faster and more sophisticated. Moreover, the Nike lacked the range of the air-breathing Talos ramjet missile.

It was no surprise that Air Force officials preferred the Talos system to Nike, and they voiced their opinion openly; in fact, the Air Force flatly refused to station the Nike around its SAC bases. In its report to the Murphee Committee, the DoD Weapons Systems Evaluation Group also recognized the effectiveness of the land-based Talos and strongly recommended its continued development. Further, the Joint Chiefs of Staff had endorsed the immediate application of Talos to meet the ballistic missile threat, and the Pentagon sanctioned a visit to Europe by Wilbur Goss to investigate the possibility of stationing Talos missiles at Air Force bases overseas.

Nevertheless, as part of a deal to assign definite areas of responsibility in the field of guided missiles to the various services, Secretary Wilson ruled on November 26, 1956, that the Army would receive cognizance of all land-based missile systems up to a horizontal range of one hundred nautical miles, while the Air Force obtained control of all land-based long-range missiles. As a result, the Army now effectively controlled the fate of the land-based Talos.

When the Murphee Committee delivered its report to President Eisenhower on December 4, it recommended that further development be carried out on both Talos and Nike, although it tended to favor the Nike system "until there has been further determination of Talos capabilities."[5] Accordingly, the Army incorporated a proposal into its supplemental appropriations request for fiscal 1957 to procure twenty-five Talos defense units immediately, modify them for land use, and install them around selected SAC bases. But the Army's prior commitment to Nike and the ever-present threat of the budget axe made the fate of the Talos Land System extremely precarious.

Again Gibson sent an urgent note to Milton Eisenhower. "I am persuaded," Gibson wrote, "that unwarranted delays in making the Talos Land System available for tactical use will involve us in grave hazards."[6] All to no avail. Early in 1957 the White House slashed the supplemental defense budget by more than 50 percent, and to help meet their service's share of the reduction, Army officials eliminated the Talos Land System.

In mid-April 1958, Wilbur Goss wrote a lengthy and heartfelt memorandum to Gibson that constituted an

138

epitaph for the Talos Land System. Although the Laboratory had never committed large numbers of staff to the program, its demise was still a bitter blow because, as Goss pointed out, "To a man we still believe not only that TALOS can do the job, but that it is the only weapon system which could have met this threat." Moreover, Goss added proudly, "We can say without fear of contradiction that we won every technical battle on the strength of logic and facts. The defeat came on the basis of national policy—a policy which apparently is based on a gamble to save money and live dangerously in the hope that the Russians will not exploit our weakness."[7]

Of course the Laboratory's efforts were not entirely in vain. In the Talos Land System, APL had developed a system concept that fully realized every performance prediction and whose advanced design would influence air defense for years to come. The program had speeded the development of the Talos 6B1, with its hundred-mile range, and the homing Unified Talos. "As a by-product of this experience," concluded Goss, "future tasks which require complexity without sacrifice of reliability can be faced with renewed confidence of success." Undaunted, Goss claimed that he would "do it all over again, even with a forehanded [sic] knowledge of the stacked odds. There must always be a few who play this defense game according to conscience, not by a pre-judgment of the winning side, or we will all surely perish."

Typhon: A Revolutionary System Concept

Goss's words certainly proved prophetic, for APL already was at work on the most complex antiaircraft guided-missile system in the nation's history. As part of its mission to provide the Navy with the maximum degree of protection possible, the Laboratory periodically staged comprehensive reviews of all potential threats facing the fleet. During the mid-1950s, the apparent growth of Soviet

139

long-range guided-missile capabilities and the speed with which those missiles could arrive at their target raised serious concerns among the APL staff. Consequently, a special task force was established at the Laboratory in 1957 under the leadership of Alvin Schulz to look ten years into the Navy's future and determine precisely where the greatest perils might lie.

After considerable study, Schulz's group reported that it recognized three major threats to the fleet: surprise from low-altitude attacks (which existing radar systems still could not detect below the horizon) or from missiles fired from submarines; saturation in the form of coordinated attacks by supersonic and high-altitude missiles and decoys in massed formation; and confusion via the use of electronic countermeasures to obscure an attack. Clearly some new defensive system was required to enable the Navy to identify and eliminate these dangers. For Schulz's study group, the answer lay in an antiaircraft system with more thoroughly integrated surveillance and fire control functions than any system developed to date. The key to the system would be a radically new type of radar, one that could provide automatic, nearly instantaneous recognition and response against multiple targets simultaneously.

Taken individually, any one of these features would have strained the state of weapons technology in 1958. Together, these innovations represented an extraordinary challenge for APL, particularly since the Laboratory had only recently taken on major new responsibilities in the form of the Polaris and Transit programs. Although Gibson liked to describe the proposed system as "the logical extension of the work of the Three T's [Talos, Terrier, and Tartar],"[8] APL was actually trying to build a system with 1960s technology well before its time. Clearly aware of the magnitude of the task that lay ahead, the Applied Physics Laboratory agreed to a request from the Bureau of Ordnance to act as technical director for the development and overall integration of an innovative missile system that

140

would be code-named "Typhon." (There had been a German missile known as "Taifun" during World War II, though there was no connection between the two weapons.)

To achieve maximum protection against enemy attacks, the Laboratory designed two separate tail-control Typhon missiles: a long-range ramjet to strike a "mother aircraft" before it released its weapons, and a medium-range solid-rocket missile, similar in size to a Tartar, that could be fired in rapid sequence, one missile every ten seconds. The long-range missile, which was slightly more than fifteen feet long and sixteen inches in diameter, grew out of a conceptual design for an advanced version of Talos. In its Typhon configuration, engineered by Bendix-Mishawaka, it could cover twice the range of a conventional Talos missile, intercepting targets at well beyond 150 miles at speeds up to Mach 4. Like its Tartar cousin, the medium-range Typhon had a diameter of thirteen and one-half inches (both were engineered by General Dynamics), but this missile could travel three times the normal distance of Tartar—that is, up to forty miles—at speeds from Mach 1.25 to Mach 4. For increased flexibility, each missile was to have interchangeable nuclear and high-explosive continuous-rod warheads. And to permit automatic handling and high-density storage, the long-range missile was designed with removable tail fins, while the medium-range missile had a folding tail.

But the real key to the Typhon system was its AN/SPG-59 "multifunction array" radar. Employing recent breakthroughs in microwave and computer technology, this system used multiple spherical lenses (known as Luneburg lenses) and electronic beam scanning instead of a movable antenna to locate potential targets. This system was designed for conducting a 360-degree scan of the horizon every second, tracking ten targets at intervals of one-tenth of a second, and guiding twenty missiles simultaneously for intercept. In the words of Alvin Eaton, who

141

Prototype of the long-range Typhon missile being prepared for flight. Successful in eight of nine missile test flights at up to Mach 4.2, Typhon nevertheless was canceled in 1962 principally because of budgetary constraints.

became the Laboratory's Typhon project supervisor in July 1962, "Typhon was the first attempt to recognize that the antiaircraft warfare problem was a total package: that you had to consider finding potential targets, sorting them out, defining which of the things you saw were proper targets for engagement, setting up an engagement process, and actually executing the engagements."

Although there were technical difficulties associated with the development of the Typhon missiles themselves, it became obvious at a very early stage that the advanced elements of the radar system would present the major stumbling block. "In truth, the radar was somewhat ahead of its time," testified Eaton, "because we were postulating the use of techniques that weren't quite ready. We'd done that before, in Talos, Terrier, and Tartar development, but this was different. It required substantial improvements in particular elements and in overall system control."

There were two especially difficult hurdles to overcome. To generate a phase-array beam, one had to install on board a ship a whole bank of transmitters, including thousands of high-voltage, delicate microwave amplifiers—a procedure that raised serious problems of reliability, stability, and durability. Moreover, as Alexander Kossiakoff explained, the radiators on the Luneburg lens had to be built around a sphere so that they faced in all directions. "To get the beam directed at a particular point in space," Kossiakoff recalled, "you had to have . . . elements that could adjust the phase, to slow down or speed up the propagation, so that they would all come out to reinforce themselves in a particular direction. That was black magic in those days." No doubt.

The second major obstacle involved the development of a computer program to direct the radar beam, telling it when to search the sky, scan the horizon, point at one of many targets, guide a designated missile, or focus in the direction from which an attack is expected, all depending on a variety of tactical scenarios. Unfortunately, neither the Laboratory nor Westinghouse, the associate contractor responsible for building the radar system, had ever written the sort of immensely complex software required. As time went on, errors continued to plague the computer program; since there seemed to be no single, readily identifiable bug in the software, a definitive solution proved elusive. Computer specialists at both APL and Westinghouse kept hoping they would turn the corner shortly, but success always remained just outside their grasp.

Despite these troubles, construction of a prototype AN/SPG-59 radar commenced in 1959, and in July 1961 a smaller, experimental, customized model at the Laboratory began simultaneously tracking multiple targets, collecting information on aircraft range, angle, and velocity. By that time, the long-range Typhon missile (the more compli-

143

cated of the two) was nearing the test vehicle phase. In February 1963, installation of a prototype AN/SPG-59 radar and weapons control system on the test ship USS *Norton Sound* was scheduled to begin. APL and its associate contractors could build at least one Typhon; the real challenge would lie in the production of this enormously complex system in large numbers.

But the Typhon program was lagging behind schedule, and costs had started to soar far beyond the original estimates. (In fiscal 1960 and 1961 the program accounted for nearly one-half of the Laboratory's annual budget.) Though the Navy continued to express interest in the system, events at sea in the early 1960s would soon overtake Typhon and cause it, too, to be canceled.

Ship Systems Troubles

Ever since the late 1940s, when the Navy began moving into the guided-missile age, responsibility for the development of the various parts of the missile systems had been divided among the various sections, or desks, of the Bureau of Ordnance. One desk had supervised the development of the launcher, a second had been responsible for the fire control system, a third had the warhead and fuze, a fourth the missile itself, and so on. Moreover, each separate part of the Talos, Terrier, and Tartar missile systems had been engineered and constructed by a different industrial contractor according to specifications provided by the Navy with input by APL. "The equipment was built," noted Kossiakoff, "but it never was really designed as a system, nor was it ever built as a system. It was designed as pieces, and each piece was optimized to do its job."

No one in BuOrd possessed the official responsibility or sufficient authority to ensure that all these different components would work together effectively; nor were there any provisions for comprehensive testing of the

144

systems before they were placed aboard ships. According to Admiral Mark Woods, who headed BuOrd's Terrier missile desk during the early 1950s, "We talked to each other, but we hadn't a clue as to how closely we had to integrate everything. This was all the learning end of the business. You were busy enough trying to make your end work, let alone worrying about whether the other guy was going to have his on time." One must remember, too, that the Navy was running its guided-missile program on an accelerated schedule, especially after 1950. The notion of spending an entire year simply checking out the systems was virtually unthinkable.

Complicating matters even further, the whole U.S. Navy research and development effort was dispersed among a number of different bureaus, each of whose chiefs zealously guarded his turf. The Bureau of Ships, for instance, designed and built the air surveillance radars while the Bureau of Ordnance independently developed fire control radars and missiles for air defense systems. Between 1920 and 1950 this arrangement had worked reasonably well, primarily because naval ordnance changed remarkably little during that time. But when the Navy inaugurated a full-scale program of missile ship construction in the postwar period, the absence of a coordinated system approach nearly proved fatal.

The danger signals first became apparent to APL in 1960, when the first of the new generation of missile ships, the Terrier frigate USS *Dewey,* underwent its operational evaluation tests. As the first vessel designed from the keel up to be a Terrier ship, the *Dewey* carried the tail-control Terrier BT missile, which was also due to be installed on all succeeding Terrier ships. But when the APL representatives, led by Thomas Sheppard, arrived to assist the Navy in these test operations, they discovered a myriad of problems in the missile equipment, many of which appeared to be due to the failure to test the weapon system as a whole.

"For example," recalled Sheppard, "the first time a fire control radar, through the computer, ordered the launcher to point was when it was put aboard a ship. You'd track a target, and the radar wouldn't necessarily track very well; it would go through the computer, which would amplify it, and the launcher was out there swinging back and forth, and it wouldn't synchronize or point in the right direction."

Another particularly vexing problem lay in the lack of alignment in the three coaxial beams of the fire control and guidance radar; that is, the tracking, guidance, and missile capture beams. Further, the highly complex fire control and launching equipment proved quite unreliable on board ship. "You couldn't keep the radar on the air," noted Sheppard, "because some component would fail. People would stay up day and night trying to get the radar to stay on the air long enough to fire a missile. Or the computer would go down, or the launcher, or the missile. So there were reliability problems and systems engineering problems."

If these difficulties had existed only in one ship, there would have been less cause for alarm. But the *Dewey* was just the first of the new generation of Terrier missile ships; the problems that were revealed in its evaluation tests would likely reappear as each succeeding ship came into service. Accordingly, as the number of guided-missile ships in the fleet grew, APL voluntarily transferred an increasing number of staff from missile to shipboard system work.

It soon became apparent to these APL representatives that the most critical source of operational breakdowns in the Terrier ships was the fire control radar, which the ships' crews simply could not maintain in working order. An emergency remedial program was subsequently established by APL, working with the fire control equipment contractors; "ship qualification assist teams" were formed to ensure that the ship systems were in full operating condition before deployment; and a "fleet failure reporting system" was initiated to acquire accurate data on the nature

146

and prevalence of equipment breakdowns. But of course the problem was far too large for the Laboratory to solve on its own. Finally, in January 1961 the APL leadership became so alarmed at the growing evidence of deficiencies that Ralph Gibson wrote a formal letter to Admiral P. D. Stroop, head of the recently formed Bureau of Naval Weapons (a consolidation of the Bureau of Ordnance and the Bureau of Aeronautics), outlining from the Laboratory's perspective the magnitude of the impending disaster.

Meanwhile, similar problems had surfaced aboard the USS *Canberra,* one of the two World War II cruisers that had been converted into Terrier ships. Between 1956 and 1957, the *Canberra's* aft guns had been replaced by two missile batteries and its magazine modified to enable it to store 144 Terrier wing-controlled missiles; the ship also carried earlier versions of the Terrier radar and weapon control equipment.

Beginning in the fall of 1960, the *Canberra* was commanded by Captain Eli T. Reich, a much-decorated World War II submarine officer with considerable ordnance experience. Reich had witnessed nearly disastrous problems with inoperable torpedoes during the war and thus was particularly sensitive to any deficiencies in the fleet's weapon systems. When Reich arrived in Norfolk, Virginia, to assume command of the *Canberra,* the ship was on its way home from an extended tour designed to show off the missile systems through demonstrations and tactical exercises with the Seventh Fleet in the Pacific and the Sixth Fleet in the Mediterranean.

After the *Canberra* docked, Reich obtained the ship's records and began reading the captain's extensive reports of the recent tour. Much to Reich's surprise, he discovered that the missile systems had failed to function as designed, suffering numerous breakdowns and displaying a disturbing inability to intercept or sometimes even approach their targets.

So Reich asked for permission to put his ship's systems through an extensive round of tests under realistic conditions and succeeded in setting up a series of rigorous, exacting exercises (code-named "Operation Springboard") early the following spring in the Roosevelt Roads area of the Caribbean southeast of Puerto Rico. During these tests, many of the *Canberra*'s missiles veered off course or failed in other ways despite the best efforts of a team of APL personnel assigned to accompany the expedition. By now, the persistent failures in the weapon systems had convinced Reich that "the Navy, and especially the technical Navy, was not paying attention. The technical Navy was concerned with the new systems, those that were going to come into being five or ten years from now. Here we had units of the fleet being advertised as the New Era, but in my view we had a paper tiger."[9] The deficiencies were not improved by an extensive ship overhaul, and Reich forwarded the dispiriting results of his latest exercise to his superiors in a report nearly two inches thick.

Within the Bureau of Naval Weapons (BuWeps), however, there was considerably less consternation about the disappointing performance of the *Canberra*'s systems than about the *Dewey*'s difficulties, ostensibly because the *Canberra* was likely to be the last converted Terrier ship, while the *Dewey* was the first of the new generation. BuWeps readily acknowledged that defects existed in both ships, but it argued that the sort of difficulties they were experiencing could reasonably be expected during any period of wholesale transition to new weaponry.

Reich's complaints and the urgent warnings of Ralph Gibson were unheeded by the top levels of BuWeps until they were supported by the findings of Milton Shaw, a former aide to Admiral Hyman Rickover. Shaw had been assigned to carry out a one-man investigation of the Navy's missile program for James Wakelin (assistant secretary of the Navy for research and development), and his conclusions about the parlous state of the missile systems on the

148

existing Terrier ships were at least as damning as Reich's or the Laboratory's.

The Get Well Program

The Shaw report finally moved the Navy to act. On January 17, 1962, Admiral Stroop called Reich (by now raised to the rank of admiral) into his office and informed him that the Navy was forming a special task force for surface missile systems whose most immediate task was to remedy the deficiencies in the 3T systems and that Reich had been chosen to head the new unit. Because the responsibilities of the special task force (which bore the code name "G" or "G division") cut across jurisdictional lines of existing bureaus, it was established as an independent organization. And like the Special Projects Office, whose management style Reich admired greatly, the chief of the surface missile systems task force (Reich) would enjoy direct access to the secretary of the Navy.

From February to June 1962, Reich recruited about a hundred of the best officers he could find to staff his task force G, which he divided into four sections: Talos, Terrier, Tartar, and Typhon. Clearly, Reich had no illusions about the challenge that lay ahead. "Here we were in 1962," he later testified, "and bits and pieces of the 3T program are spread from hell to breakfast, in the Bureau of Weapons, the Bureau of Ships, and among the contractors—fractionated. Now, how are you going to bring them all together?"[10]

Besides centralizing the responsibility for the welfare of the missile programs within the Navy bureaucracy, Reich also had to coordinate the work of his task force G with the task assignments of all the contractors involved in the 3T and Typhon programs. And that, of course, directly involved the Applied Physics Laboratory as the principal technical agency available to the Navy, particularly since task force G now had cognizance over the APL contract with BuWeps.

On May 4, 1962, Admiral Stroop informed the Laboratory that the Navy wanted it to act as the "technical agency responsible for system integration of the TERRIER, TARTAR and TALOS weapon systems."[11] (The Bureau of Naval Weapons already had given APL that assignment for Typhon in 1961.) Since no one had ever formally been awarded this responsibility before, it was necessary to spell out in detail exactly what would be required. "It is recognized," explained Stroop, "that substantial additional engineering, modification and test [sic] will be required to make this equipment meet full service requirements. In order to provide the necessary technical supervision of this effort it is requested that the Applied Physics Laboratory undertake responsibility for technical direction of development, engineering, and test effort for the weapon control portion of the TERRIER, TARTAR and TALOS systems," especially "to insure workability and compatibility of all elements of the system in a combat environment."

This charge represented a radical redefinition and significant expansion of the Laboratory's previous role in the 3T programs. With the sole exception of the Terrier production crisis, APL had concentrated almost exclusively on the creative task of blazing new trails through advanced technology, designing and developing new weapons; now the Navy was asking it to modify existing systems replete with extensive problems not of the Laboratory's making. As Stroop recognized, "The advanced stage of these programs will make this task difficult and limit the degree to which desirable changes can be effected." Indeed. "However," he added, "the importance of providing strong centralized technical guidance for this urgent effort makes this unusual assignment necessary at this time."

For APL, this new assignment meant that the Laboratory's staff would be going to sea for weeks at a time, trying to repair unfamiliar and unreliable equipment while coping with spare-parts shortages, under severe deadline pressures all the while; at the same time APL was trying to make the existing ships function effectively, more ships would be coming off the production lines. Nevertheless, APL accepted the Navy's request, making it clear that it was taking these responsibilities for what came to be known as the "Get Well" program "on a best efforts basis, since we had not developed the shipboard equipment, nor had [we] the depth of staff experienced with it that we had in programs we ourselves had built up."[12]

Actually, the Laboratory already had established in March 1962 a new unit called Fleet Systems Division to mobilize the resources of APL to meet the emergency. With Wilbur Goss (then assistant director of the Laboratory) as overall director and Thomas Sheppard as supervisor, Fleet Systems had been awarded the task of studying and seeking solutions to problems in air defense weapon systems throughout the fleet by "extending our work in this area in a hard-hitting, broadly-based and sustained effort." Eventually the majority of the professional staff associated with the 3T missile program was shifted at least temporarily to fleet systems work, joined by all available personnel in the Laboratory with relevant experience (though the Typhon, Transit, and Polaris organizations were left undisturbed). Because the most unreliable part of the missile systems was the fire control hardware, especially the shipboard radars, a complete Terrier fire control system was erected at APL's Howard County facility for test and evaluation purposes, surrounded by towers to simulate targets and measure radar performance.

Although the APL Fleet Systems team had no shortage of challenging tasks ahead of it, the technical improvements to the missile systems actually proved to be the easiest part of the Get Well program. In the next three years, while the shipboard system repairs went steadily forward at the working level, APL and task force G engaged in a protracted and occasionally heated series of negotiations over the appropriate role, rights, and obligations of the Laboratory as the Navy's primary technical resource.

Basically, the disagreement stemmed from the circumstances in which the two organizations found themselves. No one disputed that the 3T programs had not produced acceptable weapon systems. The Navy had been publicly embarrassed, and the administrative status quo simply was no longer tenable. Someone in the Navy—and Reich obviously had been chosen for the job—was going to have to institute significant and visible changes in the way the programs were managed, to demonstrate that the Navy had reestablished control of its contractors. Hence Reich decided to alter the Navy's relationship with APL and establish much tighter control over its activities. What Reich wanted, in effect, was for APL to obtain formal permission from task force G before making major decisions. Indeed, to some observers at APL he often appeared to be more concerned about the administrative policies of the Laboratory and the associate contractors than about their technical accomplishments.

The ensuing tension was exacerbated by the strong personalities who sat at the top level on both sides, notably Admiral Reich and Ralph Gibson. It seems clear that Gibson did not welcome the shift in the Laboratory's responsibilities that came with the Get Well program—he reportedly once said, "the Applied Physics Laboratory is not a repair garage"—and he certainly did not intend to let Reich or anyone else dictate how the Laboratory should best accomplish its mission.

An early indication of Reich's determination to reorient the 3T program came in July 1962, when Secretary (of the Navy) Korth (at Reich's behest) asked Bell Telephone Laboratories to serve as technical advisers, just two months after Stroop had asked APL to assume responsibility for the 3T system integration effort. By bringing Bell, whose technical capabilities he had long admired, into the program, Reich hoped to provide task force G with an independent technical agency that could help rein in the existing contractors. As Reich's senior aide, Timothy Keen, put it, "He felt that we needed our own technical muscle."

At first, the Bell management was frankly puzzled by the Navy's request, since they knew the service already had two thousand of the best technical minds in the nation at the Applied Physics Laboratory. After meeting with the APL leadership, Bell agreed to offer its assistance to the Navy on a temporary basis (two to three years) on the condition that the Navy build up its own in-house capabilities in the meantime. To avoid diluting the centralization of technical authority in the program, Bell insisted on coming in as a subcontractor to APL.

By the spring of 1964, the administrative disagreements with task force G and the continuing technical difficulties on the Typhon project had taken their toll on morale at the Laboratory. Wilbur Goss, for one, was discouraged and felt that APL should "force the reestablishment of our traditional role and a respect for it." "In a thousand different ways," he wrote, "the knowledge that APL has strong and indelible ties at the top of the Bureau serves as an armour and a shield for each of us in his daily routine. Let a vacuum be created in this tie-in and suddenly no longer can we move forward with confidence. . .; personality problems become dominant; frustration becomes commonplace; good ideas die aborning, because one is tired of arguing with people. . .who don't understand anyway."[13]

All the while, however, the APL Fleet Systems Division was continuing to improve the performance and reliability of the 3T shipboard weapon systems. As part of its systems integration responsibilities, the Laboratory obtained funds to make separate subcontracts with each of the equipment suppliers, to get them to work directly with APL and the other equipment contractors. "That," recalled Sheppard, "was a major turning point."

To further improve communication and coordination, Reich had also established a contractor steering group consisting of top-level executives (preferably with technical backgrounds as well) from each of the 3T contractors. This group met with Reich quarterly, providing a valuable forum for the exchange of information (somewhat in the manner of the APL Bumblebee technical panels a decade earlier) as well as giving Reich extra leverage, since no contractor wanted to be embarrassed by public reports of slipshod performance.

But more than organizational changes were needed to get the 3T program back on track. There was, in fact, a series of stages in the Get Well program. The first and most pressing task, of course, was to make the existing shipboard equipment function properly, both as individual pieces of equipment and as an integrated system. It was a job that required long days and nights aboard ship because, as Sheppard put it, "There simply weren't enough hours in the day to run all the tests that needed to be run."

The second phase of the program involved making the necessary changes (based on the Laboratory's testing and evaluation experience at sea) to the "improved" version of the weapons control equipment that was already in the engineering stage. Each contractor had been changing the components, design, and circuit boards of its particular piece of equipment virtually at will, until the Laboratory finally stepped in to coordinate these revisions and help decide which changes were actually worth making.

As the lead ships of each new hull class came off the production lines, the Laboratory conducted carefully controlled "development assist tests" in the shipyards or at sea, close to harbors, to check out all new and modified missile systems equipment in hope of discovering potential problems at an early stage. Because of its long experience in devising and carrying out complex testing programs, APL was asked to provide the test plan, test conductor, technical assistance, special instrumentation, data analysis, and final report for these exercises. Back at the Laboratory, meanwhile, a joint team from task force G and APL was putting together the first technical documentation of the 3T systems (both as they were and with the revisions that needed to be implemented), a study that formed the basis for future modification programs.

By the mid-1960s, sufficient progress had been made to permit the focus of the Get Well program to shift to the next generation of missiles; that is, the Laboratory used the lessons it had learned in its experiences at sea to devise new weapons with higher performance characteristics but without the weaknesses of the existing systems. Because Terrier and Tartar missiles ended up with many common parts, it became easier to periodically introduce improved components without unduly disrupting the rest of the equipment. This approach represented, of course, an extension of the principle of modularization or sectionalization originally introduced by APL in the Terrier 1B. Eventually the Terrier became known as the Standard Missile, Extended Range, and the Tartar as the Standard Missile, Medium Range.

But the fourth T, Typhon, never made it to the production line. In the summer of 1962, Admiral Reich had discovered that the Navy's budget for fiscal 1963 contained a nuclear-powered frigate that had been designated (or "called out") for a Typhon missile system. Soon afterward, when he visited a Westinghouse plant engaged in Typhon engineering work, Reich saw that the system was a long way from being ready; the same thought had occurred to the leadership of APL, for the Laboratory had kept close track of the status of the equipment. As Reich noted, there was no possible way the Navy could build a Typhon ship

155

with fully functioning hardware on schedule. "That is," Reich added, "you couldn't do it unless you wanted to repeat what had been done in the 3T business."

After investigating the status of the Typhon program for four or five months, Reich reported to Admiral Stroop that the Typhon program was lagging badly behind schedule. On the other hand, the 3T Get Well program (which Reich believed to be of equal or greater importance) desperately needed additional funds. Hence he asked Stroop for approval to ask Congress to take approximately $200 million that had been allocated for the Typhon ship and reassign it to the Get Well effort. Stroop gave Reich his blessing, Congress eventually consented, and the first nail was driven in Typhon's coffin.

Reich did not, however, want to cancel the Typhon research and development program at that time. Installation of prototype Typhon equipment on the USS *Norton Sound* already was under way and was allowed to continue, although development work on some of those components had not yet been completed (nor had they been tested), and an APL team of engineers had to spend a year on the ship while it was still in drydock, helping to put the components in working order. In late 1964 the *Norton Sound* put to sea, and the prototype Typhon unit was subsequently subjected to a comprehensive, eighteen-month test and evaluation.

But the prototype was the only Typhon system that ever came into existence. Even before the test period began, BuWeps had terminated all further work on both the long-range and the medium-range Typhon missiles. The tests on the *Norton Sound*, meanwhile, revealed that the Typhon radar still was having a very hard time detecting targets; for the overall weapon system the APL test and evaluation team obtained some good data, but performance remained below design specifications. Beset by cost overruns, opposition from certain powerful members of the Office of the Secretary of Defense, and continuing technical difficulties, the Typhon program finally was canceled.

At approximately the same time, the ongoing negotiations between task force G and APL were nearing a resolution. By early 1965 it had become clear that the Laboratory was the only resource capable of coordinating the surface missile system program; nevertheless, Reich made one final attempt to bring the Laboratory under his direct administrative control by proposing another reassessment of the APL-Navy relationship. In a letter to Ralph Gibson, Reich asked the Laboratory to establish a consolidated surface missile systems department, a suggestion to which the APL leadership was not necessarily opposed. The main difficulty in Reich's proposed scheme, however, lay in the admiral's insistence that APL should not exercise its own initiative in recognizing and solving problems within the surface missile fleet but would act only in response to "technical instructions" issued to it by BuWeps at the direction of task force G.

This was precisely the sort of restrictive relationship against which APL had been struggling for the past three years. As Gibson recognized quite clearly, the Laboratory could not function usefully if its work were "fed through, judged and utilized or discarded by Naval officers and civil servants"[14] unfamiliar with advancing technology. Gibson's assessment was seconded by the leadership of Johns Hopkins University in the persons of Milton Eisenhower and Provost F. S. Macaulay, who flatly refused to accept Reich's plan. At a meeting with the leadership of the Laboratory, Eisenhower stated that "APL exists to serve the national interests and that while we could go so far in acceding to Reich's reorganization plans, the minute we went beyond this we would be in sore trouble with the staff and with the historical objectives of the University."[15]

Despite all their administrative disagreements with Reich and task force G, however, the APL leadership still felt a strong moral obligation to continue their involvement

157

in the Navy's surface missile systems program, provided mutual confidence and a reasonable working relationship could be restored. After further discussions with Reich, a joint Navy-APL review team—including three members from task force G, two from BuWeps, and three from the Laboratory (Kossiakoff, Sheppard, and Eaton)—was established to reexamine the whole Navy surface missile systems program and APL's role therein.

From an objective viewpoint, a reorientation of the Laboratory's mission certainly appeared to be warranted, since conditions had changed drastically since the late 1940s. By 1965 there were a total of fifty Terrier, Tartar, and Talos ships already in the fleet and several dozen more on the way. Obviously those ships needed the sort of in-depth, comprehensive technical support only the Applied Physics Laboratory could provide. Moreover, it appeared that budget constraints would severely limit the number and scope of major new weapon development programs for the foreseeable future, which made improving and refining the hardware already in hand even more essential. Finally, the Department of Defense, under the leadership of Secretary Robert McNamara, had adopted a management approach (some called it micromanagement), purportedly borrowed from private industry, that laid heavy emphasis on detailed cost accounting as a means of promoting economy and efficiency. "The Navy Department must justify its requirements and report its expenditures in fine-grain detail," Reich informed APL. "This administrative load must be shared by activities such as the APL/JHU where tens of millions of dollars per year are involved. Detailed control and reporting cannot be avoided if we are to continue."[16]

During the next three months, the joint Navy-APL management study group hammered out a mutually acceptable agreement. "We spent many long days at APL working up this management plan," recalled Timothy Keen, who was one of the task force G representatives in the study group. "Basically, it was a bible as to how APL and the Navy were going to do business. It dealt with technical instructions, and plans, and what information would be sent back and forth, how money would be sanctioned and budgeted. And everybody liked it. Once we came to grips with the whole thing, there was nothing really unreasonable about what either APL or the Navy was asking for."

With the passage of time, the improved performance of the 3T systems, and the development of the next generation of missiles, the tension between the Laboratory and task force G gradually abated. In the end, the Get Well program actually strengthened the bond between the Navy and the Applied Physics Laboratory. By spending more time at sea and working more closely with the Navy than ever before, the Laboratory obtained a far better understanding of the Navy's operational needs, an awareness that it was subsequently able to translate into the design of a whole new generation of weapon systems. And once again, the Laboratory had demonstrated to the Navy—and to itself, for those who might have forgotten—that its responsibility did not end at the water's edge but extended all the way to the satisfactory operation of the fleet's weapon systems at sea.

Growth and Diversity

Beneath the seas, APL had assumed an equally broad range of duties during this period. As part of its original agreement to serve as the Special Projects Office's test and evaluation agent for the first five Polaris submarines, the Laboratory had designed a two-part series of test exercises. The first phase—the system development analysis program—took place at Cape Canaveral with Laboratory and contractor personnel present before each submarine put to sea for the first time. It consisted of a series of "demonstration and shake-down operations" (the exercises later became known as DASOs) to determine whether the systems were functioning properly, whether the instruments were reliable and accurate, what the performance parameters were, and so forth.

Then, after the submarine had been deployed for approximately a year, it went through the second phase of the process: a test firing at sea under conditions designed to simulate combat as closely as possible. This time the crew ran through the operations without any outside personnel present, going to battle stations, launching the missiles that had been deployed (with special telemetry equipment substituted for the warhead), and scoring the results. The data were then analyzed both by the Navy and by APL to reveal any significant problems in the command-control systems.

According to Luciano Montanaro, who had been a Navy test engineer on some of the earliest Polaris submarines, the exercises were deliberately designed to be as rigorous as possible. "That method of operation that was established early in the program has continued on through the years," noted Montanaro, who went on to head APL's Strategic Systems Department two decades later. "The idea was to not hide anything, to test the system as vigorously as we could to find out what, if anything, was wrong with it, and then fix it. And that was, I think, the basis for the credibility of the system."

Of course there were still bugs in the system. When the USS *Patrick Henry*, the Navy's second Polaris submarine, performed its initial missile test firings, the first missile fired straight up into the air. Unfortunately, the first stage failed to ignite properly and the missile came right back down, striking the submarine hard enough to leave a visible dent in its hull. The missile then broke in half and ignited the second stage, which roared out of the water at a tremendous speed. Luckily, no one inside the submarine was seriously injured.

Despite occasional mishaps, the Polaris system certainly was sufficiently reliable to serve as the most vital part of the United States strategic deterrent force. Even in those early days, tests demonstrated that the missiles could be delivered with remarkable accuracy, to within one mile of a target from a range of a thousand miles. Since the submarines would be able to use the Transit navigation satellite system to determine their location without surfacing, they would remain invisible to potential enemies; to demonstrate just how difficult it would be to target all these vessels, a Navy commander once took a map and drew a huge bull's-eye over an entire ocean.

Since the Laboratory had originally agreed to only a limited commitment to the Special Projects Office, Admiral Levering Smith had spent a year searching for another organization to provide him with a comparably competent, independent analysis of the Polaris system. He found none. So, at approximately the same time the fleet systems division was being formed to provide technical direction to the Get Well program for surface missile systems, the Polaris division resumed its testing and evaluation duties for the nation's submarine ballistic missile force.

For the first year, Richard Kershner remained head of the Laboratory's Polaris effort, splitting his time between that task and the newly formed Space Development Division. Early in 1963, however, Kershner decided to concentrate full-time on the expanding space program, and Robert Morton assumed leadership of the Polaris Division. According to numerous colleagues, Morton did not subscribe to textbook management theory. Instead of dividing the Polaris Division into more or less permanent groups, he assigned people to "projects," as if they were only on temporary assignment. "He wasn't the organizational type," observed Montanaro. (Nor, for that matter, had Merle Tuve been.) "In fact," added Montanaro, "a lot of folks used to describe his model of organization as similar to a wheel, with a hub [Morton] in the middle, and spokes going out to everybody else." But no one questioned the quality of Morton's leadership, and since the

161

division remained relatively small (in 1965, it consisted of only about 150 technical personnel), this sort of idiosyncratic administrative structure was able to accomplish its objectives admirably.

In other areas, however, the size of the Laboratory was becoming a very real concern. Over the previous decade, APL had grown remarkably fast. By the early 1960s, the entire Laboratory staff totaled slightly more than twenty-three hundred employees, an increase of more than 200 percent in just ten years. Clearly the cancellation of Triton, Typhon, and the Talos Land System and the difficulties encountered during the Get Well program had not had an adverse impact on the Laboratory's development, although nearly one-third of the technical staff had been engaged in Typhon-related research in the early 1960s. Instead, the extension of APL's responsibilities in space and in the Polaris program along with its expanded activities for the surface fleet had fueled the most rapid personnel growth in the Laboratory's history.

Yet this combination of program cancellations and unprecedented staff growth persuaded the leadership of the Laboratory that it would not be prudent to permit the number of employees to expand much further. Thus far, funding fortunately had kept pace with the increase in personnel (the Laboratory's Section T budget for fiscal 1961 rose to slightly more than $50 million), but no one could guarantee that it would continue to do so, particularly since the Office of the Secretary of Defense was beginning to play a much more influential role in fiscal decisions. Besides, the Laboratory had always prided itself on maintaining an atmosphere of informality and cohesiveness, and it was rapidly approaching a size where that might no longer be possible. Hence a self-imposed ceiling on the number of total staff, twenty-six hundred, was established in 1963 and has been maintained ever since with relatively little change.

162

At the beginning of 1965, almost two-thirds of the Laboratory's technical personnel were involved in one or another of the surface missile system programs, including about 200 in the fledgling fleet systems division, another 50 in the assessment division (tactical analysis and planning), and the remainder in various Bumblebee groups, including the separate 3T teams and the functional groups that supported them: guidance, aeronautics, controls, ship installation, missile test, and so forth. Since its inception in 1960 the Space Development Division had grown extremely rapidly, and at the beginning of 1965 it totaled approximately 250 professional people in four branches: research and analysis, satellite design, system engineering, and ground systems/data and control. The remainder of the Laboratory's professional staff, between thirty and forty scientists, was assigned to the Research Center. As before, more than two-thirds of the total professional staff were engineers, but by this time the number of staff members trained as mathematicians (127) nearly equaled the Laboratory's contingent of physicists (134).

To introduce new professional recruits to the increasingly varied range of projects at APL, the Laboratory administration inaugurated an associate staff training program in the late 1950s. As part of the training program, each class of twenty-five or thirty incoming employees took several months of short courses in advanced technologies relevant to APL problems: supersonic flow, advanced electronics, and so forth. Then various supervisors from around the Laboratory explained to the students the activities their particular branch or division was currently engaged in, emphasizing both the science and the practical applications in hope of attracting the best recruits to their group.

Accompanying the growth in the numbers and duties of technical personnel was an equal if not greater expansion in the Laboratory's administrative and facility support

163

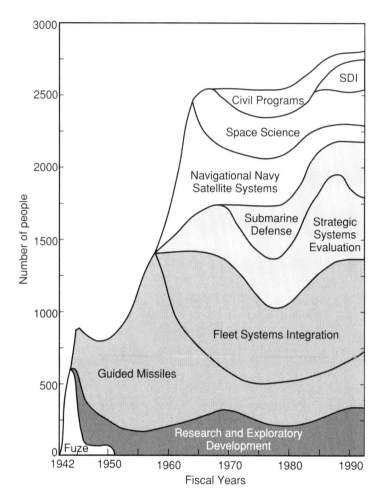

3000

2500 — SDI

Civil Programs

Space Science

2000 — Navigational Navy
Satellite Systems

Submarine Defense — Strategic Systems Evaluation

Number of people

1500 —

1000 — Fleet Systems Integration

Guided Missiles

500 —

Research and Exploratory Development

0 — Fuze

1942   1950   1960   1970   1980   1990

Fiscal Years

Growth of the APL staff and its distribution by major Laboratory activity over the Laboratory's fifty-year history. A period of sustained growth between 1952 and 1963 was fueled first by expanding efforts in surface weapons programs (1952–56), and then by new initiatives in undersea and space programs (1956–63). APL adopted a personnel ceiling of twenty-six hundred in 1963, increased to twenty-eight hundred in 1980, accounting for the relatively flat growth curve since 1965.

staff. In the early 1960s the center of APL's operations shifted to the Howard County facility, which, with the purchase of 82 additional acres in 1963, now encompassed 365 acres. By 1965 there were fifteen major buildings at the Howard County site, including a library and engineering and systems evaluation buildings, though enough Laboratory employees remained at the original 8621 Georgia Avenue offices to justify the continuation of a shuttle bus service between the two sites. The Forest Grove Station, however, was razed in 1963, following the construction of a far more sophisticated propulsion lab at the Howard County location.

Between 1957—when the Laboratory's computing operations consisted of a small section in the Bumblebee instrumentation development group—and 1960, the data processing requirements of the Laboratory grew so swiftly, nearly doubling each year, that a separate building was required to house the computer facility. A year later there were sixty full-time personnel at the APL Computing Center under the direction of Robert Rich, working with an IBM 7090 and 1401 installation that greatly surpassed the power of the Univac 1103 that Guier and Weiffenbach had used for their Doppler shift calculations. Later that year, another $400,000 computer was purchased to handle the data from the Polaris program, and shortly thereafter a microwave communications link was established to connect the APL Computing Center with various computers at The Johns Hopkins University Homewood campus in Baltimore.

During the same period, the Laboratory also broadened the scope of its involvement with the public. In 1958, members of APL's Principal Professional Staff began teaching graduate-level engineering and applied science courses at the Laboratory in the evening. At first these classes were limited to APL employees, but as the course offerings expanded, the classes were opened up first to other members of The Johns Hopkins University community and

165

then to the public at large. By 1964 the program had become so successful that the APL Education Center was formally established, thus initiating what was to become a permanent and important role for the Laboratory in graduate technical education.

Late in 1961, Ralph Gibson announced the debut of a new Laboratory publication entitled *Johns Hopkins University APL Technical Digest*, a bimonthly journal that he promised would "contain authoritative articles by members of the staff dealing with contributions from the Laboratory to fields of current interest,"[17] although the authors obviously were limited to the use of unclassified material. In its first year, nearly twelve thousand copies of the digest were produced and distributed to universities, colleges, industrial corporations, and interested individuals across the country.

Within the international scientific community, the reputation of the Laboratory was enhanced by the pioneering work being done in the Research Center. One of the most acclaimed projects was the free radical research conducted by Samuel Foner, Edward Cochran, Vernon Bowers, Frank Adrian, and C. K. Jen. (Jen, a physicist who had joined APL from Harvard University in the late 1940s, went on to serve as vice-chairman of the Research Center from 1958 to 1974.) Early in 1956, this group began a series of successful experiments to trap atoms and relatively small polyatomic free radicals in an inert solid matrix (generally argon) at very low temperatures (about 4 degrees Kelvin or minus 452 degrees Fahrenheit—the boiling point of liquid helium, the refrigerant used in these experiments). Using the recently developed technique of electron spin resonance, they detected, identified, and studied a large number of trapped radicals, including hydrogen and nitrogen atoms and numerous small polyatomic radicals of great scientific interest. Beginning with a paper in *Physical Review Letters* in November 1956, their research led to a

166

series of articles that subsequently became some of the most frequently cited publications in the history of APL, earning their authors invitations to numerous scientific conferences around the world.

During the late 1950s and early 1960s, the staff of the Research Center also performed ground-breaking research in a number of other areas: ramjet propulsion (in cooperation with the Laboratory's Aeronautics Division, a consolidation of the Bumblebee aerodynamics, launching, and propulsion groups); map-matching technology to allow cruise missiles such as Triton to guide themselves to their targets; the quantitative analysis of combustion processes (i.e., flame structure); the exploration of the properties of various types of lasers; and the unstable burning of solid-fueled rockets.

As we have seen, one of the problems that plagued the early solid rockets such as the ones that powered the Polaris missile was their unfortunate and unpredictable tendency to explode during flight. Though many explanations had been advanced to explain this phenomenon, none was altogether satisfactory. In 1957 a Research Center group led by Frank McClure and Robert Hart began an intensive study of this problem. Although they soon suspected that acoustic oscillation was somehow involved, McClure and Hart discovered that the problem involved far more numerous and complex variables than they had originally thought. Nevertheless, by 1964 they had developed a comprehensive theory that posited a connection between propellant combustion and acoustic waves: briefly, McClure and Hart proved that the burning surface of the solid propellant could amplify the acoustic waves produced within the rocket chamber, which seemed to behave like a set of flying organ pipes, until the rocket literally burst apart. After extensive experimental research, the problem was alleviated by the addition of certain chemical mixtures to the propellant.

APL Space Program Comes of Age

The space program, particularly Transit, brought APL to the public's attention in a major way. The Transit launches from Cape Canaveral attracted television network news coverage, requests for interviews with Kershner, radio broadcasts on the "sounds" of the satellites, and a host of newspaper and magazine feature stories. A model of one Transit rode on a float in President John F. Kennedy's inaugural parade; another model, accompanied by an active tracking station, appeared in a special government-sponsored science building at the Seattle World's Fair. At a time when the American people feared that the nation was falling behind the Soviet Union in scientific and engineering capabilities, the successful launchings of the experimental Transit satellites provided a welcome tonic.

After Transit 1B, in its short but fruitful life, had proved the validity of the navigation system concept, the Laboratory built and launched five more experimental Transit satellites (2A, 3A, 3B, 4A, and 4B), each designed to test different features of the system, including the power supply, the Doppler oscillator, and methods of attitude control and stabilization. Of course all these aspects of the system were interrelated. Transit 2A, for instance, employed solar cells as its primary power source (unlike the 1A, which had used a silver-zinc battery). Unfortunately, its oscillator transmitted effectively only when it was in full sunlight; in fact, there was once a six-month lapse when its signals disappeared altogether, though tracking was reestablished with no trouble at all once the solar cells began functioning again. To keep the antennae on the spacecraft always facing the earth so that its signals could be received without interruption, the satellite attitude needed to be properly controlled and stabilized, a feat that the Space Development Division accomplished through an ingenious method known as gravity-gradient stabilization, that is, the use of the earth's gravity to keep one end of the

168

satellite always pointing earthward, much as the moon is gravity-gradient stabilized so that the same face always points to the earth.

To supplement the solar cell batteries, radioactive isotope power supplies (RIPS) were placed in the Transit 4A and 4B satellites. Because the launch trajectory of the Transit 4A would carry it over heavily populated areas of Cuba and South America, the Laboratory needed special permission from the Department of State to launch the satellite. Several days before the scheduled launch on June 28, 1961, State denied APL permission to include a RIPS on the Transit 4A. The head of the Atomic Energy Commission immediately appealed to President Kennedy, who over-ruled State's veto. To get the RIPS down to Cape Canaveral in time for the launch, the APL Transit program engineer, Theodore Wyatt (an ex–World War II Marine Corps fighter pilot) had to "borrow" a Marine Corps attack plane—"I couldn't tell 'for security reasons' why I needed the plane,"[18] Wyatt later explained—and flew the equipment to the cape just in time. The Transit 4A, launched without further ado, subsequently became the first satellite to use nuclear power in space.

As planned, the next satellite in the series (the 4B, launched on November 15, 1961), was the last experimental Transit satellite; not coincidentally, it was also the most successful. It functioned effectively until late July 1962, when electrons and protons discharged into the magneto-sphere by a United States high-altitude nuclear test explosion over Johnston Island, in the Pacific Ocean, disabled its solar cells. Buoyed by the 4B triumph and knowing how to harden solar cells to avoid the damage that disabled Transit 4B, the Laboratory moved directly into the development and fabrication of prototypes of operational navigation satellites.

That process was complicated tremendously by the decision to switch from Thor-Able-Star launch vehicles to solid-fuel, four-stage Scout rockets, which were about 75

169

percent less costly but far less powerful. To get a payload into orbit using the Scout, the Laboratory had to drastically reduce the volume and weight of its satellites: they could weigh just half as much as the 240-pound Transit 4B and take up only about one-fourth the space. Since there was not sufficient room to put all the necessary solar cells on the body of the new satellites, engineers in the Space Development Division placed them instead on folded panels, or blades, which unfolded on command into a position perpendicular to the craft's axis after the satellite entered orbit.

Even more impressive was the miniaturization of the satellite's complex electronics equipment into a reliable high-density package that could fit into a compact space. This feat was accomplished by making the components compatible in diameter and length and then packing them together "like pieces of cordwood in a woodpile" before welding the connections, instead of soldering them as before. As it happened, the switch to welding also provided the system with a longer life in the environment of outer space. "That radical change in circuit assembly technique," noted Wyatt, "resulted in a substantial improvement in circuit reliability, thus repaying the investment in time, money, and turmoil many times over."[19]

Before it was ever placed in a prototype satellite, the electronics package, along with the rest of the Transit hardware, was subjected to a rigorous testing procedure at the Laboratory. "Testing was a major component right from the beginning," recalled William Guier. "Kershner learned that what you should do is build something and then test it until it fails. You find out why it fails, and then you build another one and do it again."

Along with reliable and innovative hardware, the navigation satellite system also required the development of a sophisticated computer software program. Since the science of developing large, complex computer programs was still in its infancy, this project consumed great amounts

170

of time and human resources at the Laboratory; according to Harold Black, one of the leaders of the software task group, twenty to thirty people spent about three years working on the problem before the first satisfactory computer program was produced in December 1963. At that time, the stack of punch cards containing the program stood nearly one meter high and took one and one-half hours to run on an IBM 7090. But though it may have seemed unwieldy by today's standards, the software certainly worked. In early 1964, tests demonstrated that the navigation system was accurate to within one-tenth of a nautical mile.

Meanwhile, the Laboratory had built and launched the first prototypes of the operational navigation satellites. They could no longer use the designation "Transit," however, since an overzealous Pentagon official had decided that the name was too revealing; thus the program became known only as "435." Since the Laboratory continued to use the same progressive numbering system anyway, the first operational prototype satellite, launched on December 18, 1962, was called the 5-A-1. In reality, however, the 5-A-1 was not truly operational, suffering a fatal power failure twenty hours after launch. The next satellite in the sequence never made it into orbit, and the 5-A-3 was plagued by a faulty oscillator and a memory failure during launch, though it did become the first gravity-gradient-stabilized satellite in history.

Undaunted, the APL Space Development Division proceeded to the next series of satellites, the 5-BN-1 through 5-BN-3, all of which employed nuclear power as their primary power source. Because the RIPS were heavier than solar cells, and because the Laboratory wanted to launch scientific research satellites (the 5E series, designed to measure the space environment) stacked in piggyback fashion with the navigational vehicles, the 5-BNs required a return to the more powerful Thor-Able-Star rockets. On September 28, 1963, the 5-BN-1 was successfully launched

171

and, when it was activated several days later, became the first satellite to actually provide the Navy with a limited navigational capability. Although the 5-BN-2 also did its job, the 5-BN-3 launch vehicle experienced difficulties immediately after launch and fell back toward earth before reaching orbit, releasing its radioactive power supply into the atmosphere as it descended. This procedure was consistent with Atomic Energy Commission policy at that time, which called for containment in case of an aborted launch and burnup upon reentry. Fortunately, the incident occurred while the satellite was still more than one hundred thousand feet above the ground, which purportedly rendered the chance of damage to anyone in the region virtually nil; but for a while the use of nuclear power supplies in future satellites was discontinued.

Finally, on June 3, 1964, the first 5-C navigation satellite (an improved version of the 5-A series) was launched and went into service; later that year, Vice President Hubert Humphrey officially declared the Transit navigational system operational. The 5-C-1 proved so successful, in fact, that the Laboratory elected to stop fabricating prototypes and proceed directly to the full operational series, known as Oscars (see Chapter 6). Within only four years, the Laboratory had advanced from making a satellite that weighed 223 pounds and contained no memory (the Transit 2A), to one with a 24,054-bit memory and substantial redundancy (in case of equipment failure), in a package of only 119.5 pounds. By the time the 5-C-1 ended its useful life fourteen months later, another satellite already had been placed in orbit. Since that time, the Navy has always had at least one operational navigation system satellite in operation.

While the Space Development Division at APL remained very much a one-program organization during these years, with virtually all its activities revolving at least indirectly around the navigational satellite system, an explosive proliferation of related projects led the Labora-

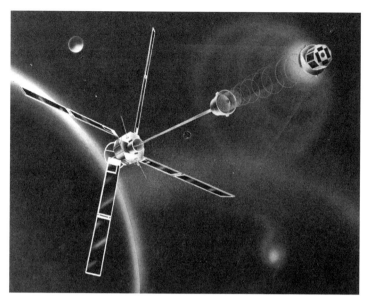

Artist's concept of an early Transit satellite in orbit with its large solar-panel blades extended. In orbit, a boom with a substantial mass at its end was extended, giving the satellite the mass distribution needed to allow gravity to align the satellite with its antenna pointing downward. In this early Transit, the deployed mass was connected to another, smaller, mass at the end of a weak spring. If the satellite tended to wobble or vibrate around its gravity-stabilized axis, the vibrational energy was quickly absorbed by the spring and the vibration stopped. Later Transits used magnetic damping to eliminate oscillations but continued to rely on gravity-gradient stabilization for primary alignment.

tory deep into the area of space science. "Transit was a program where you had to worry about all sorts of things," observed Carl Bostrom, one of the earliest members of the APL space science team: "the shape of the earth, the gravity field, the shape of the earth's magnetic field, the upper atmosphere, the ionosphere, the transmission of radio signals, the stability of oscillators, and the development of an appropriate memory system so we could store information." In short, the Transit program embodied the very

173

The Transit system in place in 1981 consisted of five satellites in circular polar orbits at an altitude of eleven hundred kilometers with a period of 107 minutes.

concept of applied physics, perhaps better than any other program on which the Laboratory has embarked before or since.

One of the earliest APL space science projects was the construction and successful launching of the TRAAC (Transit Research and Attitude Control) satellite in November 1961, simultaneous with the Transit 4B expedition. Designed in part to measure the density of charged particles in the trapped radiation belts around the earth—the better to understand forces that might affect the performance and longevity of solar cells in space—TRAAC relayed extremely significant data for nearly nine months, until the same nuclear test explosion that irreparably damaged the 4B satellite rendered it inoperable, too.

Remarkably, TRAAC had been built and launched in the brief period of only three months, an unprecedented accomplishment that was possible only because the Laboratory still retained substantial freedom of action in the field of space exploration. "There were no built-in rules for how you do things," noted Bostrom. "We worried about quality. And of course things were also simpler, so you were able to do things like that." The triumph of TRAAC, before it was disabled, helped persuade NASA to fund an $800,000 project for APL to design, construct, and participate in the launching of two more satellites for ionospheric research. Known as the Beacon Explorers B and C, these satellites went into orbit in 1964 and 1965. By that time, the first in the series of 5E satellites designed to perform various measurements in the space environment had been launched, sending back such a wealth of information that the APL space physics group had its hands full for years publishing articles based on the data.

As previously noted, the Laboratory had embarked on an intensive geodesy research effort early in the Transit program, to build better mathematical models of the earth's gravitational field so that more accurate predictions of the navigation satellites' orbits could be devised. Perhaps the most ambitious geodetic project in which APL participated was the Army-Navy-NASA-Air Force (ANNA) satellite, a joint armed services effort designed to compare the efficacy of the Laboratory's Doppler tracking equipment with ostensibly more accurate systems sponsored by the Army and the Air Force.

The first ANNA (the ANNA 1-A) was launched on May 10, 1962. Actually, the satellite that roared off the launch pad was a backup that was pressed into service just two hours before the scheduled launch, when an APL test engineer noticed that one of the meters on the original

175

satellite was behaving in an unusual manner. (A postmortem revealed that one of the transistors had been installed improperly.) Despite the pressure to get the payload into orbit, the APL representative insisted that the satellite be removed and the substitute installed in its place. "When someone sees something like that and waves the red flag," explained John Dassoulas, a longtime member of the APL's Space Development Division, "you listen to everybody. You can't get locked onto procedure too much and not use your head. The guys who have the hands-on experience can sense when things are good and when they're not." Unfortunately, the ANNA 1-A launch vehicle aborted shortly after lift-off, and the spacecraft ended up in the ocean.

That launch failure led directly to the ANNA 1-B, which was supposed to be launched on October 24, 1962, at the height of the Cuban missile crisis. "Florida was becoming an armed camp," recalled one APL engineer. "They were moving tactical airplanes down there and everything else." Furthermore, during the early stages of ascent, the path of the satellite would have passed right over Moscow and would doubtless have appeared to the Soviets as an American missile fired in anger. As soon as Dassoulas, who was running the field operation at Cape Canaveral at the time, realized where the satellite would be heading, he called Richard Kershner and contacted the local Air Force representative. The whole operation was shut down while the diplomats tried to resolve the dilemma. "They had to brief all the embassies," recalled Dassoulas, "and let the Soviets know that this was a friendly space shot. After it was all over, of course, we found out how really close to war we had come."

ANNA 1-B finally was launched on October 31, and this time the satellite made it into orbit. To keep the satellite under observation on a twenty-four-hour basis, the Laboratory had established more than a dozen fixed tracking stations around the world, from Japan to Antarctica to APL

176

headquarters in Howard County. And to the surprise of many outside the Laboratory, the ANNA experiment provided overwhelming evidence of the superiority of the Doppler tracking system over its interservice rivals.

As far as many Navy officials were concerned, however, the entire geodesy program was a waste of APL's time and talents, at least after it became apparent that the Transit navigation satellite system would soon be operational. In fact, most of the Navy hierarchy (with the notable exception of the Special Projects Office) had never been enthusiastic about the Transit program in the first place. In 1960, funding for the program had been transferred from ARPA to the newly created Astronautics Division in the Bureau of Naval Weapons. As early as February 1961, however, Ralph Gibson was complaining to Rear Admiral E. A. Ruckner, chief of BuWeps, that "a succession of unilateral actions by the Astronautics Division on matters intimately affecting the technical side of the Transit program" and the "fragmentation of this program by assignment of technical projects to other agencies without consultation with the Laboratory" had resulted in "a near-breakdown in relations between the Laboratory's technical leadership and the representatives of the Bureau of Naval Weapons with whom they must deal."[20]

By December of the following year, a high-ranking official in the DoD Development, Research and Engineering Division was attempting to withhold $5 million in Transit funds from the Laboratory on the grounds that the Joint Chiefs of Staff had gone on record that neither an accurate gravity field nor geocentric positional information was required for military purposes. Fundamentally, the Pentagon's position was that if APL wanted to continue its geodetic research, it should do so with funds obtained from NASA rather than from DoD.

And that was precisely what the Laboratory did. By broadening its range of sponsors to include the world's foremost civilian space agency, APL took a critical step

177

away from its original exclusive dependence on the Navy, BuOrd and BuWeps in particular. Like its involvement in the Polaris program and the establishment of the Fleet Systems Division, the decision by the Laboratory's leadership to expand the mission of its Space Development Division represented another step in the diversification of APL and marked a critical milestone in the transformation of the Applied Physics Laboratory into a vastly different institution from the single-minded wartime organization that had been founded in Silver Spring nearly twenty-five years earlier.

CHAPTER SIX

NEW MISSIONS

The president and the Board of Trustees of The Johns Hopkins University are convinced that the Applied Physics Laboratory has made and can continue to make highly significant contributions to the advancement of general science and technology, as well as to national security requirements. . . .

———*Statement of JHU support for APL, January 1968*

The Typhon missile system had been a controversial weapon development program, and there were many in the Pentagon, including the leadership of the DoD research and engineering organization, who did not mourn its passing. But even Typhon's detractors acknowledged that the threat Typhon had been designed to meet still seemed likely to confront the United States Navy in the very near future. In broad terms, that threat (as identified in 1957 by the APL study group under the leadership of Alvin Schulz; see Chapter 5) consisted of enemy attacks employing multiple incoming missiles approaching at high speed from all directions at various altitudes and shielded by electronic countermeasures, an imposing combination that would require an entirely new approach to antiair warfare.

When it became obvious by 1962 that the Typhon program was encountering grave technical difficulties, the Chief of Naval Operations imposed a moratorium on further large-scale antiaircraft weapon system development programs in an attempt to "establish an orderly Long Term Plan which takes into account the logistic, maintenance, and training problems of the fleet as well as the technical opportunities presented by scientific progress."[1]

In other words, the Navy wanted to step back and conduct a detailed feasibility study of the types of systems that might reasonably be developed in the technical environment of the early 1960s before deciding on any particular design approach. "It should be possible," posited Secretary (of Defense) Robert McNamara in 1963, perhaps with more hope than confidence, "to develop a new system with the high rate of fire of Typhon, [but not the] weight, size and cost penalties associated with Typhon."[2] Specifically, the Office of the Chief of Naval Operations was looking for "more flexible and standardized fire control systems for Advanced Surface Missile ships" based on three-dimensional radars and "multipurpose digital computers and digital data transmission."[3]

In pursuit of this objective, the Navy's Surface Missile Project Office, headed by Admiral Reich, awarded a series of study contracts to seven of the nation's foremost defense contractors, requesting suggestions on the type of technical design approach the Navy should follow in view of the general guidelines cited above. Six months later, the results of these studies were turned over to a special task force led by Admiral Frederick Withington, former chief of the Bureau of Ordnance. The technical director of this team was J. Emory Cook, then president of Operations Research, Inc., and formerly a member of Tuve's original team at APL. In February 1965, Withington's team of approximately 115 Navy and contractor personnel (including senior technical representatives of the Applied Physics Laboratory) began meeting to assess the various options

180

and synthesize a viable system design concept for an advanced surface missile system that would avoid both the apparent limitations of the 3Ts and the unwieldy features of Typhon.

After four months the Withington task force issued its recommendations, advocating a system modeled on the general Typhon concept as modified by the contractors' suggestions and the experience garnered during the Typhon development program. For instance, the Withington group endorsed the notion of a phased-array radar system similar to the one used on Typhon, that is, a system that employs computers to switch the beam electronically from one direction to another so that many targets can be tracked simultaneously. But this time the radar would be designed in a more conservative configuration than the original Typhon radar. The use of a flat antenna design using four planar arrays rather than a set of spherical ones reduced manufacturing difficulties and provided a more flexible arrangement. The new system would require fewer of the troublesome traveling-wave tubes by making use of phase shifters instead of individual power amplifiers. In short, the entire system was designed to be more easily producible within the current state of the art. Withington's report also insisted that the radar system be highly resistant to electronic countermeasures and that it combine the multiple functions of surveillance, tracking, and missile guidance—again, precisely the functions the Typhon radar had been designed to fulfill.

A considerable number of skeptics in the Navy still doubted that such a radar was technically feasible. Consequently, a small team at APL embarked on a program in 1965 to design a viable radar system that incorporated all the riskiest elements of the Navy's advanced surface missile system requirements. Although the radar team formally included only a handful of Laboratory personnel, other members of the Fleet Systems Division contributed their expertise by building individual parts of the system—the transmitter, receiver, synchronizer, waveform generator, and so forth.

It was a welcome assignment for those at APL who had labored so long on Typhon. "It looked like an opportunity to recover lost face," observed William Zinger, who was part of the team (headed by C. C. Phillips) that assembled the system in its final form. "It looked like this was an opportunity to achieve the objectives that Typhon had failed to achieve." By 1969 the Laboratory had devised an experimental version of a highly sophisticated signal processor known as AMFAR (advanced multifunction array radar), a six-foot rack of electronics that employed the latest developments in solid-state electronics and digital computers. Completely computer controlled (the experimental model originally used a modified National Cash Register computer), AMFAR could sort the data coming through the radar into separate tracks and perform complicated signal detection, beam switching, and frequency management tasks. It also took up far less room than the original Typhon radar; if the latter could be compared to an entire house, the newer AMFAR version would have fit comfortably on the back porch.

Countermeasures and Automation

While this research proceeded at APL, American combat pilots in the Vietnam conflict had a far more pressing concern in the summer of 1965. United States Air Force missions had recently encountered a deadly threat over the skies of North Vietnam in the form of Soviet-made SA-2 missiles. Combined with massive fire from antiaircraft batteries in North Vietnam, these missiles had begun to claim mounting numbers of American pilots, as many as 20 percent in some missions. Aware of APL's experience in countermeasures and air tactics, the director of the DoD Development, Research and Engineering Division requested

182

the Laboratory to devise at least interim protective measures against the Soviet antiair systems.

APL immediately established a working group, which eventually numbered more than one hundred people, under the leadership of Alvin Eaton and launched a full-scale testing program to develop new air combat tactics and countermeasures. Using their expertise in testing and evaluation methods, the experience gained in several decades of guided-missile system development, and their knowledge of the Soviet missile systems, Eaton's team devised a new philosophy of countermeasures that combined dispersion, formation flying, and timed maneuvers to confuse the SA-2 missiles and make focusing on one particular target extremely difficult. At times these new tactics even managed to convince the missiles to follow a misleading signal and head in an entirely different direction.

In the best tradition of the Applied Physics Laboratory, Eaton himself journeyed to the Pacific to brief the carrier pilots on the measures they should adopt to stay alive. "I had the difficult task of going to carriers, along with Navy representatives, to try to explain to the young pilots how they should best behave in the face of the Soviet SA-2 missiles," recalled Eaton. "That was a terrible responsibility." But the tactical plan worked. Within three months the effectiveness of enemy surface-to-air missiles dropped from 20 percent to 2 percent, and it remained under 2 percent for the duration of the conflict in Southeast Asia. In fact, the modified version of these tactics that is still in use in the U.S. military helped keep losses in the 1991 Persian Gulf War to a minimum. This exercise also led APL even further into the study of countermeasures and their effects on U.S. defenses and forces, and it paid dividends in the design phase of the next generation of weapon systems by making them even harder to counter. To develop and test tactics on a continuing basis, a formal Navy program known as Fleet Operation 210 was established with APL acting as technical agent, and APL was also made responsible for developing a major new test range (Echo Range) at the Naval Weapons Station at China Lake, California, to support the operation.

As one part of the Laboratory dedicated itself to the countermeasures effort in Vietnam, another substantial working group was formed to aid the United States naval forces engaged in combat operations in the Gulf of Tonkin. In simulation exercises, these ships had been plagued by the persistent failure of their search radars to detect incoming missiles and the accompanying inability of their fire control radars to acquire the missiles early enough to successfully intercept them. Their manually operated systems seemed especially vulnerable to interference from bad weather, enemy jamming, and land clutter. Officials in the Bureau of Ships who had responsibility for these shipboard surveillance systems insisted that a new search radar then under development, the AN/SPS-48, would alleviate the problem for the modern class of Terrier ships, but since this system would not fit on Tartar destroyers, some alternative clearly needed to be found.

Stepping outside its traditional area of responsibility, APL obtained permission to conduct an exercise code-named "Project Snapshot" in the Gulf of Tonkin under actual combat conditions to assess the nature of the problem and point the way toward a solution. Led by Ralph Robinson, a veteran of the VT fuze and Bumblebee programs, an APL Snapshot team spent a month on board the USS *Mahan*, the air control ship in the Gulf region, using a specially developed radar video recorder to take a continuous picture of the surveillance radar scopes while making a separate recording of the operator-developed radar tracks. In one memorable episode, Robinson and his colleagues monitored an "alpha" assault—an all-out, combined Navy-Air Force attack authorized by Congress—on a major North Vietnamese ammunition depot at the north

184

end of the Gulf of Tonkin. In this sort of operation, which employed 175 aircraft, it was imperative to get the planes into and out of the assault area with the greatest possible speed to avoid retaliation, using approaches from different directions and at different altitudes to avoid mid-air collisions.

When the Snapshot data were analyzed at the Laboratory, they demonstrated conclusively that the major flaw in the radar operations was the inability of the ship's operators to handle more than a few target tracks simultaneously. "You had people looking at radar scopes with grease pencils, trying to find targets, and then they would manually measure the position of the target, and tell people in weapons, 'This is your target, he's located *here*,'" recalled George Emch, one of APL's leading radar experts. "Then they'd go out and search around, and fire control, of course, has a very narrow beam. You could take a couple of minutes finding the target," and a couple of minutes was far too long, even in 1965. The presence of natural clutter made the situation even worse, especially in the case of low-altitude attacks, with the attendant radar echoes from the surface of the water and land. Here was a clear indication that warfare had passed beyond the capabilities of manual systems under human control; to be effective in combat, shipboard radar systems henceforth would need to be automated.

So in 1967, APL launched a two-pronged effort to develop an automatic detection and tracking system that could be used to upgrade existing Navy radars. First, some means had to be found to permit the radar to distinguish between real targets and natural or artificial interference. The Laboratory's solution was a device known as the adaptive video processor, a signal processor that was able to filter out clutter and electronic jamming while maintaining a steady fix on incoming air targets. The signals from the processor were then fed into a digital minicomputer; when the computer recognized "hits" from correlating successive radar scans of the horizon, it identified the blips as air targets and tracked them for identification and, if necessary, for designation to the fire control system.

In December 1970 the Laboratory's experimental computerized radar detection system demonstrated a startlingly successful ability to detect and track simulated attacks in land tests at Mare Island, California. Aware that previous attempts to devise such an automated system had failed miserably, Navy observers were surprised by the excellent performance of the APL system. But then, unlike the systems developed by others, APL's system had been based on a thorough practical understanding of environmental interference and developed under real-life operating conditions. After the Mare Island tests, APL was given approval to construct a shipboard model of its automatic radar system, now renamed AN/SYS-1. The system made its seagoing debut in early 1973 aboard the USS *Somers* and again performed virtually without a flaw. Acting as the system design and integration agent, APL subsequently supervised the incorporation of the AN/SYS-1 system into the modernization package for the Navy's guided-missile destroyers during the next several years, testing it under operating conditions in environments around the world.

A New Director

By 1966 both Ralph Gibson and Johns Hopkins University president Milton Eisenhower were approaching retirement age. Before he left office, Eisenhower wanted to secure the leadership succession at the Laboratory; at the same time, he did not want to put a deadline on the transfer of power, and so he asked Alexander Kossiakoff, then associate director, if he would be willing to serve as director when Gibson retired.

According to Kossiakoff, he "frankly was not overjoyed" at the prospect of stepping into the director's role. Ever since Gibson had assumed that post in 1948, Kossiakoff

Alexander Kossiakoff, seated, and James R. Austin with monitor on which changing combat situation data gathered by AN/SYS-1 would be displayed. They are inventors of the system, which brought automatic detection and response capabilities to naval combat ships. Kossiakoff became APL director in 1969, and Austin became head of the Submarine Technology Department in 1977.

had been acting essentially as the director's alter ego; during his long tenure as assistant and associate director, Kossiakoff had supervised the technical operations of the Laboratory, allowing Gibson to concentrate on representing APL to the Navy, the University, Congress, and the public. "I really enjoyed the job of being number two," Kossiakoff later acknowledged. "It gave me a lot of responsibility, but also some freedom from playing front man." Although he hesitated briefly (and understandably) before accepting the appointment, Kossiakoff could hardly have refused to take on the job for which he had understudied for more than twenty years. To fill his position as associate director, Kossiakoff recommended Frank McClure.

At the end of the year, Eisenhower decided to make the appointment of Kossiakoff public, still without designating any effective date for the transfer of authority. During the interim (which unexpectedly lasted for two and one-half years), Kossiakoff was named deputy director, while McClure moved up to become associate director. In effect, three men were filling two positions. Fortunately, any awkwardness that might have resulted from this arrangement was tempered by the long years of association and personal friendship shared by Gibson, Kossiakoff, and McClure. When Gibson did retire in the spring of 1969, Kossiakoff officially became director and McClure assumed the position of deputy director, a title never used before or since at APL.

Given his long experience in managing the internal operations of the Laboratory, it was not surprising that Kossiakoff chose not to disrupt the existing structure of the organization. Ever since the establishment of the Polaris, Fleet Systems, and Space Development Divisions in the early 1960s, APL had operated as a sort of loosely held federation, with each division (later becoming departments) enjoying considerable independence within its own specific area of responsibility. While they were encouraged to explore new directions or discuss projects with potential sponsors, the departments were not, however, free to commit the Laboratory without specific authorization from the director's office. This procedure had been adopted for two reasons: first, to ensure that any new tasks met certain stringent criteria defining what might be appropriate projects for the Laboratory, in keeping with APL's special relationship to the Navy; and second, to guarantee that any new commitment requiring additional staff would be matched by a corresponding reduction somewhere else in the Laboratory so that the overall personnel ceiling would not be violated.

While the director held a formal veto over the acquisition of new tasks, the Laboratory leadership had always functioned as a collective decision-making body, meeting periodically (usually weekly) to review current programs, assess new initiatives, and discuss management issues. Originally this group—usually consisting of six to eight individuals, including the director, assistant directors, and division or department heads—had been known as the Technical Policy Board; by the time Kossiakoff assumed the directorship the name had changed to Program Review Board.

This collegial type of arrangement proved quite successful, largely because most of the members of the board were longtime friends who respected each other immensely. As late as 1969, the leadership of the Laboratory consisted almost exclusively of men who had come through the wartime years together, sharing a common history and sense of mission. Gibson, Kossiakoff, McClure, Avery, and Kershner had all been at Allegany Ballistics Laboratory together; Sheppard had been on Tuve's original staff at APL; Eaton had been a leading missile system engineer at the Laboratory since the immediate postwar period; and Robert Morton had come to APL from the Harvard Underwater Sound Laboratory. Since they were also enormously capable and independent individuals, they—like many of their colleagues in the academic and scientific world—shared a distinct aversion to formal management theory or structures. In fact, the word "management" was almost never heard in the Laboratory; instead, the much less tainted term "leadership" was employed.

With each department free to pursue its own particular mission, the centrifugal tendencies that had first appeared in APL during the late 1950s increased, accelerating the process of diversification. Since the experience gained through each new project tended to open avenues to multiple additional opportunities, the Laboratory found itself pursuing an ever wider range of programs, generally in areas even farther removed from its original Navy antiaircraft mandate. In many ways this development was very welcome, but it also complicated tremendously the

189

task of maintaining any effective centralized control over the Laboratory as a whole.

Such was the organizational nature of the Laboratory when Alexander Kossiakoff became director in 1969. Born in Saint Petersburg, Russia, in 1914, Kossiakoff had fled with his family into China through Siberia in 1917 during the Russian civil war. After living in China for six years, the family emigrated to Seattle. Trained as a physical chemist, Kossiakoff graduated from the California Institute of Technology and subsequently received a doctorate from The Johns Hopkins University. But like Gibson, McClure, and Kershner, Kossiakoff's experience at the Allegany Ballistics Laboratory and APL had broadened his technical interests and expertise far beyond any formal academic training. Indeed, Kossiakoff was so deeply immersed in the technical aspects of the Laboratory's operations that even after he became director he retained for a time his position as head of the Laboratory's Surface Missile Systems Department, the unit that had been formed in 1964 to oversee the Fleet Systems (Sheppard) and Missile Systems (Eaton) Divisions.

As director, Kossiakoff eschewed rigid formulas and restrictive procedures for decision making, choosing instead to decide each issue on its own merits. "He used to like to say, 'Our policy is to have no policies,'" recalled Timothy Keen, who joined APL as Kossiakoff's assistant after leaving the Navy in 1966. "He didn't want to be pinned down." In this, Kossiakoff was clearly following the lead of Tuve and Gibson before him. As Kossiakoff explained in a recent interview, "I always felt that too many policies are an excuse for not thinking."

If this type of "situational" leadership style did not necessarily lend itself to long-range strategic planning, it is equally true that it would have been extremely difficult to do any long-range planning anyway, given the nature of the Applied Physics Laboratory in 1970. The major departments operated on wholly different time scales. Fleet Systems, for instance, enjoyed a certain amount of stability

190

in its work, but since the fleet's requirements were not entirely predictable, budgets and staffing requirements could be planned only tentatively several years into the future. Polaris Division, on the other hand, operated virtually as a branch of the Special Projects Office, and since SP formulated detailed plans six years in advance, the Polaris Division had a great deal of certainty built into its mission.

At the other end of the scale, meanwhile, was the Space Department (until 1966, called the Space Development Division). After Transit became operational the Navy decided that it really had very little business in space, and so the Laboratory's Space Department staff had to scramble constantly for new projects, most of which had only a three-year life at best.

Clearly this trend toward diversity was not going to be reversed in the near future, for one of the first challenges confronting Kossiakoff was the development of a broader base of sponsorship for the Laboratory. The recent administrative disagreements with Admiral Reich and task force G had taught APL the wisdom of not placing all its budgetary eggs in one basket, and the Navy's decision to slow down the development of new weapon systems provided a clear indication that APL needed to seek out a wider range of sources of funding wherever possible, especially in nonmilitary research projects.

Birth of Aegis

In the meantime, however, the Laboratory's work in fleet defense represented about half the total APL effort and continued to demand top-level attention. Uncertainty concerning the stability of program support after the cancellation of Typhon was heightened by the fact that the whole decision-making process for weapons research and development in the Department of Defense had bogged down severely, a victim of the sort of excessive analysis of

191

programs and options that had originally begun during the tenure of Secretary Robert McNamara. "We were just crippled," complained Admiral Wayne E. Meyer, then a guided-missile specialist in the Bureau of Naval Weapons. "We couldn't decide anything." The situation was further complicated by the fact that the emerging digital computer technology was still imperfectly understood, and it was obviously going to take considerable time to sort out its implications for combat systems.

It was the 1967 sinking of the Israeli ship *Elath* by a Soviet-made Styx cruise missile fired from an Egyptian boat during the Six-Day War in the Middle East that finally pushed the Navy into action. The realization that the "future" threat that had long been predicted by APL analysts (basically, an unmanned extension of the principle of the Japanese kamikaze airplanes) was no longer a matter of speculation forced a major restructuring of the Naval Operations organization and spurred the development of the new defensive system recommended in 1965 by the Withington study

In 1968 the Navy gave the Surface Missile Project Office the go-ahead to select a contractor to build the proposed system. Radio Corporation of America (RCA) was chosen as the prime contractor, and Wayne Meyer (then a captain) was named to head the program. The new system was christened Aegis, after the shield of Zeus. Meyer, who had been familiar with APL's antiaircraft expertise ever since his training days in the Terrier missile program at Fort Bliss, Texas, selected the Laboratory to act as the program's technical adviser. In that role, APL was responsible for ensuring that the contractor's design satisfied the Navy's technical requirements, identifying potential areas of risk, proposing alternatives where necessary, and conducting tests to evaluate each option.

Meyer was determined to keep Aegis closely aligned with the recommendations of the Withington study. As he often explained, the system was based on three basic

192

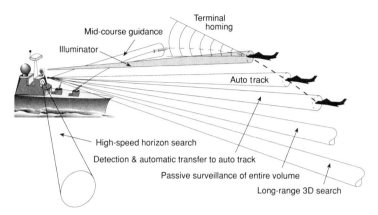

Mid-course guidance

Terminal homing

Illuminator

Auto track

High-speed horizon search

Detection & automatic transfer to auto track

Passive surveillance of entire volume

Long-range 3D search

The Aegis weapon system is designed to permit automatic sequencing from target detection to kill while maintaining continuous horizon search and passive surveillance, efficiently meshing all weapon systems to permit a continuous defense in depth.

functions and five performance requirements. "The three basic functions are detection (that is, you must first find the target [in] such terms that a weapon can engage it); engagement (the killing of it); and the control of the other two. . . .Performance factors, which we subsequently in Aegis came to call the cornerstones, consisted of reaction time (how much time is allotted from detection until first motion to attack); countermeasures (God-made, and man-made, and what kind of resistance must a design have); firepower (lead in the air, not in the magazine . . .); availability (what does the performance have to be, from a manpower, reliability viewpoint?); and coverage (how much area must it embrace?)."[4]

Meyer's criteria seemed to mesh perfectly with the automated radar design that APL had developed in the previous five years. In fact, soon after RCA began working on an engineering development model of Aegis, it decided to adopt the Laboratory's AMFAR design virtually intact; modified to meet the specific requirements of the Aegis system, the radar system later became known as AN/

193

SPY-1 and AN/SPY-1A. Though the Aegis program itself nearly perished in the early 1970s because of funding disagreements between Congress and the Pentagon and squabbles within the Navy bureaucracy over whether Aegis ships should be nuclear or conventionally powered, development and engineering work on the radar progressed so quickly that the AN/SPY-1 radar system was installed at an RCA test site in Moorestown, New Jersey, in the spring of 1973.

To help solidify congressional support for the Aegis program, Meyer moved the land-based prototype radar and computer system from New Jersey to the venerable *Norton Sound* in the spring of 1974 so that the SPY-1 could be tested at sea. In May, the system automatically detected, tracked, engaged, and successfully intercepted with Standard missiles two drone aircraft targets over the Pacific Ocean. By December the *Norton Sound*'s tracking and fire control capability had conclusively demonstrated its superiority to every other Navy ship. Deeply impressed, the secretary of the Navy released Aegis funds that had been withheld pending the outcome of the sea-based trials, and in October 1976 the program moved into the shipbuilding phase.

Considering the complexity of the Aegis system, the research and development phase of the program had proceeded remarkably swiftly and without undue difficulty. Behind its success, of course, lay the experience and knowledge gained so painstakingly through the Typhon project both at APL and at sea and the Laboratory's years of experimental work on the AMFAR system. "Without Typhon," concluded Alvin Eaton, "I don't think Aegis would have existed in the same form, or in the same time scale, or even at all."

The same episode that spurred the development of Aegis (the sinking of the *Elath* in 1967) also convinced the Navy that it needed cruise missiles of its own. In the late 1960s, the Laboratory began conducting homing guidance

Silhouetted against its own blast-off exhaust, Standard Missile SM-2 accelerates straight up from one of the cells in the vertical launching system, flush with the deck of USS Norton Sound.

experiments for a cruise missile later known as Harpoon, which would be capable of being launched from ships, submarines, airplanes, or land batteries. Recognizing APL's unmatched expertise in countermeasure technology, the Navy asked the Laboratory to test Harpoon repeatedly against the most sophisticated jamming and deception equipment available until all its weaknesses had been discovered and corrected. In 1971, APL joined an ongoing program to develop an even more powerful cruise missile, the Tomahawk, with a range of nearly 250 miles. Using the knowledge of map-matching guidance systems obtained during the early years of the Triton program, the Laboratory was able to help design a similar, albeit far more sophisticated, terrain-contour-matching system to guide the Tomahawk to its target with absolutely no assistance after launching.

The Laboratory continued to concentrate its cruise missile research efforts on Tomahawk and Harpoon guidance systems until mid-1982, when Rear Admiral Steven Hostettler, who had taken charge of Tomahawk development, recognized that his program needed the same sort of comprehensive system engineering support that APL had provided to the 3T program. Accordingly, Hostettler asked APL to accept the role of technical direction agent for the Tomahawk program, a responsibility the Laboratory has executed ever since for the Joint Cruise Missile Project Office and its successor, the Cruise Missile Program Executive Office.

Deeper into Space

The successful demonstration of all the essential elements of a Transit operational satellite in 1964 led the Navy to select a contractor to fabricate a constellation of satellites for deployment of an operational system. The Naval Avionics Facility in Indianapolis (NAFI) was chosen and awarded a contract to build satellites to the latest APL design, designated "Oscar." (Adhering to a strict interpretation of the original Transit plan, the Navy waited until 1968, when four navigation satellites were in service at the same time, to officially declare the system operational.)

Unfortunately for the Navy, the first Oscar satellites produced by NAFI were so flawed that they ceased to operate after only a few weeks, a far cry from the program's goal of five-year satellite lifetimes. So APL was brought back into the program to build ten of the first sixteen Oscars. After suffering some "life-time" problems with the first APL-fabricated Oscars because of an unannounced design change by the solar cell manufacturers, Oscar 12 (which was the sixth in the Laboratory's series and contained modified solar cells) was launched on April 14, 1967, and remained in service for more than twelve years. The next Oscar satellite proved even more reliable, lasting for more than sixteen years. Meanwhile, the development of a more accurate model of the earth's gravitational field (the result of APL's early geodetic studies) allowed the Laboratory to introduce refinements into the navigation system that gave users the ability to determine their position with remarkable accuracy: to within one-tenth of a mile.

While the second-generation Navy navigation satellites were plying the heavens, the Laboratory's Transit computer software staff was encountering unwonted problems. In 1966–67, a short time after the APL Space Development Division's computer group had overcome all the initial programming obstacles and put together a viable software package, the eleven-year solar ultraviolet flux cycle reached its peak; that is, the level of solar radiation reaching the earth rose significantly, heating the upper atmosphere and increasing the amount of drag on the satellite. A revision of the computer program was required to compensate for the altered orbit, and it was nearly 1970 before Harold Black and his team of specialists were finally able to get their orbital calculations back to their previous degree of accuracy.

When Frank McClure first broached the concept of a navigation satellite system in 1958, he had predicted that it would prove to be even more of a boon to commercial maritime interests than to the military. By the early 1980s, McClure's forecast appeared to have come true: at the beginning of 1983 there were about 36,350 shipboard navigation sets in the hands of private and commercial users, dwarfing the number in the U.S. Navy. One of the most well-publicized nonmilitary applications of the satellite navigation system was the exploration of the famous Northwest Passage by the icebreaker *Manhattan* as part of an experiment to determine the best way of bringing oil from the North Slope of Alaska to the lower forty-eight states. And when the USS *Hornet* had to rescue the Apollo 12 astronauts from their splashdown in the Pacific, it too used Transit to find them. In later years the system was employed by the governments of Brazil and Canada to map wilderness areas and by Britain and Norway to settle a dispute over their respective boundaries in the North Sea oil fields.

By the very nature of its work, the Space Department has always been required to regularly generate innovative

Vice President Hubert H. Humphrey presents the Distinguished Public Service Award to Richard B. Kershner in October 1967 for his role in developing the Transit navigation system.

ideas that may lead to new projects. Each project, especially those that involve the construction of a specific piece of hardware, is necessarily finite in duration; as one member of the Space Department noted, "You've got to launch the damn thing sometime." Consequently, the department has repeatedly endured peaks and valleys in obtaining task assignments. According to Carl Bostrom, "The trick over there [in the Space Department] has always been to have a whole bunch of programs, each of which has a bell-shaped funding curve, and make them all add up so they come out as a flat line. You've only got four hundred people [as of 1991], and you want them all to be busy all the time, so you don't want a peak that carries you to six hundred and then a valley that carries you to two hundred. That's always been the challenge."

It became even more of a challenge whenever projects were delayed by a year or more, thereby knocking all the Laboratory's staffing plans into a cocked hat. And since the Space Department was usually applying its expertise to problems that were still on the cutting edge of space technology, it could not always offer sponsors the comfort of a firm cost estimate. "We have to create our own work," noted John Dassoulas. "If we see that the government has a problem, and we think we have a solution to it, we have to convince them that we recognize their problem, that we have a fix for it, and that they ought to let us work on it. And that's in some ways more difficult than responding to a request for proposal. It's both challenging and it's difficult, between an unknown problem and an unknown definition. They want to know exactly what it's going to cost. So you have to have understanding sponsors." Even so, the Space Department has turned down projects that were not sufficiently challenging from a technical point of view, eschewing any routine or operational activities.

Members of the Space Department also needed sufficient patience to wait years and sometimes decades before learning the results of their handiwork. For instance, the

Galileo spacecraft that was launched in 1989 bore an energetic particle detector that had been designed largely at APL in the preceding decade, but the final data from the experiment would not arrive back on earth until 1995. Nevertheless, the Space Department staff has always enjoyed the luxury of actually building its own experimental equipment, a pleasure that much of the rest of the Laboratory no longer shares. "That's what makes it so much fun to work here," noted Dassoulas. "We've got the hands-on experience, and we stay with [a project] from the time it's conceived until the time it's launched, and even after that to assess the data from it, write the papers, and all the rest. We've maintained that tradition through all the years."

When funds from the Navy began to dwindle after the Transit system went into operation, the Laboratory naturally turned first to NASA for support for potential space research activities. A series of successful NASA-APL space science projects followed, including the geodetic satellites GEOS-A (1965), GEOS-B (1968), and GEOS-C (1975). The APL-NASA collaboration continued with the IMP (Interplanetary Monitoring Platform) series of satellites, which carried proton detectors to obtain data on concentrations and composition of various types of solar particles, particularly between earth and the moon, that might be encountered by astronauts during the Apollo missions. And in June 1978 came the launch of SEASAT, an ocean dynamics satellite designed to provide all-weather, day-night global data on the world's oceans. The most critical piece of SEASAT equipment developed at APL was a radar altimeter that helped the satellite carry out detailed measurements of ocean surface topography, wave height, and surface wind speed.

Defense-sponsored space research did not disappear entirely after 1965, however. On July 1, 1967, the Department of Defense Gravity Experiment (DODGE) satellite, designed and built at APL, was sent into orbit to study and demonstrate the principle of gravity-gradient stabilization—a procedure to keep one face of the satellite always pointing at the earth—at synchronous altitudes (i.e., the altitude at which a satellite takes exactly one day to circle the earth). The DODGE experiment produced an artistic bonus as well, after the fashion of the original wide-angle photograph of the southwestern United States taken from a V-2 rocket in the late 1940s. To help make certain that the satellite was pointing toward the earth, DODGE carried a camera; by rotating three color filters in front of the lens, the Laboratory was able to produce the first color picture ever made of the entire earth. The photographs were so stunning that they were later featured in the November 1967 issue of *National Geographic* magazine.

In the early 1970s the Laboratory embarked on the "Transit Improvement Program" (TIP), designed not to improve the accuracy of the system (as noted above, it could already identify one's location to within one-tenth of a mile) but to make the system virtually self-sufficient in terms of orbital accuracy for at least a week at a time in case the ground stations were ever disabled by natural catastrophe or war. To maintain the satellite in a stable orbit in the face of environmental forces that were constantly producing drag, TIP spacecraft carried a neat little device known as DISCOS (disturbance compensation system), developed jointly by APL and Stanford University. This system operated via a free-floating sphere that rested within a cavity in one section of the satellite. While the outer walls of the satellite were subject to drag and hence were continually slowing down, the protected sphere was able to maintain a constant speed in a true ballistic orbit. With the aid of sensors that measured the relative motion of the sphere relative to the cavity, the satellite was able to recognize the resulting difference and take remedial action; that is, it fired a jet in the proper direction to speed up the craft so that the sphere would once again be located in the center of the cavity, thereby keeping the satellite moving in a drag-free orbit. After successfully demonstrating this principle, APL

201

designed a simpler version for the operational satellites in which the floating mass was free to move along track (the direction in which drag was acting) but was constrained magnetically in the other directions.

The first experimental TIP satellite developed at APL, known as Triad, was nuclear powered and proved very successful. But the TIP-2 and TIP-3 satellites, which employed solar power cells, were not. In both cases, the enfolded blades that carried the solar cells failed to open. "We struggled to find out why for a couple of years," recalled Harold Black, "and we couldn't figure out why they didn't open."

At one point the investigators grew so frustrated that a Space Department staff meeting deteriorated into personal recriminations, a situation that Richard Kershner refused to tolerate. "I have a vivid recollection of that meeting," noted William Frain. "There was one individual who was clearly hell-bent on finger pointing. Kershner said, 'I want this discussion to stop. We're not here to assign responsibility.' He said, 'I'm responsible for this mission, and I'm responsible to the Navy, and I will take that responsibility. Let's put our energies into finding out the cause of the problem.'" As it turned out, the problem was caused by the heat shield of the launch vehicle deploying too soon. As a result, the nylon loops that held the tiny antennae stowed between the solar cell blades had melted, fusing the tips of the blades together and rendering them immobile.

Certainly the most widely publicized space science ventures in which APL has been involved were the Voyager and Galileo programs. Launched in the summer of 1977, the Voyager I and II spacecraft contained instruments to conduct low-energy charged-particle (LECP) experiments in the environments of the planets Jupiter, Saturn, Neptune, and Uranus. When the two Voyagers reached Jupiter in 1979, the LECP instruments sent back a remarkable array of data indicating that the plasma sheet around the planet registered temperatures near 100 million degrees Fahren-

202

heit (more than six times hotter than the center of the sun). Those numbers might have been impressive enough, but Saturn's plasma sheet proved to be even more searing, with temperatures ranging from 600 million to one billion degrees Fahrenheit. Combined with their extensive research on the earth's magnetosphere, these results established the Space Department's space physics division, under the leadership of Stamatios (Tom) Krimigis, as one of the nation's leading centers for both terrestrial and interplanetary particles and fields research.

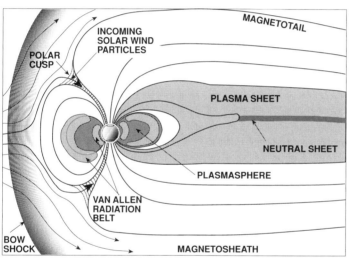

Simplified schematic of the earth's magnetic field and its interaction with the solar wind. The solar wind is a continuous stream of particles emitted by the sun, most of which escapes into interstellar space. Some of the solar wind, however, interacts with the earth's magnetic field and produces the complicated state of affairs shown here. The magnetic field and the charged particles near the earth are responsible, among many other phenomena, for the great radiation belts that surround the earth, named the Van Allen belts after their discoverer, James A. Van Allen, a former APL scientist. Instruments and complete satellites developed at APL have provided important contributions to the understanding not only of the earth's magnetosphere, but also of the magnetospheres of Jupiter, Saturn, Uranus, and Neptune.

But all those experiments almost never took place. In the mid-1970s, with the deadline for the Voyager launches rapidly approaching, it became clear to the leaders of the APL Space Department that the Laboratory's hardware was simply not going to be ready in time. "It was an extremely complex instrument," noted Carl Bostrom, "and very tightly packaged." So Bostrom went to Kershner and volunteered to serve as project manager for the next nine months to try to get the program back on schedule. "We worked up a very detailed schedule," explained Bostrom, "and we put a lot more people on. One of the problems was that we required multilayer printed circuit boards, circuit boards with ten to fourteen layers of separate circuits that were then stacked together and interconnected at the proper places. Then the components were mounted on." Normally, one drafter laid out all fourteen layers; instead, Bostrom assigned seven or eight drafters to work simultaneously on different layers, a process that naturally increased the risk of the whole unit failing to function

Carl Bostrom (Voyager project manager) and Stamatios (Tom) Krimigis (principal investigator), surrounded by the Voyager project staff. Bostrom became Laboratory director in 1980, and Krimigis was named head of the Space Department in 1991.

properly. Nevertheless, the gamble paid off, and Bostrom managed to bring the project in on schedule with a product that performed flawlessly.

The Biomedical Program

Perhaps the most intriguing possibility for APL civilian projects, however, lay in the area of biomedical research. The Johns Hopkins University—with its School of Medicine, the School of Hygiene and Public Health, and one of the best university teaching hospitals in the nation—had long enjoyed a well-deserved worldwide reputation for its medical facilities, and it seemed only natural that the University's medical institutions should join forces with the Applied Physics Laboratory to develop new biomedical technology and instrumentation.

In 1964, Frank McClure and Richard Johns, M.D., a professor at the Johns Hopkins Medical Institutions (the collective name for the University's medical schools and the hospital), began meeting informally to discuss potential areas of collaboration. Shortly thereafter, APL's Alvin Schulz was assigned to The Johns Hopkins School of Medicine for a year as a sort of roving medical physicist to learn more from the inside about the needs and opportunities in the field. But the real breakthrough came when officials at the National Institutes of Health launched a full-scale effort to encourage the application of modern technology to the practice of medicine. When Johns Hopkins officials were approached about the possibility of conducting such projects, they responded enthusiastically and got in touch immediately with Frank McClure.

McClure subsequently asked Joseph Massey, who had been heading up the Research Center's investigations into laser technology, to help him establish a biomedical program at the Laboratory. According to Massey, McClure initially told him that the job would take only three weeks. As it turned out, Massey spent the next eighteen years

205

managing the collaborative program, both from the APL side and, after his appointment to the medical school faculty, from that side as well.

After a series of preliminary meetings in which medical school personnel acquainted APL senior staff with the current state of medical knowledge and technology, the two organizations got down to specifics. "The first area they decided to look into was ophthalmology," explained Massey, "since the ophthalmologists already had some optical technology with their instruments. So Alvin Schulz, Frank McClure, Richard Johns, and I met with Edward Maumenee, the director of the Wilmer Institute [Johns Hopkins's world-renowned opthalmological institute] and in the course of our conversation he became very enthusiastic." As a means of establishing initial lines of communication, McClure and Massey set up a day-long meeting at APL between the Wilmer Institute staff and interested members of the Laboratory staff. At that time, institute representatives had an opportunity to explain any problems they had encountered that might be amenable to technical solutions. Several weeks later, a similar meeting was held to give the APL participants an opportunity to recommend solutions to those problems.

In the next six weeks, a series of follow-up meetings between members of the two staffs resulted in a list of eight prospective projects, including the development of noncontact methods of measuring the internal pressure of the eye, methods of analyzing slices of neural tissue, and the use of lasers to provide an indication of retinal activity behind cataracts. In May 1967, APL received its first collaborative biomedical grant, and after the National Eye Institute was established in 1968, it became one of the leading sponsors of the Laboratory's projects in optical technology.

In the meantime, Massey, McClure, and Johns had launched similar programs in the fields of cardiovascular and neurosensory diseases, each time starting with exploratory meetings between APL and medical school personnel. Whenever new department heads joined the medical school faculty, they were invited to attend similar orientation meetings to acquaint them with the expertise that existed at the Laboratory.

For the first eight years the Laboratory operated its biomedical program out of the Research Center without establishing a separate, formal organization. In fact, as a matter of policy, virtually all the APL personnel who lent their talents to the program did so on a part-time basis (often voluntarily giving up their evenings and weekends to work on biomedical projects) while retaining their positions in other divisions of the Laboratory. "Very few people—just myself and two or three colleagues—were charged with fostering this program, getting it up and running, getting money for it, and so on," said Massey. "Every technical person, to my knowledge, at that time worked only part-time on it, with the full realization and understanding of his group supervisor. It was encouraged from Gibson's level right on down."

This arrangement allowed APL personnel to contribute to the program without jeopardizing the progress of their regular projects or falling behind technical advances in their own fields of expertise. For most Laboratory staff members, working on biomedical projects was personally rewarding as well as professionally stimulating. The Navy, which was fully aware of these cooperative ventures, gave them its blessing along with blanket permission to use any and all government-owned equipment developed at the Laboratory so long as its own programs were not adversely affected. In fact, during this period the Pentagon expressly encouraged the use of military-based technology for non-military purposes.

NASA, meanwhile, was similarly promoting the application of space-based technology to civilian needs through its Technology Transfer Office. Under this program, Robert Fischell, a talented APL engineer who served as assistant head of the Laboratory's Space Department from 1978 to 1988, developed a number of medical devices that could be implanted in the human body, including the rechargeable cardiac pacemaker and a programmable implantable medication system (PIMS).

As part of a reorganization of the Research Center in 1973 after the appointment of Robert Hart as chairman, Alexander Kossiakoff established the Laboratory's biomedical effort as a separate program office under the aegis of the director's office. Massey continued to serve as head of the program, spending much of his time at the University's medical facilities with a few colleagues from the Laboratory, searching for new opportunities for collaboration. "It was basically a person-to-person approach," said Massey. "I took care of most of the neurosensory projects; Bill Guier, who was helping me, was the contact for cardiovascular problems, and Barry Oakes was the hospital man."

During the next decade, APL's biomedical effort developed into one of the largest and most productive programs of its kind in the United States. By 1982 the Laboratory had helped design more than a hundred new instruments for research and clinical applications. Among its most noteworthy inventions were a rechargeable cardiac pacemaker; an argon laser photocoagulator to treat the special ophthalmological problems of diabetics; an implantable device to measure intracranial pressure; powered prosthetic limbs; special-purpose equipment to facilitate research on the central nervous system; and a range of computerized clinical information systems for hospitals.

Strategic Systems and Submarine Security

Although the Applied Physics Laboratory's work for the Navy's Special Projects Office did not involve the development of similarly innovative hardware, it did provide a constantly expanding range of opportunities for employing and enhancing the Laboratory's expertise in the field of strategic systems testing and evaluation. APL continued to serve as the SP's independent analyst, participating in DASO exercises for each new class of Polaris submarines and certifying them for deployment, collecting and analyzing data from their patrol and operations tests at sea, and providing annual reports to the naval commanders in chief on the reliability, accuracy, and response time of the strategic submarine fleet's weapon systems.

At one point early in his tenure as director, Kossiakoff considered subcontracting some of this seemingly routine systems analysis work to outside organizations. That work appeared to be far removed from APL's original mission of designing and developing new weapon systems, although the testing and evaluation work was supplemented by occasional technological breakthroughs such as the invention of hover control devices and special sonar systems for the Polaris submarines.

Before taking any precipitous action, however, Kossiakoff spent several weeks with Robert Morton and the other leaders of the Polaris Division (which became the Strategic Systems Department in 1973). After listening to Morton and his colleagues explain the full extent of APL's involvement in the strategic nuclear ballistic missile submarine (SSBN) program, Kossiakoff learned just how critical the Laboratory's role really was. Anytime there was a change in missile design, for instance, a host of changes reverberated throughout the rest of the system with implications for test equipment and instrumentation, operational procedures, maintenance, training, documentation, and so forth. As the only organization that fully understood the entire submarine guided-missile system, APL was responsible for identifying all those changes for the Navy. "So," recalled Kossiakoff, "I said to myself, if we start delegating some of these menial-looking jobs to other organizations and they foul up when it's still our responsibility, it's not going to be on my watch."

For the most part, SP managed the development of each new generation of SSBN missile systems—first Polaris, then Poseidon, and finally Trident—so well that few major problems remained to be resolved by the time the systems were actually deployed. Still, the systems were sufficiently complex that some difficulties inevitably occurred, and those that did crop up invariably were discovered at an early stage by APL's rigorous testing procedures. "The whole point of the test program," noted Donald L. Eddins, who joined the Polaris Division in 1963 and went on to become head of the Strategic Systems Department, "is to find the problems and fix them before they get bad."

In 1968 a whole new range of challenges suddenly arose when the Navy, acting on instructions from the Pentagon, inaugurated a program in the Special Projects Office to ensure the survivability of the strategic submarine fleet. The Navy's objective was to examine every conceivable means of detecting submarines and understand every physical phenomenon that might afford a detection opportunity. "The purpose of the program," noted Gary Smith, one of the first members of APL's SSBN security team, "was to be out in front of any potential adversary in knowing how a submarine might be detected and, further, in countering that detectability before that adversary could ever build a system that could detect it."

Given its close relationship with APL and the Laboratory's intimate knowledge of the Polaris system, it is not surprising that the SP chose APL to serve as technical director and central laboratory for this submarine security program. Following the model of the original Bumblebee program, APL subsequently assembled a team of university laboratories, industrial corporations, and Navy labs with the most expertise in this area, all acting under the direction of the Laboratory.

Initially, SP and APL embarked on the SSBN security program on the basis of little more than a handshake—the contract for work tasks totaling several hundred thousand

210

dollars ran only about three lines or so—because of the trust that had grown up between the two organizations. As the Laboratory embarked on a recruiting effort to staff the program, it conducted its first series of detection exercises, pitting one team of U.S. subs against another to determine how vulnerable the fleet was to its own sonar systems.

From the beginning, SP (and particularly Levering Smith) insisted that the program be firmly focused on the future and not dedicated merely to devising defenses against existing detection technology, since the Laboratory would then have been in the uncomfortable position of always reacting to new technical advances made by potential enemies. Thus the program was grounded in a thorough understanding of the physical characteristics of the ocean environment, which naturally meant that the Laboratory would need to conduct a wide range of in-depth experiments on a long-term basis to advance the state of oceanographic knowledge. In other words, the emphasis was placed on the fundamentals of ocean physics, which do not change, rather than on specific technology, which changes frequently. For precisely that reason the Laboratory staffed the program with the best scientific minds available, regardless of any specialized training in submarine technology.

The program expanded rapidly. By the late 1970s, when it was spun off from the Strategic Systems Department to form the Submarine Technology Department under the leadership of James R. Austin, nearly two hundred APL employees were involved in the program, as were an equal number of contractors.

From the start, the submarine security technology program attacked every conceivable means of submarine detection, from the traditional acoustic and magnetic methods to the detectability of hydrodynamic, chemical, and other disturbances produced by the passage of an operational submarine. The objective was to systematically investigate each class of phenomena to determine whether

211

the likelihood of its providing a means of detecting SSBNs was sufficient to warrant developing countermeasures. Each investigation was led by an APL team working with contract personnel and Navy laboratories especially well versed in the respective fields. Together they carried out critical experiments, often using operational submarines, to quantify the present and potential threats. For those threats that were already well recognized, such as active and passive acoustic detection (water being an effective medium for transmitting sound but a poor medium for transmitting virtually anything else), operational strategies and countermeasures were devised and tested to minimize the risk of detection.

Along the way, the submarine security technology program also discovered a number of potential vulnerabilities that might conceivably have created problems in the future, all of which were eventually remedied through operational practice changes, redesigns, countermeasures, and so forth. Moreover, there were a few scares during the 1970s and 1980s when the actions of the Soviet navy gave certain indications that the Soviets might be able to track part of the U.S. SSBN fleet. But, according to Gary Smith, at no point since the program began has even a significant fraction of the Navy's deployed submarines been vulnerable to enemy attack at any one time.

Civil Programs

In the late 1960s, as discontent with the American role in the Vietnam conflict spread rapidly through college campuses across the nation, the Applied Physics Laboratory's intimate and long-standing ties with the U.S. military establishment made it a natural target for local student antiwar protests. Although the main undergraduate campus of The Johns Hopkins University was slow to join the nationwide student movement, sufficient discontent existed to lead the University administration to issue a formal statement supporting the national defense mission of APL.

Nevertheless, the connection between the University and the Laboratory continued to draw criticism from a substantial number of JHU students. In May 1969, the University's undergraduate student council suggested a reevaluation of APL, including its possible separation from the University. University president Lincoln Gordon, who had assumed office upon Milton Eisenhower's retirement in June 1967, rejected the council's demands, but his response failed to satisfy some of the more radical members of the student antiwar alliance, particularly one group that called itself "the Committee for the Conversion of APL." Insisting that "society has too many pressing environmental and social problems needing solutions for Johns Hopkins to be harboring a $50 million-a-year partner in the military industrial complex,"[5] the committee insisted in the spring of 1970 that if the University would not divest itself of APL, then the Laboratory should be converted to "socially useful" activity.

Of course the University administration had always— save perhaps for the brief period after World War II— believed that APL was in fact performing "socially useful" activities by promoting the defense of the United States. Accordingly, President Gordon refused to accept the committee's recommendations. But in his reply to the committee, Gordon pointed out that both the Laboratory and the APL Advisory Board were greatly interested "in expanding the work of APL in such fields as health, urban affairs, and transportation."

While the student protestors might have remained skeptical, much of the Laboratory's leadership was in truth willing and even eager to increase the Laboratory's participation in civilian research programs beyond the space and biomedical projects already in existence. This sentiment meshed nicely with the federal government's attempt in the late 1960s and early 1970s to encourage the application of

213

aerospace technology to social problems. If they could put a man on the moon, went the contemporary reasoning, why couldn't they clean up the cities, or safeguard the environment, or discover cheap and clean energy supplies?

One of APL's first opportunities for expanding into civil work arose in 1968, when a former Navy commander who had joined the U.S. Department of Housing and Urban Development (HUD) asked APL to assess the feasibility of a proposed underground rapid transit system that employed a combination of gravity and pneumatic power. Using a hypersonic gun tunnel that the Laboratory had constructed for the Navy on the theory that subway trains in underground tunnels were subject to the same physical forces as missiles in a gun barrel, an APL team headed by Robert A. Makofski ran a thorough series of practical experiments on the system and produced a report for HUD within six months. (A competing organization had eschewed the experimental approach and tried to analyze the system using computer studies alone; after a year it had produced nothing of consequence.)

Officials of the recently formed Urban Mass Transit Administration were so impressed with APL's performance that they invited the Laboratory in 1969 to evaluate ten of the most promising mass transit proposals they had received from companies seeking federal funding. Most of these projects involved personal rapid transit systems, that is, attempts to transport people with the convenience and privacy of automobiles in a more efficient manner, usually through some form of computerized automation. Unfortunately, virtually all the proposed systems underestimated the complexity of computer control of an automated transportation network, and so only a few proved to be even remotely viable.

Meanwhile, a representative of the National Academy of Sciences had suggested that the Laboratory develop its own solution to the problems of urban mass transit by

214

applying its extensive expertise in propulsion theory. Intrigued by the challenge, William Avery, one of APL's leading propulsion experts, investigated the possibilities and decided that a system based on the same fundamental principles as a ski lift offered the best chance of building a low-cost, convenient, and comfortable alternative. By 1972, Avery and a colleague had developed an ingenious accelerating walkway that enabled pedestrians to get on and off moving vehicles at transit stations. Unfortunately, the program never received funding once officials at the Department of Transportation had decided to solve the problem of urban traffic congestion by simply buying more buses.

The Laboratory's contributions in the environmental area paid more immediate dividends. In 1970 the Coast Guard commissioned the Laboratory to use its knowledge of radar automation systems to help develop a harbor traffic control system that could monitor hundreds of ships simultaneously and prevent collisions that might release pollutants into the water. The system proved so successful that it was installed in San Francisco Bay, which had suffered precisely such an environmentally catastrophic accident several years earlier. Farther out in the ocean depths, an APL team led by William Avery launched an intensive study in 1975 of the concept of ocean thermal energy conversion (OTEC), an intriguing attempt funded by the U.S. Maritime Administration to employ sun-warmed surface seawater to vaporize liquid ammonia, thereby providing power to drive a turbine generator before turning the ammonia back into a liquid through the infusion of cold seawater. Experimental OTEC "plantships" (not unlike cruising power-generating stations) were constructed and tested in Hawaii and the Gulf of Mexico. Although their success demonstrated the viability of the concept of ocean thermal energy conversion and led to an enthusiastic request by JHU president Steven Muller (who had assumed office in February 1972) for further governmental investigation of the benefits of OTEC technology, the falling price of petroleum supplies in the early 1980s caused the program to be shelved, at least temporarily.

APL's most extensive environmental program was a twelve-year effort to evaluate prospective power plant sites in the state of Maryland. In the early 1970s, utility companies throughout the state experienced a dramatic upsurge in power usage. Anticipating continued increases, the Maryland Department of Natural Resources asked APL, along with the Chesapeake Bay Institute and The Johns Hopkins University Department of Geography and Environmental Engineering, to study the effects of power plant construction at a variety of likely locations. Using large-scale data collection, laboratory experiments, and modeling techniques, APL researchers were able to deliver detailed predictions of the impact of power plant construction on aquatic environments, air quality, noise levels, aesthetic considerations, soil chemistry, and so forth. These studies, along with the Laboratory's recommendations for alleviating negative impacts, helped the utilities determine which sites should be preserved for future power plants.

Although these civil projects certainly provided socially beneficial results, they always remained very much a peripheral part of the Laboratory's total mission. "The biggest problem with civil programs," explained Robert Makofski, "was the uncertainty and unpredictability of being funded. You would be funded quite well for a period of maybe a year, or a year and a half, and then it would be time for new funding. You could have gaps that ran anywhere from a month to three or four months between those funding periods. As a program manager, you'd have to spend all your time looking for other work so you could keep your people together for the remainder of the program. It's a very difficult type of activity."

216

Crisis and Commitment

Still, additional civilian projects represented a very attractive prospect in the period from 1967 to 1977, because an ill-advised congressional attempt to govern defense-related research institutions had brought APL to the edge of one of the severest crises in its existence. In the late 1960s, the House Ways and Means Committee had launched an investigation of the Aerospace Corporation, a nonprofit (albeit lavishly funded) organization established primarily to conduct ballistic missile system engineering for the U.S. Air Force. The president of Aerospace, though an excellent administrator, refused to cooperate with the congressional inquiry, declining to explain some of his company's expenditures and cost allocations.

Angered by Aerospace's refusal to cooperate, congressional investigators asked the Department of Defense for a list of all the nonprofit organizations working primarily for the Pentagon. After further review, the list was narrowed to seventeen institutions, most of which were university-operated laboratories of varying size, including The Johns Hopkins University Applied Physics Laboratory, along with several free-standing, nonprofit corporations engaged in system engineering and operations analysis for the military services.

An objective, impartial assessment would have revealed that these organizations really had little in common other than their reliance on DoD funding. Certainly there was a vast difference between a university laboratory such as APL and a corporation such as Aerospace. Aerospace existed solely to support its sponsor, the Air Force, and received in effect a guaranteed annual budget; APL, on the other hand, had numerous military and civilian sponsors, possessed no guaranteed funding support, and was, besides, part of one of the nation's foremost academic institutions.

217

Nevertheless, Congress grouped all seventeen institutions in the category of federal contract research centers (FCRCs), and demanded that DoD provide a report on their activities every year. This requirement might have been burdensome but not terribly serious. The affair took a far more ominous turn, however, when Congress imposed a ceiling on the annual budget of each of these institutions in an obvious effort to restrain their growth. There was also a limit on the total FCRC funding, so that an increase in one FCRC's budget required a corresponding decline in another's. To make matters worse, congressional committees that were dissatisfied with one or two individual FCRCs adopted the practice of levying across-the-board decreases in budgetary ceilings for the entire group.

At the outset of the FCRC debate, the Executive Committee of The Johns Hopkins University Board of Trustees reaffirmed its support of APL as an integral part of the University community by unanimously adopting a resolution on January 8, 1968, that stated, "The relationship of the Applied Physics Laboratory with the other divisions of the University is mutually beneficial and appropriate to the central purpose of the University." The resolution continued:

> The mutual goal of pushing forward science and technology, [the resolution continued] and a common desire for public service, provide a strong community of interest. The top staff of the Laboratory is an outstanding and dedicated group of scientists which has remained together for over twenty years in large part because of the environment and support which The Johns Hopkins University has provided. . . .The president and the Board of Trustees of The Johns Hopkins University are convinced that the Applied Physics Laboratory has made and can continue to make highly significant contributions to the advancement of general

science and technology, as well as to national security requirements, through its functioning as part of the University.[6]

Any doubt about the University's commitment to the Laboratory should have been erased with the signing of a new contract between the University and the commander of the Naval Ordnance Systems Command (the successor organization to BuWeps) on December 13, 1968. In that agreement, the University and the Navy agreed on the following mission statement for APL:

> The mission of the Laboratory is to provide, within the contractual authority provided by the navy, support of specific Navy and other Governmental programs through research, development, engineering, test, and evaluation in the areas of surface missile systems, space systems, astronautics, electronic warfare systems, ballistic missile systems, advanced propulsion systems and their subsidiary technologies, ordnance devices and other areas in which the need for the Laboratory's assistance arises.[7]

While this statement should have erased any doubts about the University's determination to maintain its association with APL, the continuing congressional surveillance combined with the decision of other academic institutions (including Cornell University, MIT, Columbia University, and Stanford University) to sever their ties with defense-related research laboratories in the face of the growing student antiwar movement led the director of the DoD Development, Research, and Engineering Division to ask the president of Johns Hopkins to confirm yet again the University's commitment to the Laboratory.

Accordingly, on May 8, 1970, the Executive Committee of the University's Board of Trustees approved another formal statement on the Applied Physics Laboratory, reaffirming its policy as expressed in the January 8, 1968, declaration. The committee also reiterated its "continuing support both of the national security mission and of the basic science and civilian technology mission of the Laboratory" and endorsed a recent statement by the Principal Professional Staff of APL in which the Laboratory's leadership expressed its abiding conviction that "the revolutionary advances in technology made in the past thirty years have rendered national security and perhaps survival critically dependent on the continued mastery of the most advanced modern technology."[8]

But as the Laboratory moved into the 1970s, the congressionally mandated ceilings on FCRCs were causing the APL staff difficulty in fulfilling APL's defense mission to the best of its ability. Even when Congress relented slightly and allowed the FCRC ceilings to creep upward during that severely inflationary decade, the increases that were granted never kept pace with the rapidly spiraling cost of living. "The only thing that saved us," observed Kossiakoff, "was that we went into that period with a very sizable carryover, which was due to the fact that we always had more jobs than we could do, and the money at that time could accumulate and last for a number of years. So we were able to use that and gradually work down through it."

By 1975, however, the Laboratory had run into a wall. Unable to delay the inevitable, APL instituted a hiring freeze and even began laying off personnel for virtually the only time in its history. Although the numbers were never large in relative terms, affecting perhaps 5 to 10 percent of the Laboratory staff, the unfortunate episode placed a strain on APL's leadership and diverted administrative resources that should have been more productively employed elsewhere. As Kossiakoff noted, "When you're involved in that kind of thing, it takes a tremendous amount of management effort, because you have to do it in such a way as to preserve the integrity and the vitality of the place. You can't let this kind of thing become a general oppression. . . .You have to shield the bulk of the Laboratory from it."

220

Aided by members of the Maryland congressional delegation, who worked diligently within the House and Senate committee structure to remove APL from the list of FCRC organizations, DoD finally persuaded Congress to exclude the three Navy university laboratories from its FCRC guidelines. Freed from these arbitrary restraints, APL returned almost immediately to its previous personnel levels and, in fact, added a small number of employees to handle tasks to which the Laboratory was already committed.

Coincidentally, it was also in 1976 that the final contingent of APL employees left the Laboratory's original 8621 Georgia Avenue location and completed the exodus to Howard County. On the evening of June 30, APL security guards turned over operation and maintenance of the building to the Naval Surface Weapons Center. But before the last Laboratory personnel departed, someone stopped in the office of the director and wrote a brief message on a blackboard; it read simply, "There were great men here." Fourteen years later, the building was demolished to make room for a parking garage.

CHAPTER SEVEN

THE FIFTH DECADE

The world is not a friendly place,
and I doubt that it ever will be.

———*Gary Smith*

At a meeting of The Johns Hopkins University Board of Trustees in the autumn of 1978, Alexander Kossiakoff approached Carl Bostrom and informed him that University president Steven Muller wished to confer privately with him. Since Bostrom had recently been appointed head of the APL Space Department and assistant Laboratory director for space systems as well, he assumed that the meeting with Muller was merely a matter of routine, the sort of conference the president of the University might hold with any new assistant director.

But Bostrom was mistaken. When they sat down behind closed doors in Kossiakoff's office, Muller asked Bostrom if he would be interested in becoming the next director of APL upon Kossiakoff's retirement in the summer of 1980. "I said, 'Gee, I guess I'd like to think about that a little bit,'" Bostrom recalled. "He said, 'Take your time. Take a week.'"

Bostrom's hesitation stemmed primarily from the fact that he had taken over the Space Department only a few months earlier and was concerned about finding a replacement on short notice. Fortunately, George Weiffenbach, a longtime member of the APL space team who had left the Laboratory in the early 1970s, agreed to return as head of the department. After spending many hours discussing the matter with Kossiakoff, Bostrom decided to accept the appointment. Again the Laboratory passed through a lengthy transition period, and in July 1980 Carl Bostrom became the fourth director of the Applied Physics Laboratory.

Since Bostrom had not even been head of a department before 1978, his rather meteoric rise to the highest echelon of the Laboratory's leadership took many at APL by surprise (including Bostrom himself, who had received no indication of the impending appointment before his conversation with Muller). Further, Bostrom came from outside the Laboratory's traditional mainstream mission of fleet defense. His work in the Space Department had not even focused on the Transit navigation satellite system, but on the sort of space science experiments that were only marginally related to the Navy's requirements. But Kershner had moved Bostrom rapidly through the APL hierarchy because he recognized in him precisely the sort of leadership qualities that the Laboratory would need to prosper in the changing defense research environment of the 1980s. Bostrom's appointment carried a symbolic significance as well, for it clearly reflected just how far the diversification of the Laboratory had proceeded by 1980.

On his last day as director, Kossiakoff was sitting in Timothy Keen's office when Bostrom walked by. "So we chatted for a little while," said Bostrom, "and then, just as we were leaving, Kossy reached out his hand and said, 'Don't screw it up.' That was the change-of-command ceremony."

Although Bostrom did not arrive in the director's office bearing any grand design to change APL's mission priorities or take the Laboratory into radically new areas of research, he did intend to alter its internal administrative procedures, to delegate responsibility and authority, and to decentralize the structure of the decision-making process so that more people would be involved. Soon formal committees began to assume responsibilities previously held by individuals; supervisors were kept fully informed of the Laboratory's administrative policies through special seminars; and management by consensus continued even more strongly as the preferred method of operation. To some at APL, this change represented a loss of technical direction and the imposition of an unwieldy bureaucracy that discouraged creativity. To others, it promised an opportunity to finally conduct the sort of participatory long-range planning they felt the Laboratory had lacked for quite some time.

Since Bostrom's assumption of the directorship coincided roughly with the retirement of most of the wartime generation of APL leaders (including Kossiakoff, Kershner, Avery, and Morton), one of his first and most pressing official tasks was to select their successors. Fortunately, there was no shortage of qualified candidates. When Alvin Schulz retired as associate director in 1986, he was replaced by Alvin Eaton, who previously had been assistant director with responsibility for program review. Eaton in turn was succeeded in 1989 by James Colvard, a longtime veteran of the Navy laboratory establishment and one of a handful of outsiders to assume a leadership position at APL. In the Space Department, Vincent Pisacane took over the reins from George Weiffenbach; when Pisacane subsequently became assistant director for exploratory development, Stamatios (Tom) Krimigis, a former protégé of James Van Allen at the University of Iowa, took his place as head of the Space Department.

Luciano Montanaro, whose first acquaintance with APL had come in the early days of the Polaris experiments when he was a naval officer, succeeded Robert Morton as chief of the Strategic Systems Department and served in that position until 1990, when he became assistant director and turned Strategic Systems over to Donald Eddins. In 1986, Thomas Sheppard, whose years of dedicated service at the Laboratory spanned five decades, stepped down as head of Fleet Systems, and Eugene J. Hinman took over the

224

leadership of the Laboratory's oldest department. And, in the Aeronautics Department, Richard Suess succeeded Gordon Dugger, who had earlier replaced William Avery.

While APL was experiencing its greatest period of change in the top leadership of the Laboratory since the late 1940s, significant changes were being made in the area of technical and administrative support activities as well. Ever since the late 1950s, APL had been building extremely reliable spacecraft; by 1980, however, its facilities were obsolescent and simply too small for many advanced applications. To preserve its future as a hands-on laboratory and ensure that APL would enjoy the most advanced facilities for engineering design, experimental fabrication, and testing in extreme environments, Bostrom and his colleagues decided to completely modernize and consolidate the Laboratory's technical services operations. Accordingly, he sought and received approval to construct a large, modern spacecraft engineering and test building, equipped with the latest cleanrooms, vacuum chambers, and numerous other facilities necessary to support topflight space programs. Fittingly, the building was named after Richard Kershner.

Shortly thereafter, the Laboratory's leadership decided to completely modernize APL's general mechanical and electronic design and fabrication facilities. The new Technical Services Department, headed by Robert Makofski, was established by combining the Computing Center, the library, the reports office, and the engineering services division. The department was staffed with personnel and top-level supervisors drawn from the various technical departments. Over the following decade, Technical Services personnel played an integral role in projects ranging from submarine detection to space systems and from biomedical implants to ramjet research. The department also introduced a computer-aided engineering network that allows all parts of the Laboratory to transmit designs to one another electronically, and a computer-aided manufacturing program that allows products to be fabricated to very strict tolerances without operator error.

To provide office and laboratory space for these operations, the Executive Committee of the JHU Board of Trustees approved a major new building, APL's largest, to replace a block of the "temporary" metal buildings that had housed such activities ever since the Laboratory first moved to Howard County. Upon its completion in 1990, this structure was named the Steven Muller Center for Advanced Technology, in honor of retiring JHU president Steven Muller, who had provided the Laboratory with such staunch support throughout his eighteen-year tenure.

By the time Bostrom had moved into the director's office, the Laboratory had begun to recover from the deleterious effects of the FCRC program. The number of professional staff had risen to slightly more than twelve

Retired Johns Hopkins University president Steven Muller viewing an exhibit describing the Steven Muller Center for Advanced Technology. The center was completed in 1990 and dedicated on March 11 of that year.

hundred; because of the ceiling on the total staff size, the percentage of professionals on the total laboratory staff had increased since 1965, from 38 percent to nearly 49 percent. Engineers were still three times more numerous at APL than any other group of scientists or technicians, but physicists were making a comeback (19 percent) vis-à-vis mathematicians (11 percent) and chemists (only 4 percent).

On the Surface

Fleet Systems remained the largest department (it had become a department in 1973), with approximately 450 professional staff members. As the new decade began, Fleet Systems's attention was still firmly focused on its assignment as technical support agent to the Aegis program office, headed by Admiral Wayne Meyer. In sea combat tests, a prototype Aegis system aboard the USS *Norton Sound* had already demonstrated its ability to find, identify, and track hundreds of hostile weapons simultaneously at ranges up to 250 miles. On May 16, 1981, the first Aegis ship, the USS *Ticonderoga*, was officially launched with considerable ceremony.

Remarkably, considering that it was the first product of an innovative and tremendously complex technology, the *Ticonderoga* was delivered on time and on budget. Because of the intense attention paid to systems integration throughout the entire research, engineering, and production process—and because of Wayne Meyer's energetic and determined leadership of the program—Aegis never experienced the sort of technical failures that had plagued the 3T systems. Aside from a temporary problem with ship stability and a few minor computer programming difficulties, the Aegis system functioned with extraordinary reliability from the outset, detecting and tracking every incoming "enemy" test aircraft within a radius of 250 miles.

In the meantime, a substantial segment of APL's Fleet Systems Department had shifted its primary focus from the

227

design of combat systems for individual ships to the problem of coordinating the actions of an entire battle group. Back in 1978, the Laboratory had been designated technical direction agent for the battle group antiaircraft warfare coordination effort sponsored by the Aegis program office. The objective, of course, was to multiply the effectiveness of a task group in combat by employing its firepower in concert via a computer network, as if a single, central intelligence were directing the battle group's actions. APL's fleet effectiveness analyses had recently demonstrated that such coordination could substantially eliminate duplicate engagements, thereby decreasing missile "wastage," and dramatically improve each ship's air-target information—and lessen the chances that incoming enemy missiles might somehow slip through the outer defenses—through the integration of all ship data into a fused track data base.

At first, the concept of coordinated action met considerable resistance from the fleet. In particular, there was concern over the potentially disastrous possibility that disabling the command ship in the battle group might render the whole group vulnerable. Others feared the effect of enemy electronic countermeasures (jamming) on the data link between ships. But the advent of automated tracking systems based on AN/SYS-1 technology aboard all combat vessels—with Aegis ships providing complete coverage within their radar range—demonstrated the viability of such a system. To tie the ships together, however, and make the concept of coordinated action feasible, the system required the design and production of several other components: (1) a means of accurately aligning each ship's radar tracks into a self-consistent network, (2) a secure communication system with an unprecedented data rate, and (3) high-speed processors to allow each ship to combine and reconcile data into a single accurate air picture indexed to its own combat systems.

By 1987, each of these components had been developed, and the Navy appointed APL as technical direction agent for its new cooperative engagement capability program. In this role, the Laboratory first conducted a prototype engineering test at APL, using three buildings in the role of ships to demonstrate the effectiveness of prototypes of each of the components cited above. APL also developed the complex software programs that controlled the surveillance and combat coordination functions. A year later, the Laboratory carried out a demonstration and validation of the cooperative engagement capability concept at sea aboard operational ships. This exercise, known as Milestone 90, was an unqualified success, even though one of the Aegis cruisers participating in the venture was detached to the Persian Gulf to join Operation Desert Storm in the midst of testing.

The achievements of Milestone 90 brought widespread support within the Navy to the cooperative engagement capability program, and the service subsequently embarked on a full-scale program to introduce the technology into the fleet by the mid-1990s. Moreover, other branches of DoD began to discuss the possibility of extending this capability to joint applications, such as Navy and Air Force surveillance aircraft and fighters, and the Patriot and Hawk air defense systems. Thus the Laboratory, largely through the Fleet Systems Department, has played a major role in ushering in a new era in military warfare in which the major defense units in any given region are networked to function as a single, organic system.

In any engagement, of course, Navy vessels must first determine whether any aircraft that ventures into the range of its detection system is a friendly or an enemy craft. When offensive missiles can reach their targets within seconds, this identification must be done quickly and accurately. Unfortunately, the process of identification is often hindered by limited information, by the heavy traffic of commercial aircraft in any given area, and by the complex circumstances in which Navy vessels often find themselves. Accordingly, in 1987 APL conceived an automatic identification (AutoID) system to aid ship personnel in making such decisions in a swift and accurate manner.

AutoID employs a collection of encoded rules that represent the decisions an operator would make given certain tactical situations and directives, taking into account such variables as track speed, altitude, and heading. In 1988, the first AutoID system was deployed on the USS *Forrestal* and proved an immediate success, both in identifying Navy planes posing as bandits and in detecting actual drug-smuggling flights. Two years later, the original AutoID system was removed and placed on another carrier deployed in Operation Desert Shield.

While APL had been a major contributor to cruise missile development ever since the Navy evidenced real interest in such ordnance following the sinking of the *Elath* in 1967, it was not until 1982, when the transition of the Tomahawk system into production encountered grave difficulties, that APL was asked by the Navy to assume a major responsibility in the program. Rear Admiral Steven Hostettler, who was brought in to manage the troubled program, acted promptly to reorganize and strengthen the program's infrastructure. Acting on his experience in the 3T program and his knowledge of the Laboratory, Hostettler designated APL as his technical direction agent.

This new responsibility broadened the APL charter to embrace all elements of the Tomahawk weapon system. Admiral Hostettler formed a small team that spearheaded efforts to solve problems hampering Tomahawk's transition to production; specifically, the Tomahawk team introduced and enforced a new discipline in the program by establishing design baselines, firmly controlling changes, and focusing management attention on solving the most pressing difficulties. With APL providing leadership in

Launched from surface ships and submarines, the Tomahawk cruise missile provides a long-range autonomous strike capability. Guidance for the land attack variant uses terrain and scene matching to achieve exceptional accuracy. The antiship variant employs a radar seeker to attain its high success rate.

several critical areas the initial problems were solved, and Tomahawk went into production successfully.

Meanwhile, in 1982 Carl Bostrom had combined two units of the Fleet Systems Department with the Laboratory's Assessment Division to establish the APL Naval Warfare Analysis Department. Headed by Fleet Systems Department veteran Richard J. Hunt, the new department was designed to maintain and broaden the Laboratory's work in systems analysis over the entire spectrum of naval warfare, using computer modeling and simulating techniques to develop insights into antiair, antisurface, strike, and antisubmarine issues.

Strengthened by the addition of extra staff and aided by state-of-the-art electronic displays and data, the department developed the Warfare Analysis Laboratory (WAL), a general-purpose seminar wargaming facility that creates an information processing and display environment where high-ranking naval officers and APL operations analysts can examine tactical situations and conduct mission and requirements analysis while "playing through" various operational scenarios.

Typically, WAL exercises consist of two playing teams (Blue and Red), an analysis team, and a moderator. In August 1989, for instance, the Laboratory conducted an exercise to compare the relative cost and operational effectiveness of land-based, sea-based, and mixed land-and-sea-based antisatellite operations. Among those participating in the senior advisory group for this exercise were the deputy commander of the U.S. Space Command, five senior civilian officials of the Department of Defense, and seven flag officers from the various services. The Blue team consisted of three retired flag officers with recent command experience and personnel from the relevant U.S. Army and Navy commands; the Red team included space experts from six U.S. intelligence agencies along with a number of WAL personnel.

Although APL's advanced ramjet development programs for Triton and the long-range Typhon missile were terminated in the mid-1960s, the Laboratory has continued to carry out research in air-breathing engine technology in its Aeronautics Department (until 1984, the Aeronautics Division). During the 1970s, when APL was the principal preserver of interest and knowledge of hypersonic ramjets in the United States, the Laboratory succeeded in designing a ramjet combustor that successfully sustained burning in an air stream at supersonic speeds. When incorporated in a missile configuration, this supersonic combustion ramjet (also known as a scramjet) provided significant net positive thrust at hypersonic speeds, a landmark event in the history of jet propulsion.

In the mid-1980s, the federal government established an ambitious program to develop a demonstration model of the National Aerospace Plane (NASP). Envisioned as "the ultimate airplane," NASP would be capable of taking off from conventional airfields and reaching speeds up to seventeen thousand miles per hour, twenty-five times the speed of sound, while routinely flying from earth to space and back. Since the primary propulsion system that would take the plane from Mach 3 to nearly orbital speeds would be a dual mode ramjet engine transitioning to a scramjet at hypersonic speeds, it is not surprising that the government enlisted APL as an integral member of the national team of industrial corporations and laboratories established to develop such a vehicle. Specifically, a task group from the Laboratory, headed by Frederick Billig of the Aeronautics Department, was awarded the responsibility of performing critical path technology development and transferring its unique experience in advanced ramjet technology to the two engine development contractors, much as APL had done back in the days of the Section T program.

Under the Surface

In support of the nation's undersea forces, the Laboratory's Strategic Systems Department continued its traditional testing and evaluation work for the Special Projects Office, though its tasks grew increasingly complex with the introduction of each new weapon system. Starting with the original Polaris program in the late 1950s, a new SSBN missile system had been introduced into the submarine fleet every five to seven years: the Polaris A1, A2, and A3, the Poseidon C3, and the Trident C4. But before Special Projects brought into the fleet the next generation of submarines and missiles, the Trident II, the Laboratory embarked on a program designed to provide even greater precision to its tracking and measurement systems.

This endeavor, known as the Improved Accuracy Program, was designed to provide the capability of tracking a missile with extreme accuracy throughout its powered flight. The requirements of this mission were beyond

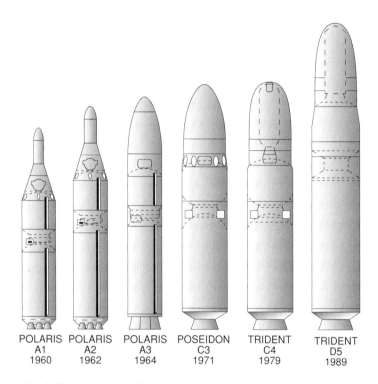

POLARIS	POLARIS	POLARIS	POSEIDON	TRIDENT	TRIDENT
A1	A2	A3	C3	C4	D5
1960	1962	1964	1971	1979	1989

Fleet ballistic missiles (FBMs) have grown in size and changed in shape since the first Polaris was launched from a submerged submarine in 1960. As this drawing indicates, the missiles have become larger so that they can carry more fuel and travel greater distances. As missile range increases, so does the ocean area within which the FBM submarines can operate, thus reducing the danger of their being detected.

the capability of existing range radars, and APL decided to use satellite navigation as the basis for measurement. Enlisting the assistance of their colleagues in the Space Department, a team of Strategic Systems Department engineers developed a technique known as SATRACK, initially using Transit until that group of satellites was superseded by the Global Positioning System. As SATRACK developed, it gave the Laboratory the capability of measur-

234

ing position to within a few feet and velocity to within hundredths of a foot per second, thereby contributing to the achievement of a delivery accuracy for the Trident II weapon system that approached the limits of the best land-based intercontinental ballistic missiles.

Before the Trident II missiles could take their place in the Navy's strategic arsenal, however, they had to overcome a series of spectacular test firing failures. In the late 1980s, the Trident II program successfully completed a series of land-based launches from Cape Canaveral and moved into the underwater test phase. But when the first submarine-launched Trident II missile broke through the surface of the water, it went into a series of spiraling loops and crashed back into the sea. Although the cause of the failure was not immediately clear, suspicion focused on the greatly increased sea-related forces acting on the first-stage motor during the launch of the missile, which was, after all, nearly twice the weight of previous submarine-launched ballistic missiles.

Strengthening some of the first-stage motor components led to a successful second sea launch, but when a third missile was fired under more severe launch conditions, the missile again failed shortly after launch. Now the possibility of a potentially disastrous flaw in the missile's basic design seemed very real; unless the problem could be identified and solved, the entire Trident II program would suffer extensive delays and cost increases. With attention from the highest level of government focused on the problem, the Special Projects Office placed the highest priority on resolving this crisis, appointing a high-level investigating committee of nine industry specialists headed by retired Vice Admiral Levering Smith. At Smith's request, the APL Strategic Systems Department provided the committee with direct assistance in the form of flight data analysis, dynamic simulations, and analysis of proposed modifications that enabled the experts in the fleet ballistic community to analyze the complex effects of underwater travel on the missile. Based on these sophisticated data, the missile-water dynamics were finally understood to the point where suitable design changes could be made to the missile's first-stage motor to enable the Trident II to take its place at last as the nation's latest and most advanced submarine-based missile system.

The Submarine Technology (Sub Tech) Department, which had been spun off from the Strategic Systems Department in 1977, continued to grow, reaching a peak in personnel in 1979, when it completed an initial review of the Navy's submarine security program. However, the very size and potential military importance of the rapidly expanding SSBN program raised questions in DoD and in the Office of Naval Operations (OPNAV) as to the prudence of delegating such broad program management responsibility to any organization outside the Navy, even one with the proven track record of APL. As a result, an oversight office was established in OPNAV in 1979; three years later, management responsibility for the entire SSBN security program was transferred from the project office in APL's Strategic Systems Department to the OPNAV deputy for submarine systems.

In managing the SSBN security program, OPNAV elected to bring in a number of additional participants, gradually reducing the funding and program responsibility of the APL Sub Tech team. Aware that APL's role in the program could diminish significantly in the near future, Sub Tech launched a concerted campaign to expand its technical concentration beyond the SSBN security program, building especially on its skills in submarine detection technology and ocean physics. Within two years this effort began to achieve results as the Laboratory was awarded new assignments with several Navy systems commands and the Defense Advanced Research Projects Agency (DARPA). These initiatives more than offset subsequent decreases in the level of SSBN security funding and simultaneously provided a healthy degree of diversification in APL's sponsor base.

Over the next few years, Navy officials had second thoughts about the central management of the SSBN security program. In 1989, after Sub Tech had achieved several significant successes in expanding the limits of understanding in the field of antisubmarine warfare, OPNAV asked APL to resume its leadership role in the program. In addition, the Navy's attack submarine community decided that it required a similar program to anticipate threats to the security of its vessels and subsequently asked APL to fulfill this need as well. These requests presented the Laboratory with the problem of responding to these vital national security requirements without abruptly reducing the level of its commitments in other areas. In the end, APL chose to accept these additional responsibilities by relaxing the Laboratory's self-imposed personnel ceiling for a two-year period.

Facing the need to develop a quantitative understanding of the physics of submarine detection in the extraordinarily dynamic ocean environment, with its complex array of fronts, eddies, turbulence, and internal waves, APL created a methodology for large-scale ocean experiments capable of dealing with phenomena extending for tens or hundreds of miles. In these experiments, Sub Tech has employed an array of vessels, aircraft, and submarines equipped with instruments and innovative sensors, many of them developed at the Laboratory, coupled with computerized measuring and recording systems.

During the 1980s, APL further improved the efficiency and productivity of its at-sea investigations by linking its research vessels via satellite communications networks to an operations center at the APL facility in Howard County, where computing resources and scientific personnel were available to support the experiments. During the past few years, the operations center has been used to analyze data

Deployment of the APL-developed temperature-conductivity-fluorometer chain from the aft deck of the MV Acadian Mariner, under way in the Sargasso Sea in October 1984. The chain instrument system, which is used to study oceanic internal waves, microstructure, and current shear, is wound on a winch in the center of the picture and passes through the "donut" guide before being lowered into the ocean by the knuckle boom crane.

during tests, assess the impact of unexpected environmental conditions, revise test plans, troubleshoot systems and components, modify system software, and prepare and deliver graphic data packages for use aboard ship.

One specific area in which these at-sea experiments have played a crucial role is the use of active sonar to detect submarines that are too quiet to be detected by passive means. This problem has become especially critical with the advent of a new generation of superquiet submarines. Despite doubts voiced by some skeptics that "backscatter" from the ocean floor would mask the weak echo returned from a distant submarine, Sub Tech has been able to adapt radar techniques developed at APL to prove that under favorable conditions, low-frequency sonar is in fact capable of detecting even absolutely quiet submarines at great distances.

Research in the 1980s

The APL Research Center, too, has continued to evolve. In the early years (see Chapter 3), the Research Center's areas of concentration were largely limited to spectroscopy, chemical kinetics, high-altitude research, and wave physics. In the 1960s and 1970s, however, the center's activities broadened to include research in such areas as plasma physics, map-matching technology for cruise missiles, flame structure, laser technology and unstable burning of solid fueled rockets (see Chapter 5).

From time to time Research Center projects that had substantial immediate practical application were expanded and accommodated in other areas of the Laboratory. Some notable examples include the space satellite tracking project that led to the invention of the Transit navigation satellite system and spawned the APL Space Department, and the Laboratory's biomedical and fire research programs, which operated out of the APL Director's office as quasi-independent units.

Funding sources for the Research Center have also shifted during the years. For the first fifteen years of its existence, the center's work was funded by the Navy as a separate task. Beginning in 1963, however, the Navy required that the Research Center's work be charged to "independent research and development" (IRAD), a category that the government had established to support relevant research by defense contractors.

At that time, the Laboratory's IRAD funds were split approximately equally between the Research Center's work and exploratory research projects in other APL divisions. But IRAD funds were subject to a ceiling, which for APL in the early 1970s was approximately two million dollars. By the time Robert Hart replaced Frank McClure as chairman of the Research Center in 1972, the total Laboratory IRAD spending had reached its ceiling, and even though the Research Center maintained a constant staffing size, inflation caused the center's costs to creep upward at the expense of exploratory development elsewhere. Caught in a financial squeeze, APL could have sought additional IRAD funds above the ceiling limit, but then the Laboratory would have been required to submit detailed justifications for all its research projects for Navy review, a process that, being foreign to APL's traditional mode of operations, appeared onerous to the Laboratory's leadership at the time.

Instead, the Laboratory chose to aggressively pursue funding for the Research Center from external sources. During the latter half of the 1970s, this effort succeeded in securing nearly half the support for the Research Center's programs from outside sponsors, yet it barely kept pace with the skyrocketing inflation of that period. Finally, in 1979 the Laboratory decided to submit to the justification and review process for IRAD for fiscal 1980, enabling it to qualify for additional funds. Fortunately, the review process proved to be less burdensome than anticipated, and APL's exploratory development programs accordingly began growing significantly again.

Theodore Poehler, who became director of the Research Center in 1983, encouraged an emphasis on research projects with manifest practical applications while simultaneously seeking to strengthen the Research Center's position in the outside world of sponsored research. The results of Poehler's initiatives may be seen in the wide variety of projects the Research Center undertook during the 1980s. For instance, in the late 1980s a group of APL scientists involved in the rapidly growing field of high-temperature superconductors discovered and refined a set of techniques that have provided a unique means of probing important aspects of these materials.

Another Research Center team has focused on the increasingly critical problem of corrosion in the nation's aging natural gas pipeline system. By combining electrochemical studies of corrosion with sensors (large, dynamic range magnetometers) developed for space and submarine applications, these scientists have developed a new method of monitoring the condition of a buried pipeline without resorting to excavation. Using these sensors, APL has helped develop a theory of environmentally related corrosion as a dynamic process, changing surprisingly rapidly with location and time.

In the field of ophthalmological research, an APL Research Center team devised a novel theory of the structure of the human cornea and, through extensive experimentation, provided conclusive evidence to support that theory. Along with its implications for the study of healthy corneas, this endeavor has led to a better understanding of structural alterations in pathological corneas.

Shortly after Donald Williams assumed the helm of the Research Center in 1990, he led a full-scale planning effort to determine what sort of projects the center should pursue in the coming decade. The result was a comprehensive document known as "Research Center 2000," which recommended such projects as wave propagation and scattering, nonlinear dynamics, computer and information sciences, materials science and evaluation, and biomedical research.

Frank McClure's untimely death in 1973 not only deprived the Laboratory of one of its most brilliant and forceful leaders, but it also took some of the heart out of the collaborative JHU-APL biomedical program that McClure had founded and championed. Reductions in federal appropriations for National Institutes of Health research grants during the late 1970s and 1980s delivered another serious blow to the program.

Nevertheless, the Laboratory's biomedical research effort continued to produce significant results. One of the more intriguing projects of the 1980s was known as PIMS (programmable implantable medication system). An early application of space technology to biomedical problems, this system allows physicians to implant in a patient a drug

241

reservoir (e.g., insulin for the control of diabetes) and a pump, along with electronics to control the pump and communicate with the external world via an implanted transceiver. After a number of successful experiments with animals, human trials with this device began in 1990, and the Laboratory expects the Food and Drug Administration approval for general use in 1993.

To help alleviate the suffering caused by the AIDS epidemic, particularly in Third World and developing nations, APL researchers and their colleagues in the School of Medicine devised a syringe that could not be used more than once, on account of the presence of a thin polymer plug that swells upon exposure to liquids, making the syringe inoperable after a single use. Other recent APL biomedical innovations have included SIBIS (self-injurious behavior-inhibiting system), which effectively suppresses the compulsive head-beating behavior of autistic children; an ingestible encapsulated temperature probe that transmits its reading via a radio link; and a variety of instruments and advanced techniques to investigate the human nervous system.

In 1991, Carl Bostrom decentralized the biomedical program by disestablishing the central office and vesting responsibility for its research projects in the various departments. According to Robert Flower, who had assumed the leadership of the biomedical programs office in 1982 upon the retirement of Joseph Massey, "We decided that after all of its history, that these kinds of collaboration had matured ... and that it made better administrative sense to place the responsibility for overseeing the work in the specific departments of the Laboratory in which the participants resided, because that is where the authority lies, and that is where the responsibility for maintaining priorities resides." In the early 1990s, APL moved to strengthen its biomedical program further with a program to address the specific medical needs of the military services, with sponsorship from the Department of Defense.

242

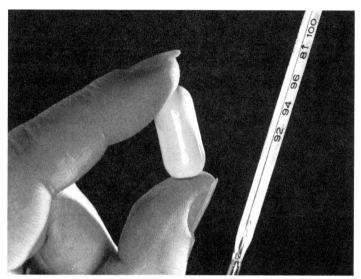

Ingestible temperature capsule, developed at APL and marketed commercially, is being applied in a variety of uses that require continuous, remote monitoring of body temperature—for example, in deep-ocean devices and firefighting.

Space—New Initiatives

In the early 1960s, when the first Transit satellites were soaring into orbit, Ralph Gibson praised the APL Space Development Division for giving the Laboratory "a shot in the arm" by providing it with an entirely new mission, one that has since played an increasingly prominent role at APL. Progressively broadening its perspective from the largely navigation and geodesy-related problems of the 1960s and 1970s, the APL space effort attained department status in 1966 and by 1985 employed a professional staff of 280 individuals.

In one of the Space Department's most successful ventures, APL joined with research organizations in West Germany and Great Britain in a collaborative experiment to study the origins, composition, and dynamics of the

243

radiation zone around the earth. The project had originated at APL, and the Laboratory assumed the responsibility for obtaining funding from NASA and putting together a prestigious international team that included scientists from the Max Planck Institute for Extraterrestrial Physics in Munich and from Britain's Rutherford Appleton Laboratory and Mullard Space Science Laboratory. For this experiment, known as AMPTE (Active Magnetosphere Particle Tracer Explorer), each nation built its own spacecraft. The American satellite, known familiarly as the Charge Composition Explorer, was designed and constructed by APL to determine first how much of the energy from the solar wind actually makes its way into the earth's magnetic field and then how much of that energy is deposited over the polar ice caps, where it helps produce the well-known phenomenon the aurora borealis.

Ever since the early days of Transit, APL's space science experts had made a special study of geodesy, and in the early 1980s the Laboratory once again made a major contribution in that area with an APL satellite known as Geosat. Built for the Navy and launched in March 1985, Geosat carried a radar altimeter capable of measuring a relatively calm ocean surface with the precision of a few centimeters.

As a sequel to the Voyager experiments, the APL Space Department also built portions of an energetic particle detector for the Galileo mission, launched in 1989. Although Voyagers I and II had passed near Jupiter, Galileo was designed to send a probe deep into that planet's atmosphere, where the particle detector would help measure the composition and dynamics of the searingly hot plasmas that swirl around the planet, before the spacecraft resumed its voyage past the four largest Jovian satellites.

Valuable as these projects were to the advancement of knowledge about the space environment, however, they did not seem likely to lead the Laboratory into any new large-scale, long-term research programs. Then, unexpect-

Geosat undergoes a final check at the Richard B. Kershner Space Systems Integration and Test Building. Dedicated on October 11, 1983, the Kershner Building has made possible a lead role for APL in important space programs for NASA and DoD, including the Delta 180 and 181 space experiments for the Strategic Defense Initiative.

edly, a major new source of research funds appeared. On March 23, 1983, President Ronald Reagan announced that his administration intended to investigate the possibility of constructing a highly effective airborne defense against ballistic missiles, a speculative concept that had been bruited about ever since the 1950s. "I call upon the scientific community in our country," the president declared in a nationwide television address, "those who gave us nuclear weapons, to turn their great talents now to the cause of mankind and world peace, to give us the means of rendering these nuclear weapons impotent and obsolete."

Before committing the nation to an unrealistic objective that could require decades to achieve, consuming billions of dollars in the process, Reagan directed a blue-ribbon panel of scientists and engineers led by James Fletcher, former head of NASA, to assess the technology required for a ballistic missile defense system. In late 1983, Fletcher's team reported that such a system appeared to be technically feasible; the panel concluded that powerful new technologies were becoming available that could justify a major technological development effort to implement a defensive strategy.

Accordingly, on January 16, 1984, President Reagan authorized a national research program to evaluate and demonstrate the technical feasibility of intercepting offensive nuclear missiles. Three months later, the administration consolidated all the new and ongoing research projects in this area under the Strategic Defense Initiative Organization (SDIO), headed by General James Abrahamson, a graduate of MIT who had previously successfully managed the space shuttle and F-16 fighter aircraft programs. Abrahamson's staff, however, remained relatively small, forcing SDIO to rely on outside organizations for technical expertise and counsel.

Meanwhile, certain members of the APL leadership recognized that SDIO now represented the best available source for funding the type of innovative, advanced technology research programs in which the Laboratory had always excelled in the past. An initial APL proposal to apply its expertise in high-level computing systems to the Strategic Defense Initiative (SDI) never got off the ground, but

246

shortly thereafter a high-ranking member of the SDIO staff contacted Samuel Koslov, assistant to the director for technical assessment at APL, to see if the Laboratory could supply his office with technical specialists in such fields as guidance, control, electronics, and thermodynamics on a small-scale, as-needed basis.

After an April 17, 1984, meeting between APL officials and representatives of SDIO, the Laboratory undertook to determine whether the Laboratory could make a useful contribution to the program under those conditions. At first, the prospect of participating in the SDI effort only in an advisory role did not appeal to many at APL. But in the very last paragraph of its formal request for technical assistance, SDIO had included a suggestion that APL's experience in space systems, especially its reputation for building and launching satellites under tight deadline constraints, might also prove valuable. By that time, the Reagan administration was coming under heavy pressure from critics of the SDI program to provide some tangible evidence that the whole concept of an antiballistic missile defense was not just some "star wars" fantasy, and General Abrahamson desperately wanted to conduct a successful in-space experiment within two or three years at the latest.

There was considerable resistance among the Laboratory's leadership to the suggestion of a near-term launch for SDIO on the grounds that it was simply too risky a project. Yet the concept aroused terrific enthusiasm within the APL Space Department, which was the one department of the Laboratory with significant recent experience in putting together just this sort of experimental venture under tight time constraints. Besides, the department had just completed the launch of the AMPTE mission and hence had staff resources available.

In November 1984, a team under the leadership of program manager John Dassoulas started to devise an experiment for assessing the feasibility of the concept of tracking, intercepting, and destroying an intercontinental ballistic missile (ICBM) during powered flight in space. Meanwhile, Carl Bostrom established an internal advisory committee, chaired by Alvin Eaton and including Alexander Kossiakoff (who had become the Laboratory's chief scientist since his retirement as director), to review the Space Department's plans. "I wanted to make sure," Bostrom explained, "that we weren't just doing something because [SDIO] said they wanted something done quick." At the same time, though, Bostrom realized that if the experiment were successful it might well represent a welcome first step toward the development of the sort of permanent test platform for space experiments that could complement the Laboratory's historic involvement with land- and sea-based missile testing.

Originally, SDIO had asked APL to devise an experiment that could be carried out in two or three years. "Then all of a sudden, the classic telephone call came," recalled Koslov. Instead of a twenty-four-month deadline, SDIO wanted APL to be ready to launch within twelve months. "Then all hell broke loose," Koslov added. "It was sort of like, 'Tell us what you need in terms of money and we'll get it for you.'"

Facing an accelerated schedule, which later was negotiated to fourteen months, Dassoulas and his group concluded that they would need to be extremely creative in adapting existing technology, since there was no time to develop anything entirely new. Complicating matters further, the whole experiment had to be conducted in compliance with the guidelines of the Anti-Ballistic Missile Treaty, which meant that it could employ no ICBM components nor involve any object that would travel on an ICBM-like trajectory or velocity.

Calling on their colleagues in Fleet Systems Department for advice, the Space Department planned at first to employ a tactical missile with an active homing guidance system as an interceptor. Conventional radar would be used to get the spacecraft to within a hundred feet of its target, where its warhead would explode and saturate an area of several hundred square feet with lethal pellets. For a rocket booster, the APL team selected McDonnell-Douglas's two-stage Delta vehicle, and henceforth the project was known familiarly as Delta 180. Eventually the interceptor evolved into a hybrid comprised of elements of the Phoenix missile, Delta second-stage components, and tankage from a communications satellite. As the project proceeded, both the Hughes Corporation and McDonnell-Douglas became essential members of the Delta 180 team, combining forces to build the interceptor itself and participating in mission planning and implementation.

At a meeting in Washington on February 20, 1985, the APL system engineer for Delta 180, Michael Griffin, presented the experiment design to SDIO officials and representatives of most of the nation's major aerospace contractors. Virtually all the contractor representatives expressed hearty skepticism that APL could meet either its schedule deadline or the proposed $200 million budget. Nevertheless, SDIO told the Laboratory on the following day to proceed with its planning, and on April 12, General Abrahamson gave final approval to the Delta 180 project, for which APL, with its excellent reputation for systems engineering, was awarded the role of technical leader.

The final design of the experiment as devised by APL featured the launching of two spacecraft atop a single rocket. Once in orbit, the two vehicles would separate, drift apart, and then turn to face each other, nose to nose. When they were separated by a distance of 220 kilometers, the rocket engines on the two spacecraft would be ignited. At 60 kilometers, the terminal radar homing system on the intercepting spacecraft would begin to track the target vehicle, guiding the interceptor toward it.

After running simulations with the aid of the Fleet Systems Department, the APL Delta 180 team concluded that the encounter would need to be almost exactly head-on, since the interceptor lacked any significant acceleration advantage over its target. At the same time, the team had to design a spacecraft essentially without propulsion, which would be supplied by the second stage of the Delta rocket. And though there was no time to build complex new sensor or guidance systems (most of the material was off-the-shelf equipment), the Space Department did build a special visible and ultraviolet sensor for the mission, which it integrated onto the sensor module with the other instruments.

Fortunately for APL, General Abrahamson proved to be an understanding and sympathetic sponsor. "He gave us a challenge and sent money, and let us alone and let us work," testified Dassoulas, who viewed the general as a younger version of Ralph Gibson. Without interfering, Abrahamson kept close tabs on the progress of the project at the working level, meeting frequently with the APL team at the Pentagon on weekend afternoons, boosting morale by visiting the Laboratory to personally interview virtually everyone involved in the Delta program and participating personally in the final preflight reviews of the project hardware. Although he remained under heavy pressure to meet the administration's deadline, Abrahamson never accepted any technical risk to maintain the program's schedule.

In June 1986, one month ahead of schedule, APL shipped its spacecraft to Cape Canaveral for the start of launch preparations. On September 5, 1986, Delta 180 was launched, and less than three hours later the interceptor spacecraft accelerated toward its target and scored a direct hit.

From a global perspective, this remarkable demonstration may well have intensified the pressure on the Soviet leadership to negotiate a new arms control agreement. Closer to home, APL's ability to carry out a successful and complex mission in such a short time brought a flood of requests for other similar experiments. During the next five years the Laboratory conducted two more launches for

250

SDIO, including the Delta 181 mission to observe and collect data on various defense-related phenomena in the space environment (including rocket exhausts and test objects), and Delta Star, an even more ambitious observation and tracking experiment that was completed within a nine-month deadline.

By late 1991, the Laboratory's Strategic Defense Initiative program had expanded so rapidly that funding from SDI projects made up approximately 75 to 80 percent of the APL Space Department's annual budget. The most ambitious SDI project currently under way at APL is the Midcourse Space Experiment (MSX), a venture planned for a mid-1993 launch. As devised by APL, the MSX project will feature a massive fifty-five-hundred-pound satellite designed to provide the first documentation of technical capability to identify and track incoming ballistic missiles in space during their mid-course flight phase.

During the past thirty years, each technical department of APL has evolved largely according to its own mission, and each has developed an identifiable culture of its own. The Fleet Systems Department, of course considers itself (along with the Aeronautics Department and the Naval Warfare Analysis Department) the heir to the historic APL mission to protect the nation's surface fleet from air attacks. Yet the focus of that mission has obviously shifted in an age when all parts of the nation's defense structure are spending less on the development of new weapon systems and concentrating more on the enhancement of existing systems.

Beginning with the 3T Get Well program, Fleet Systems has become intimately associated with the day-to-day operations of the Navy. This association has allowed the department to understand in detail the real operating environment and problems of Navy weapon and combat systems and has contributed substantially to Fleet Systems' ability to conceive and develop effective new engineering solutions. This association, however, has required the

251

department to assess and balance its commitments to solving pressing short-term requirements of the fleet, while at the same time meeting its traditional obligation of looking into the future to ascertain what new systems or materiel the Navy might need to defend itself against future threats.

While the fundamental mission of the Strategic Systems Department has changed little since its inception at the start of the Polaris program, the department has continued to expand the scope of its activities. Unlike Fleet Systems and the Space Department, Strategic Systems produces reports rather than exotic hardware, and its staff requires the ability to deal with a complex array of variables and a high tolerance for ambiguities, which is not precisely the quality most engineers possess. Yet, perhaps more than any other group in the Laboratory, the members of the Strategic Systems Department enjoy the satisfaction of knowing that their work represents a vital contribution to the safety and effectiveness of the nation through the continued well-being of the submarine deterrent force.

As we have seen, the work of the Research Center in the past decade has become more closely integrated with the rest of the Laboratory's programs. With its continuing experiments in oceanography and its theoretical investigations in submarine detection technology, the Submarine Technology Department has retained much of its original focus on understanding the fundamentals of ocean physics. And of course the Space Department, which represents nearly one-seventh of the Laboratory's professional staff, continues to excel in the design and construction of new satellites and spacecraft, both for SDIO and for civilian sponsors such as NASA.

The Johns Hopkins University
Applied Physics Laboratory

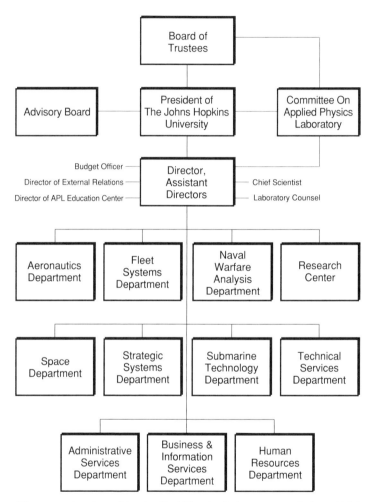

The organization of the Applied Physics Laboratory on July 1, 1992.

253

At the end of 1991, the Navy still directly supplied approximately two-thirds of the Laboratory's $400-million annual budget. The number and variety of projects have grown, of course, from the simpler days of the Bumblebee program, when there were fewer than twenty accountable tasks, to the current list of 250 programs with nearly four hundred separate tasks. Nor is there any longer a single individual in the Navy with the same close personal ties to APL as Admiral Levering Smith or the early chiefs of BuOrd and BuWeps, who considered themselves responsible for the Laboratory's welfare.

Undoubtedly the most significant change in the operating environment of the Applied Physics Laboratory—indeed, of all government contractors—in the past thirty years has been the steadily growing intrusion of bureaucratic administrative procedures. Not for nothing did Bostrom complain in the summer of 1991, "Our biggest problem for the last five years has been dealing with the bureaucracy."

Yet the changing environment of DoD research has not prevented the Applied Physics Laboratory from continuing to play a vital role in the United States' defense structure, as witnessed by the Laboratory's contributions to the allied victory in the recent Persian Gulf conflict. The Navy battle groups in the gulf employed the Aegis air defense system, an experimental command support system developed at APL, and surface-to-air Standard missiles to defend themselves against air attack. The land attack variant of the Tomahawk missile that struck targets deep in Iraqi territory relied on guidance systems developed in large measure at APL (in fact, APL had been called in as technical direction agent for the entire Tomahawk development program in 1982). The battle plans for the Navy and Air Force electronic countermeasure aircraft that gained and retained control of the skies made extensive use of APL tactical recommendations. And the Patriot missile that earned such high marks in defending Israeli and Saudi cities and allied military bases against Iraqi tactical ballistic weapons (SCUDs) benefited greatly from the advice and expertise of a small group of individuals at APL who had been working steadily with the Army and the prime Patriot contractor, Raytheon, during the past decade to bring the missile to its maximum effectiveness.

In the autumn of 1991, Carl Bostrom announced his intention to retire. To succeed Bostrom as director of APL, Johns Hopkins president William C. Richardson selected Gary Smith, then serving as associate director, saying, "Gary's excellent credentials as an experimental physicist and as a proven leader at the Laboratory superbly qualify him to steer APL into a new era of service to the nation and to The Johns Hopkins University." Smith's appointment was confirmed by the University's Board of Trustees on November 11, 1991, and on July 1, 1992, he became the sixth director of the Applied Physics Laboratory, with a mission to lead it into the uncharted waters of the post–cold war world to the twenty-first century.

Gary L. Smith, sixth director of the Applied Physics Laboratory, with William C. Richardson, president of The Johns Hopkins University (November 5, 1992).

DIRECTORS OF THE
APPLIED PHYSICS LABORATORY

Merle A. Tuve
1942–1946

Lawrence R. Hafstad
1946–1947

Ralph E. Gibson
1948–1969

Alexander Kossiakoff
1969–1980

Carl O. Bostrom
1980–1992

Gary L. Smith
1992–

APPENDIX: SOURCES

Oral History Interviews

Much of the material for this study came from a series of oral history interviews conducted between March and November 1991. Most, but not all, of the participants were present or former staff members of the Applied Physics Laboratory. To all of the individuals listed below, I express my heartfelt appreciation for their invaluable contributions.

Benjamin E. Amsler
Harry C. Anderson
Clarence E. Andrews
James R. Austin
William H. Avery
Shirley Biberstein
Harold D. Black
Carl O. Bostrom
Rachel Branthover
William E. Buchanan
Elmore R. Chatham
Edward L. Cochran
Richard N. Creswell
Lester L. Cronvich
John Dassoulas
Alvin R. Eaton
Donald L. Eddins
Richard T. Ellis
George F. Emch
Robert W. Flower
Samuel N. Foner
William E. Frain
Robert M. Fristrom

Betty W. Gadbois
William H. Garten
Walter A. Good
Wilbur H. Goss
Robert H. Grauel
William H. Guier
Robert W. Hart
Eugene J. Hinman
Robert L. Hutchins
Chih Kung Jen
Timothy J. Keen
James L. Keirsey
Robert E. Kemelhor
Bernard Kornblit
Samuel Koslov
Alexander Kossiakoff
Stamatios M. (Tom) Krimigis
Mary D. Lasky
James B. Maddox
Robert A. Makofski
Joseph Massey
Mark O. Mathews
Wayne E. Meyer

257

Luciano P. Montanaro
Milton L. Moon
Cyril J. O'Brien
Marion E. Oliver
Fletcher Paddison
Charles S. Perry
Theodore O. Poehler
Edward M. Portner
Frank B. Proctor
Eli T. Reich
Robert P. Rich
Ralph O. Robinson
Conrad J. Rorie
James N. Schneider

Alvin G. Schulz
Thomas W. Sheppard
Helen L. Sherbert
William B. Shippen
Gary L. Smith
Levering Smith
Arthur C. Stucki
Richard P. Suess
E. Leon Virts
George C. Weiffenbach
Donald J. Williams
Mark W. Woods
William H. Zinger

Documentary Sources

For this project, I enjoyed complete access to all the unclassified files in the APL archives. By far the most useful papers were located in Dr. Gibson's director's office files. As one might expect, documentary sources of the past twenty-five years were under much more severe classification restrictions.

Further vital documents on matters of national security policy for the period 1942–60 were found in the documentary series *Foreign Relations of the United States* published by the U.S. Department of State. In addition, background information was obtained from the *APL News*, the *Johns Hopkins APL Technical Digest*, the *New York Times*, *Newsweek*, *Science*, *Time*, and the *Congressional Record*. Additional documentary sources include the following:

APL: The First Forty Years (APL, 1983).
Armacost, Michael H., *The Politics of Weapons Innovation* (New York: Columbia University Press, 1969).
Baar, James, and William Howard, *Polaris! The Concept and Creation of a New and Mighty Weapon* (New York: Harcourt, Brace & Co., 1960).
Baldwin, Ralph B., *The Deadly Fuze* (San Rafael: Presido Press, 1980).
Ball, Desmond, *Politics and Force Levels* (Berkeley: University of California Press, 1980).
Hezlet, Sir Arthur, *Electronics and Sea Power* (New York: Stein and Day, 1975).
Sapolsky, Harvey M., *The Polaris System Development* (Cambridge: Harvard University Press, 1972).

NOTES

For the most part, annotation is provided only for substantive, direct quotations. Quotes from the oral history interviews are typically not attributed, since their source should be obvious. References to DOF numbers are references to the director's office files of The Johns Hopkins University Applied Physics Laboratory.

Chapter One

1. P. A. Abelson, "Merle Anthony Tuve," *Year Book 1982* (Philadelphia: American Philosophical Society, 1983), 525.

2. J. B. Phinney III, *Scientists Against Time* (Boston: Little, Brown, 1946), 224.

3. W. Goss, interview with author, October 1991.

4. Phinney, *Scientists Against Time*, 235.

5. Ibid., 236.

6. *New York Times*, 22 September 1945, 21.

7. *The First Forty Years* (Laurel, Md.: The Johns Hopkins University Applied Physics Laboratory, 1983), 11.

Chapter Two

1. W. G. Berl, "Annotated Bumblebee Initial Report," *Johns Hopkins APL Technical Digest* 3(2):173 (1982).

2. *APL News* 38(2):6.

3. *APL News* 18(11):8.

4. *The First Forty Years*, 23.

5. J. Goss, "History of Staff Growth and Evolution of the APL Organization," (Laurel, Md.: The Johns Hopkins University Applied Physics Laboratory, July 1984), E3-11.

6. Ibid.

7. J. Goss, "History of Staff Growth," E3-15.

8. W. Goss, J. Van Allen, W. Good, et al., to M. Tuve, memorandum dated 7 September 1945. Copy provided to the author by W. Goss.

9. J. Goss, "History of Staff Growth," E3-10.

10. F. A. Long to Lt. Col. C. N. Pruden, memorandum dated 26 November 1945, DOF No. B-50.

11. "Missiles Versus Missiles," *Newsweek*, 21 February 1949, 52.

12. R. E. Gibson, memorandum to files dated 25 June 1947, DOF No. B-49.

13. R. E. Gibson, memorandum to files dated 24 November 1947, DOF No. B-49.

14. A. G. Noble to I. Bowman, memorandum dated 25 October 1947, DOF No. B-49.

15. *New York Times*, 1 June 1947, 9.

16. *The First Forty Years*, 79.

17. *New York Times*, 3 September 1947, 27.

Chapter Three

1. R. E. Gibson, "Reminiscences," *Johns Hopkins APL Technical Digest* 4(4):227 (1983).

2. W. G. Berl, "Introduction, R. E. Gibson Retrospective," *Johns Hopkins APL Technical Digest* 4(4):225 (1983).

3. R. E. Gibson to A. Kossiakoff, memorandum dated 27 March 1978, published in *Johns Hopkins APL Technical Digest* 4(4):246 (1983).

4. R. E. Gibson, Christmas message to staff, December 1948, DOF No. B-46.

5. R. E. Gibson, memorandum of conversation with A. G. Noble dated 10 November 1949, DOF No. B-45.

6. U.S. Department of State, "National Intelligence Estimate, Nov. 15, 1950," *Foreign Relations of the United States* 1:414 (1950).

7. *New York Times*, 26 October 1950, 1.

8. A. Kossiakoff to F. D. Boyle and P. H. Girouard, memorandum dated 20 November 1953, DOF No. B-38.

9. *The First Forty Years*, 45.

10. W. Goss to R. E. Gibson, memorandum dated 27 March 1952, DOF No. B-39.

11. "Special Report to the Trustees of The Johns Hopkins University," 23 May 1955, 13, copy in DOF No. B-35.

12. U.S. Department of State, "Memorandum of Discussion of National Security Council, 25 March 1953," *Foreign Relations of the United States* 2:260 (1952-54).

13. Minutes of meeting of Trustees Committee on the Applied Physics Laboratory, 10 October 1951, DOF No. B-40.

Chapter Four

1. W. Guier, interview with author, September 1991.

2. F. T. McClure to R. E. Gibson, memorandum dated 18 March 1958, published as Appendix A, *History of the Space Department*, (The Johns Hopkins University Applied Physics Laboratory, Laurel, Md., January 1979).

3. R. E. Gibson, interview with Cyril O'Brien, undated, Public Information Office, The Johns Hopkins University Applied Physics Laboratory, Laurel, Md. (Audiotape).

4. Ibid.

5. Ibid.

Chapter Five

1. U.S. Department of State, "Memorandum of Discussion of the National Security Council, 3 July 1957," *Foreign Relations of the United States* 19:537 (1955-57).

2. R. E. Gibson to M. Eisenhower, memorandum dated 6 September 1957, DOF No. B-22.

3. Ibid.

4. Ibid.

5. C. F. Meyer to R. E. Gibson, memorandum dated 21 December 1956, DOF No. B-27.

6. R. E. Gibson to M. Eisenhower, memorandum dated 22 January 1957, DOF No. B-23.

7. W. Goss to R. E. Gibson, memorandum dated 14 April 1958. Copy provided to author by a former APL employee.

8. R. E. Gibson, memorandum to the files dated 2 May 1962, DOF No. B-11.

9. Eli T. Reich Oral History, Naval Institute Press, undated manuscript provided to author by Eli Reich.

10. Ibid.

11. P. D. Stroop to The Johns Hopkins University, memorandum dated 4 May 1962, DOF No. B-5.

12. A. Kossiakoff to F. S. Macaulay, memorandum dated 17 May 1963, DOF No. B-4.

13. W. Goss to R. E. Gibson, memorandum dated 6 March 1964, DOF No. B-4.

14. R. E. Gibson to F. S. Macaulay, working paper dated 6 April 1964, DOF No. B-4.

15. Minutes of 5 March 1965 meeting with M. Eisenhower at The Johns Hopkins University, Baltimore, in unsigned memorandum dated 9 March 1965, DOF No. B-4.

16. E. Reich to Distribution, memorandum dated 22 March 1965, DOF No. B-4.

17. *APL News* 18(12):3.

18. "The Gestation of Transit," *Johns Hopkins APL Technical Digest* 2(1):36.

19. Ibid.

20. R. E. Gibson to E. A. Ruckner, memorandum dated 2 February 1961, DOF No. B-13.

Chapter Six

1. T. C. Hone, "Aegis Combat System Case Study" (Annapolis, Md.: U.S. Naval War College, undated), 2. Copy provided to author by Wayne E. Meyer.

2. Ibid., p. 3.

3. Ibid., p. 4.

4. Wayne E. Meyer, interview with J. Marchese, 30 April 1990.

5. R. P. Sharkey, *Johns Hopkins Centennial Portrait of a University* (Baltimore: The Johns Hopkins University, 1975), 50.

6. Statement on the Applied Physics Laboratory: Resolution adopted by the Executive Committee of the Board of Trustees of The Johns Hopkins University (JHU), in memorandum dated 8 January 1968 from L. Gordon, president of JHU, to P. R. Ignatius, Secretary of the Navy, DOF.

7. Contract between the U.S. Government and The Johns Hopkins University (JHU) dated 13 December 1968, signed by L. Gordon, president of JHU, and A. R. Gralla, commander, Naval Ordnance Systems Command, Department of the Navy, DOF.

8. "The University and the Applied Physics Laboratory: Statement by the Executive Committee, Board of Trustees, The Johns Hopkins University," 8 May 1970, DOF.

NAME INDEX

Abrahamson, James 246, 247, 249, 250
Adrian, Frank 166
Austin, James R. 187, 211
Avery, William H. **60**, 105, 106, **109**, 111, 189, **215**, 224, **225**

Billig, Frederick 233
Black, Harold D. 111, 171, 197, 202
Bostrom, Carl O. **111**, **173**, 175, 199, **203**, **205**, **222–224**, 225, 226, 231, 242, 248, **254**, **255**
Bowers, Vernon 166
Bowman, Isaiah **8**, 35, 36, 37, 48, 54, 55, 56, 57, 59
Burchard, John E. 3
Burke, Arleigh 115
Bush, Vannevar 2, 7, 8, 20, 59

Campbell, Levin 19
Carlton, George 105
Chatham, Elmore R. **4**, 11, 12, 13, **15**
Cochran, Edward L. 84, 166
Colvard, James 224
Cook, Earnshaw 47, 48, 49
Cook, J. Emory 180

Dahlstrom, Kirk 25, 31
Dassoulas, John 176, 199, 200, 247, 248, 250
Draper, Charles 110
Dugger, Gordon 225

Eaton, Alvin R. **30**, 53, **65**, **94**, **99**, 100, **101**, **141**, 142, 158, 183, **189**, 194, **224**, 248
Eddins, Donald L. 210, 224

Eisenhower, Dwight D. 91, **108**, 109, **133**, 134, 138
Eisenhower, Milton **123**, 135, 138, 157, **186**, 187, 213
Ellis, Richard T. 51, 52, 83, 97, 98
Emch, George F. 185

Fletcher, James 246
Flower, Robert W. 243
Foner, Samuel N. 32, 49, 85, 86, 87, 166
Forrestal, James **35-37**, 52, 53
Fous, Albert 23
Frain, William E. 112, 202

Gamow, George 85
Garten, William H. 78
Gibson, Ralph E. **37**, **38**, 41, 42, **48**, **49**, 53, **54**, **58-61**, 63, 64, 66, **67**, 75, **79**, 84, **87**, 111, 117, **121**, 122, 123, 125, 128, 130, 131, **134**, **135**, 138, 140, **147**, 148, 152, 157, 166, 177, 186-190, 207, **243**, 250
Goddard, Robert 3
Good, Walter A. 34, 35
Gordon, Lincoln 213
Goss, Wilbur H. **10**, 11, **16**, 23, **25**, 27, 31, **32**, 34, **35**, **38**, **68**, 78, 79, 87, 105, **138**, 139, **151**, **153**
Griffin, Michael 249
Guier, William H. **119-123**, 125, 127, 165, 170, 208

Hafstad, Lawrence R. **3**, **8**, 25, **33**, **34**, 35, **43**, **48**, 49, 54, **55**, **57**, 62
Hart, Robert W. 167, 208, 239
Hensel, H. Struve 20
Hickman, C. N. 2
Hinman, Eugene J. 224
Hitler, Adolf 3
Holliday, Clyde T. 46
Hopkins, D. Luke **8**, 38, 47, 49, 54
Hostettler, Steven 196, 230

Hudson, Richard L. 85, 86, 87
Humphrey, Hubert H. 172, 198
Hunt, Richard J. 231

Jen, Chih K. 166
Johns, Richard, M.D. 204, 206

Keen, Timothy J. 153, 158, 190, 223
Keller, Kaufman T. 68, 69, 76
Kemelhor, Robert E. 115, 116
Kennedy, John F. 168, 169
Kershner, Richard B. **38**, 51, 53, **72**, **73**, 97, 105,
    106, **111**, **112**, **124**, **127**, **130**, 161, 168, 170, 176,
    189, 190, 198, 202, 203, 223, 224, **225**
Kistiakowsky, George 19, 116
Kongelbeck, Sverre (Steve) 103
Korth 152
Koslov, Samuel 247, 248
Kossiakoff, Alexander **37**, **38**, 40, 53, 60, 66, 70, **71**,
    72, 75, **85**, **105**, 106, **109**, 110, 111, 113, 143,
    144, 158, **186–191**, 208, 209, 220, 221, **222**,
    223, 224, **248**
Krimigis, Stamatios M. (Tom) 203, 205, 224

Larson, Roland W. 73
Lear, Ben 18
Lorin, René 23, 27

Macaulay, F. S. 157
Maddox, James B. 10, 89
Makofski, Robert A. 214, 216, 225
Marshall, George C. 68
Massey, Joseph 87, 205, 206, 207, 208, 243
Maumenee, Ed 206
McClure, Frank T. 38, 53, 84, 85, 87, 105, 111, **117**,
    119, **122–124**, **167**, 187, **188**, 189, 190, **197**,
    204, 205, 206, 239, **241**

269

McNamara, Robert 158, 180, 192
Meyer, Wayne E. 192, 193, 194, 227
Montanaro, Luciano P. 160, 161, 224
Morton, H. S. 64
Morton, Robert 93, 113, 116, 161, 189, 209, 224
Muller, Steven 215, 222, 223, 226
Murphee, Eger V. 136

Noble, A. G. 51, 67

Oakes, Barry 208
Osborn 116

Paddison, Fletcher 136
Parsons, W. S. 8
Patton, George S. 19
Petersen, Robert P. 44
Phillips, C. C. 182
Pisacane, Vincent 224
Poehler, Theodore O. 240
Porter, Henry H. 63, 88

Raborn, William F. 109, 115, 116, 126
Rae, Randolph S. 80
Reagan, Ronald 245, 246
Reich, Eli T. **147-149**, **152-158**, 180, 191
Rich, Robert P. 165
Richardson, William C. 255
Rickover, Hyman 148
Roberts, Richard B. 21, 22, 25, 38
Robinson, Ralph O. 97, 112, 184
Roosevelt, Franklin D. 2, 8
Ruckner, E. A. 177

SUBJECT INDEX

8621 Georgia Ave.   9, 10, 16, 89, 165, 221

Aberdeen Proving Grounds (Aberdeen)   17, 83
Advisory Board (APL)   (*see* APL Advisory Board)
Aegis system   191-194, 227, 254
Aerobee sounding rocket   45, 46
Aerojet Corporation   45
Aeronautics Department (Division)   225, 251
Allegany Ballistics Laboratory   2, 37, 38, 39, 40, 60, 189
AMFAR (advanced multifunction array radar)   182, 193
AMPTE (Active Magnetosphere Particle Tracer Explorer)   244
AN/SPG-59 radar (Typhon)   141, 143
AN/SPY-1 radar (Aegis)   194
AN/SYS-1 automatic detection and tracking system   184-187, 228
ANNA (Army-Navy-NASA-Air Force satellite)   175-177
APL Advisory Board   56, 213
Apollo 12   198
ARPA (*see* Defense Advanced Research Projects Agency)
Associate Staff Training Program   163
Atomic Energy Commission   54, 169, 172
Automatic Identification system (AutoID)   230

Battle Group Coordination   228
Battle of the Bulge   19
Beacon Explorer satellite   175
Beam-riding guidance   42
Bell Telephone Laboratory   152, 153
Bendix Corporation   28, 78, 79
Biomedical program   205-208, 241, 242
Board of Trustees (JHU)   8, 22, 36, 47, 55, 60, 85, 90, 218, 222, 226

V-1 "buzz bombs"   17
V-2 rockets (Vergeltungswaffe-2)   21, 43-46
Vitro Corporation   60
Voyager I and II spacecraft   202, 203, 244
VT fuze (*see also* proximity fuze)   4-7, 11-20, 25, 39, 43

Warfare Analysis Laboratory (WAL)   231, 232
Westinghouse Electric Corporation   143
White Sands Proving Ground   43, 79, 137
Wilmer Institute (Johns Hopkins)   206
Withington task force   180, 181
Wolfe Motor Company   9

XPM (experimental prototype missile)   63, 77

Young Turks Committee   34, 35

About the Author

William K. Klingaman holds a Ph.D. in history from the University of Virginia and is a specialist in 20th century American affairs. He was co-editor of the Department of State's *Foreign Relations of the United States* series and has served as an editorial consultant to the Department of Defense.

Among Dr. Klingaman's other books are the following:

1919: The Year Our World Began (St. Martin's Press, 1987).
1941: Our Lives In a World on the Edge (Harper & Row, 1988).
1929: The Year of the Great Crash (Harper & Row, 1989).
The First Century: Emperors, Gods, and Everyman (HarperCollins, 1990).
Turning 40 (NAL/Dutton, 1992).

Dr. Klingaman lives in Columbia, Maryland, with his wife and two children.